Stop Counseling!

Start Ministering!

Martin and Deidre Bobgan

Scripture quotations are taken from the
Authorized King James Version of the Bible

Moskowitz, Eva S. *In Therapy We Trust: America's Obsession
with Self-Fulfillment.* © 2001 The Johns Hopkins University Press.
Reprinted with permission from The Johns Hopkins University Press,
pages indicated in the endnotes.

Peck, Janice. *The Age of Oprah.* © 2008 Paradigm Publishers.
Reprinted with permission of Paradigm Publishers, pages indicated in
the endnotes.

Stop Counseling! Start Ministering!

Copyright © 2011 Martin and Deidre Bobgan
Published by EastGate Publishers
4137 Primavera Road
Santa Barbara, CA 93110

Library of Congress Control Number 2010942279
ISBN 978-0941717-22-9

Printed in the United States of America

Table of Contents

What This Book Is All About

As every man hath received the gift, even so minister the same one to another, as good stewards of the manifold grace of God. If any man speak, let him speak as the oracles of God; if any man minister, let him do it as of the ability which God giveth: that God in all things may be glorified through Jesus Christ, to whom be praise and dominion for ever and ever. Amen.

1 Peter 4:10-11

Our greatest joy in ministering is to lead those who are suffering from problems of living away from sinful problem-centered conversations to a daily walk with the Lord. We emphasize the daily walk because walking closely with the Lord, spending time in His Word and prayer, and being mindful of Him during the day will serve to enable believers to know and follow God's will as difficulties occur. **We pray that this book will give you confidence to minister in such a way as to strengthen fellow believers in their daily walk with Christ.**

Throughout this book we voice a two-pronged concern about problem-centered counseling, both of which we will be describing in detail. One is what we call "sinful problem-centered counseling" during which the conversation and questions lead to sinful communication, which we call "the Jeremiah 17:9 syndrome." The other we simply call "ongoing problem-centered counseling," during which problems are continually discussed meeting after meeting with little or no spiritual growth through the Word of God and the empowerment of the Holy Spirit. **Both are sinful and they often occur together** throughout psychological and biblical counseling, The one generates sinful communication and the other continues to empower the flesh rather than nurture the new life in Christ. In place of such sinful and on-going problem-centeredness, we recommend and describe Christ-centered ministry, during which problems may be discussed, but the direction is towards Christ Himself and His life in the believer.

Stop Counseling!

Why would anyone want to stop counseling? We give reasons throughout this book as to why Christians should be opposed to counseling, literally stop it, and start ministering. We choose the word *counseling* because it is generic enough to cover both psychological (psychotherapy) and biblical counseling. This is the type of counseling where those with personal and interpersonal problems of living seek help through psychological or biblical problem-centered conversations. The problems discussed at length are those personal and interpersonal problems of living that are normally taken to one who is designated as a psychological or biblical counselor. **The commonality for both psychological and biblical counseling is that both are sinfully problem-centered!**

Our concern is what the counselee and the counselor say as they pursue the problems presented and discussed.

Start Ministering!

Central to ministering to individuals in need is to overcome their fixation on their problems, turn their attention to Christ, and encourage spiritual growth. This is not an easy task as sinful problem-centeredness is the default position of people raised in the American therapeutic culture. It is a constant battle that one who ministers will need to deal with if spiritual possibilities are to be accomplished. As one ministers biblically this battle must be won in order to spiritually enable the one in need. **As ministry increases, problem-centeredness must decrease** so that the one in need develops a solid, dependent daily walk with the Lord whereby current and future problems of life can be confronted spiritually. This book is meant to enable you to **Stop counseling!** and **Start ministering!** by helping those in need become more Christ-centered and Word-centered, equipping them with the truths of Scripture, and encouraging them **to live the daily life** that will be honoring to the Lord and beneficial for meeting life's problems.

Use of Terms

Throughout this book we use the terms *counselor, counselee*, and *counseling* when what we say is related to the psychological or biblical counseling movement, because these are their preferred terms. We use the terms *psychotherapist* and *counselor* to designate the person who counsels. Also, we use the terms *psychotherapy* and *counseling* to indicate the process, and we sometimes use them interchangeably. Whenever we use the term *counseling* by itself in reference to biblical counseling, it refers to problem-centered biblical counseling, and when we use the designation "problem-centered counseling" by itself, it can refer to both psychological and biblical counseling. **We will not repeatedly use quotes around the word *biblical* when used with the word *counseling*, but let it be understood that, as we demonstrate in our writing, biblical counseling is not biblical because it is sinfully problem-centered like the psychological movement.** In addition, we use the terms *client* and *counselee* when referring to the one receiving the counseling. Finally, two terms that we use interchangeably throughout the book are *sinful* and *evil* in reference to verbal communication, as in "sinful talk" and "evil talk." **Because counseling is essentially a female friendly activity, which we will demonstrate later, and because women comprise the large majority of the counselors and counselees, we will often use the feminine gender alone when referring to the counselors and counselees, as is the common practice today.**

Overview of Chapters

In **Chapter One** we reveal how the privacy of private lives became public and how the therapeutic mentality became ubiquitous throughout America. Early marriage education classes prior to World War II mandated a move from lives being private to a need to reveal as much as possible about one's personal life, thoughts, and relationships in order to be helped. **It was primarily women who sought the help.** During the post-World War II era women's magazines carried and conveyed a so-called necessity to express publicly what had previously been unexpressed and private. Also during the pre-war and early post-war periods the psychotherapeutic gospel, in which private lives are made public to the counselor, was the leaven being infused into marriage education and women's magazines that eventually came to full loaf with licensed therapists and the therapeutic gospel permeating all of society and even the church. We briefly describe how the sinful problem-centeredness began with the psychological counseling movement after World War II and was later adopted by the biblical counseling movement.

Alongside the post-World War II counseling movement came the almost simultaneous arrival of the media driven exposure of personal lives becoming publicly proclaimed and drastically displayed in a new and unprecedented way. While men and women are both guilty of the publicizing of private lives, men were instrumental in initiating such exposure in therapy, but **women led the way and are primarily responsible for its current popularity and expansion**. Complementary to the counseling movement was the rise of media moguls like Oprah and others who capitalized on women's interests by corrupting women's strengths to their own detriment. All of this gave rise to all of life in the United States being viewed through the lens of the psychotherapeutic gospel. At the same time the media madness with its expression and often sinful practices moved into the online availability of almost everything from benign banter to devilish debauchery through such social networking sites as YouTube, Facebook, Twitter, and MySpace and through search mechanisms such as Google and Yahoo.

We discuss the "Jeremiah 17:9 syndrome" in **Chapter Two** and the ramifications of the deceitful heart. We reveal various ways the deceitful heart of both the counselor and counselee affect psychological and biblical counseling. Popular biblical counseling approaches are discussed in **Chapter Three** to demonstrate the sinful problem-centeredness of biblical counseling and to reveal that biblical counseling, even at its best, involves sinful conversations through its unbiblical practice of problem-centeredness. **In spite of the fact that many biblical counselors are often very biblical in their teaching of Scripture, we reveal how unbiblical they are in what they do.** We discuss the rise of problem-centered counseling in **Chapter Four** and reveal how it infiltrated Christian schools, Bible colleges, seminaries, Christian universities, denominations, and mission agencies. We reveal the erroneous use of Proverbs 18:13, which is the lynchpin for much of the problem-centeredness in biblical counseling. **We also demonstrate that counseling is a female-friendly environment, which is loathed by most men, who are often reluctantly forced into it.**

The unbiblical practice of cross-gender counseling, with women counseling men, men counseling women, and a woman or man counseling a married couple, was "inherited" by biblical counselors from the psychological counseling movement with little thought or challenge and is practiced throughout the church. **Chapter Five** enumerates biblical and practical reasons why this practice should be discontinued.

Although problem-centered counseling itself is **not** a scientific or biblically supported activity, it can be evaluated scientifically to test its claims of efficacy or usefulness. The predominant reasons why psychological and biblical counseling **may be** somewhat successful are found in the scientific literature. The results of the scientific examination are surprising and little known to the average person. These surprising and little-known reasons for the positive results are discussed in **Chapter Six** along with the detrimental effects of many counseling approaches.

Two major unbiblical practices in the biblical counseling movement are charging for counseling and counseling in a separated-from-the-church counseling center. These two unbiblical practices are typically found together as community counseling centers usually charge fees for their services. In **Chapter Seven** we name some names of the many who are in cahoots with respect to either directly or indirectly supporting this practice.

One of the greatest difficulties in personal ministry in the Body of Christ is overcoming the common practice of problem-centeredness. In **Chapter Eight** we describe the unbiblical nature of psychological and biblical problem-centered counseling and suggest what can be done when it occurs. Many will not know what to do if problems are not pursued and discussed in detail. Many will **not** know what to do to avoid getting bogged down in such sinful talk. Though we have criticized problem-centered counseling as being sinful, because both the counselees and counselors converse sinfully about problems, we have made it clear in our past writings that **"We are not saying 'Do not talk about problems.'"**[1] **We do listen to problems; but the way we respond and the direction we take differ from those in the biblical counseling movement.**

Chapter Nine informs those who desire to minister biblically, but may not know what can be done absent problem-centeredness. **One of the most powerful spiritual disciplines is an intentional daily walk with the Lord and all that implies.** Lack of a purposeful daily walk with the Lord is one of the biggest shortcomings in a Christian's life and often happens during times when one is experiencing personal and interpersonal problems. **Chapter Ten** discusses elements of the daily walk for Christians to consider as they are bombarded with the issues of life. The last chapter titled **"Stop Counseling! Start Ministering!"** gives a summation of the prior ten chapters and also includes recommendations of "Do Not's" and "Do's."

Conclusion

The entire thrust of this book is to explain biblically, practically, and scientifically why Christians should Stop Counseling! and to provide suggestions for Christians who may need encouragement and guidance to Start Ministering! As a result of reading this book, we pray that you will become totally turned off to psychotherapy and contemporary biblical counseling, which are both sinfully problem-centered, and totally turned on to the traditional biblical ministry that preceded the Johnny-come-lately biblical counseling movement.

1

The Public Undressing
of Private Lives

**There is a way which seemeth right unto
a man, but the end thereof are the ways of
death.   Proverbs 14:12**

Throughout church history the Bible has been sufficient
to minister to the personal and interpersonal problems of living without resorting to the very wisdom of man about which
God warns His people (1 Cor. 2:5, etc.). How did the church
move from the comfort and confidence in the Word of God
and the work of the Holy Spirit in the fellowship of the saints
to its current condition where solutions to the issues of life
are found in the unbiblical evil speaking (Eph. 4:31) that
takes place in problem-centered counseling and in the public
undressing of private lives? In attempting to provide something better than the world, Christians nevertheless followed
the problem-centeredness of worldly counseling along with
its sinful speaking. Not only have these Christians opened
Pandora's Box, but apparently they believe that its evil contents of exposing the sins and failures of others are necessary in the process of helping people who are suffering from
the trials of life. Like the Israelites during the time of the

13

Judges, they are doing what is right in their own eyes (Judges 21:25).

Two main streams of influence occurred historically to promote this evil, both of which began in the secular society and eventually weaseled their way into the church. Like the proverbial camel's nose in the tent, unbiblical evil speaking became the common parlance of God's people. God's Word was first replaced by the "camel" of communication called "counseling," and then Christians went public by expressing instead of suppressing their private emotions, thoughts, and lives. The first stream is counseling gushing forth with the psychological counseling movement and followed by the biblical counseling movement, where sinful speaking became part and parcel of the lingua franca of the people of God in the counselor's office. The second and tandem stream is the progression from personal privacy regarding thoughts and lives, once considered sacrosanct and kept private from public disclosure, to public exposure with sinful speaking and its ptomaine touchy-feely talk, with grumps and grumbles rumbling beneath a facile façade of pseudo righteousness. **The publication of private lives first began in the confines of counselors' offices and eventually evolved into the broadcast blather of talk shows.** The Jeremiah 17:9 syndrome, described later, reveals the human depravity from which the sinful problem-centered mania began and is the dreadful abyss of mankind out of which the publicizing of private lives erupted.

This chapter briefly documents the movement in the United States from private thoughts about self and others being shared in the counseling office to private lives becoming publicly proclaimed with many defamed. Both of these streams will be examined in this chapter to set the stage for biblical reasons why counseling conversations have run roughshod over the "faith which was once delivered unto the saints" (Jude 3) and corrupted biblical admonitions regarding the tongue to the contrary (James 3).

Publicizing Private Lives

Once upon a time there was no licensed problem-centered counseling as we know it today, except for psychoanalysis. There were no degreed and licensed counselors who charged money for ongoing conversations about the issues of life. That was sixty years ago. Now this sinful problem-centered counseling has become so much a part of our culture that speaking out against it, as we do, raises eyebrows and hackles. However, the problem we have with counseling is that it is problem-centered and inevitably leads to sinful speaking, which we will describe in detail later.

We begin by revealing what problem-centered counseling is. The kinds of problems we are talking about in this book are **those personal and relational troubles, difficulties, and dilemmas normally taken to a psychological or biblical counselor and discussed in detail and at length with the counselor.** They are the mental-emotional-behavioral problems of living that are normally surfaced in counseling and constitute the center of the conversation. We will reveal some of these problems later as we elaborate on what it is and what is wrong with problem-centered counseling and why it inevitably leads to evil speaking (Eph. 4:31). **While the counselees generally come in with a problem-centered mind-set, the counselors are the ones who are primarily responsible for the corrupt conversation that follows, through their questions and responses.**

Next we describe what problem-centered counseling **is not**. We are not Roman Catholics, but give the following as an example. Problem-centered counseling is **not** like a Catholic confessional in which a person comes alone as a penitent, sorrowful about some sin or wrongdoing on her part and seeking forgiveness.[1] Note the person (penitent) is confessing **her own sin and not that of others.** Contrary to the Catholic confessional, **problem-centered counseling generally flows in the opposite direction in that the counselee is typically confessing sins of others who are usually not present, thus making public to a third party what was formerly private and at the same time violating biblical admonitions to the contrary.** The Catholic confessional does not consist of repeated meetings about problems with on-going discussions comprised of confessing the sins of others, unbiblically accusing and blaming them, and publicizing their personal and private lives. **The repentant sinner who confesses her own sins rather than those of others is the exception in biblical counseling.** While in many instances it would be beneficial if the one in need would first confess her own sins before discussing the reason for seeking help, it is unlikely to happen because we live in a 2 Timothy 3, last-days era. At least it has not happened in all the biblical counseling we have seen, heard, and read. And, it has not happened in almost forty years of our own ministry to others.

Conversations between and among people have been going on ever since the Garden of Eden. Conversation is the sharing of thoughts, feelings, and ideas by spoken communication and includes both informal and formal sharing of words. The kind of conversation to which we are referring is both. It will sound informal and casual at times. It is formal in that it is the kind of conversation that occurs when one or more persons with a personal or interpersonal problem come to a particular person known as a counselor or psychotherapist in order to receive help. The help is given within the formal framework of the counselor's particular theory, techniques, and training. **But the backdrop is that**

the counselee generally reveals confidences and confesses sins of others. The counselor enables the counselee to do so through particular learned theories and techniques, which generally expand the confidences revealed, but fails to find out the truth behind what is said. When one crosses the line from confessing one's own sins to confessing the sins of others, the fleshly tendency in such a setting will inevitably turn to revealing confidences and private matters resulting in speaking evil of others. As we describe later, the depravity of one's flesh generally takes over in such a problem-centered setting.

In future chapters we describe in greater detail what is wrong with problem-centered counseling and reveal what is unbiblical about it, with **the counselor being the one who promotes, produces, and draws forth the sinful conversation.** Here we will deal solely with the fact that, from its origin in contemporary counseling, conversations about problems of living and the people involved moved from being private, normally restricted to family and close friends, to semi-public with professional counselors, who are generally unfamiliar with the counselee, with the understanding that what is said is to remain confidential.

Pre and Post World War II

Prior to World War II only problem-centered psychoanalysis existed, along with various attempts at marriage counseling and education. Following World War II and less than sixty years ago marked the beginning of more popular and much more affordable forms of counseling. However, these various forms of counseling were all problem-centered, just as the various forms of psychoanalysis are. **This was a turning point from private lives staying private to the expectation (and so-called need) for the undressing of people's personal lives in the privacy of the counselor's office.**

The United States is the international seedbed of the evolution from maintaining privacy in thought and confidentiality in what one says to becoming public both in the counselor's office and in personal and public relationships. Our nation reached this precarious pinnacle of public exposure through a series of unusual events. The story begins strangely enough with Franz Anton Mesmer (1734-1851), an Austrian physician who declared, "There is only one illness and one healing."[2] Mesmer thought he had discovered something entirely new, never before detected by medical science. He believed he had discovered an invisible energy or fluid that he called "animal magnetism," which when imbalanced causes illness and when rebalanced brings cure. In his book *Mesmerism and the American Cure of Souls*, Robert Fuller explains Mesmer's theory: "Since there was only one cause of illness, it followed that there was only one truly effective mode of healing—the restoration of equilibrium to the body's supply of animal magnetism."[3]

Of interest here is how mesmerism's method of cure **evolved** into a public puffery of one's private life with a public maligning, humiliating, and vilifying of one's friends and relatives, typically behind their backs. Mesmer's method began with utilizing magnets as a means of cure and began with bodily manipulation, but evolved from concentrating on the bodily affects on the mind and on bodily manipulation to speaking, with conversation being the means of healing through the mind. This seemingly minor change was the dramatic commencement of **conversation as the medium of cure and problem-centeredness as the method of cure.** Though mesmerism at first dealt primarily with physical healing, it later expanded to spiritual and personal growth through conversation. These conversations that occurred with mesmerism became the open-sesame into the private lives and thoughts of those who sought such services.

The three main offspring of mesmerism in the United States were hypnosis, New Thought, and psychotherapy. The New Thought movement in America, also known as positive thinking and Mind Cure (including Christian Science) evolved over a period of time until as Fuller describes it:

> The latter New Thought authors, sometimes referred to as the positive thinkers, attempted to systematically apply mind cure principles to the routine affairs of everyday life. In practice this resulted in an uncritical use of mind cure psychology for deriving surefire solutions to difficulties arising in home life, interpersonal relationships, and business.… In other words, mesmerism eventually evaporated into a fairly uncritical cult of the power of positive thinking.[4]

Eva Moskowitz, in her book *In Therapy We Trust*, says, "New thoughters named specific states of mind and described their psychological effects. In doing so they introduced considerable specificity to America's therapeutic gospel."[5]

Professor of psychiatry Thomas Szasz describes Mesmer's influence this way:

> Insofar as psychotherapy as a modern "medical technique" can be said to have a discoverer, Mesmer was that person.… Mesmer stumbled onto the literalized use of the leading scientific metaphor of his age for explaining and exorcising all manner of human problems and passions, a rhetorical device that the founders of modern depth psychology subsequently transformed into the pseudomedical entity known as psychotherapy.[6]

The book *History of Psychotherapy: A Century of Change* says:

Historians have found several aspects of mesmerism and its offshoots that **set the stage for 20th-century psychotherapy**. It promoted ideas that are quintessentially American and have become permanent theoretical features of our 20th-century psychological landscape.[7] (Bold added.)

Problem-centered counseling was a movement from mesmerism to Freudian free-association, which required one to say to the therapist without reservation **everything** that came to mind, to later counseling approaches that encouraged counselees to say whatever they wished, without reservation and without any verification or need for any proof of what is said. **In other words, the counselee is encouraged to speak about whomever, whatever, and whenever, and the counselor regularly accepts it as true.** The mistaken idea is that in order to help someone in need it is necessary to hear extensive, detailed information about the problems and the people involved. This includes the counselor accepting as truth whatever is said, discussing it in as much detail as deemed necessary without challenging or contradicting what is said, and then applying her point of view regarding the problems and solutions. This encourages counselees to share their innermost thoughts, opinions, and accusations.

Such conversations inevitably lead to sinful speaking, which we will describe later as we document the biblical prohibitions against it. We will also demonstrate that the counselors are primarily responsible for the direction of the conversation and later we will show what can be done to help individuals in need without hearing or knowing the problems in such detail or discussing at length the problems and the people involved. Those who minister must seriously consider their responsibility as they listen to the problems that are brought up so as not to amplify or augment the sinful talk of the one in need.

Influence of Freud

Many regard Freud as the godfather of modern psycho-therapy. Moreover, his influence has significantly intruded into the biblical counseling movement regarding its problem-centered conversation. E. M. Thornton, a lay Fellow of the Royal Society of Medicine, says in her book *The Freudian Fallacy*:

> Probably no single individual has had a more profound effect on twentieth-century thought than Sigmund Freud. His works have influenced psychiatry, anthropology, social work, penology, and education and provided a seemingly limitless source of material for novelists and dramatists. Freud has created a "whole new climate of opinion"; for better or worse he has changed the face of society.[8]

One of the legacies of Freud and psychoanalysis is the concept of repression. Repression is "the **involuntary** psychological act of excluding desires and impulses (wishes, fantasies or feelings) from one's consciousness and holding or subduing them in the **unconscious**" (bold added).[9] Freud's psychoanalytic theory of repression was popular and highly influential in the thinking and writing of many. Most important was the accompanying assumption that repression was pathological.[10] **The Freudian influence led many to believe that, if repression is pathological, then expression is healthful, and thus created a climate where people feel free to express their negative emotions, speak sinfully about others, and seek emotional healing through talking about their problems and the people involved.**

Even though there is a difference between Freudian repression, which is supposedly **involuntary** and **unconscious**, and the general use of the word *repression*, which means **voluntary** and **conscious**, people still assumed that any repression was harmful. Therefore, **it was concluded that it is better to express than to repress.** (See Chapter Four for evidence to the contrary.) Couple this with the fact that the patient in psychoanalysis is to "free associate," which means to say whatever comes to mind without restraint, and you eventually end up with the express-all and tell-all environment currently prevalent both inside and outside of the counseling room. **Expression became the Siren call that set the stage for the psychotherapies and biblical counseling that followed.**

The Therapeutic Gospel

The therapeutic gospel is all about self. Eva Moskowitz's book *In Therapy We Trust* is subtitled *America's Obsession with Self-Fulfillment*. Her main theme has to do with the "therapeutic gospel." She says:

> There are three central tenets to this "therapeutic gospel." The first is that happiness should be our supreme goal. Wealth, public recognition, high moral character—each of these achievements is held valuable only to the extent that it makes us happy. Success, in the final analysis, must be measured with a psychological yardstick....
>
> The second tenet of our therapeutic faith is the belief that our problems stem from psychological causes. Problems that were once considered political, economic, or educational are today found to be psychological....

> The third and final tenet of the therapeutic gospel is the most important, but it is so universally accepted, so seemingly self-evident, that we hardly notice its existence. This tenet is that the psychological problems that underlie our failures and unhappiness are in fact treatable and that we can, indeed *should*, address these problems both individually and as a society. This is the essence of the therapeutic gospel.[11] (Italics in original.)

Last-days lovers of self seek personal happiness as the supreme goal and the therapeutic gospel convinces people that unhappiness is "treatable."

"Tell it down to the last detail."

Moskowitz begins her chapter titled "Marriage: A Science of Personal Relations" by saying, "Between 1920 and 1940 experts dedicated to a **psychological vision** of marriage banded together to form the new profession of marriage counseling"[12] (bold added). Dr. Paul Popenoe, who opened the first marriage clinic in the United States, reported that **eighty percent of the time it was the wives who brought the cases to the clinic**.[13] Moskowitz reveals that Popenoe's approach to marriage counseling was "talking it out" and that there was a necessity of "hearing the rest of it." According to Popenoe, the counselor needed to "get below the surface" in order to save a marriage.[14] Moskowitz reports on the rising number of marriage centers early on and says:

> Marriage experts founded these centers because they believed that the real problems of marriage "must be dragged out into the open." Their private consultations were part of a fight against silence and reticence. Marriage counselors believed that frank and

open discussion of marital discord was critical if the nation was to ensure mastery over drift.[15]

Moskowitz says that Ernest Groves, an early marriage counselor who preceded the current counseling craze, believed that:

> People could be helped simply by teaching them to face their problems. Grove's mantra became, "**Tell it, down to the last detail** which you have confided to no man, and which nearly chokes you to bring out. Don't stop with this year, or the year before, but keep digging back into your life. It will be hard. It will hurt" But Groves promised that it would be cathartic.[16] (Bold added.)

Now there is no longer a need to encourage people to be cathartic, because people now do it automatically and reveal all without needing much encouragement.

According to Moskowitz, in order to attain the therapeutic gospel of happiness early marriage counselors deemed it necessary to go through the psychological labyrinth of "talking it out," "hearing the rest of it," "get[ting] below the surface," and "tell[ing] it, down to the last detail." The transparency mantra of letting it all hang out came to full bloom as a hoped-for means of achieving happiness and self-fulfillment, spread its tentacles throughout all of American society, and morphed itself into the church, both through Christian psychological counselors and biblical counselors. Moskowitz says, "It is practiced in every conceivable institution."[17] Worse yet, it is practiced in nearly every conceivable Christian institution.

In her book Moskowitz describes the beginning post-World War II era of the therapeutic gospel in her chapter "Home: The Unhappy Housewife." She says:

During the era of the cold war (1945-1965) the therapeutic gospel laid claim to a new realm: the American home.... The public, but **especially American housewives**, learned an entirely new way of thinking about their lives, and a new language that went with it. Terms such as ego, inferiority complex, and self-esteem, which had been obscure before the war, became, quite literally, household words.

This domestication of the therapeutic gospel was an important episode in America's journey to the therapeutic altar. Psychological professionals, many of whom had played a key role in World War II, led the way. They sought to translate their wartime investments into peacetime dividends.[18] (Bold added.)

Central to her chapter on the home is a section on "Women's Magazines and the Therapeutic Gospel." She says:

Although the champions of the therapeutic gospel during the 1940s and 1950s were many, **none were more devoted or more influential than women's magazines**. In the 1950s and early 1960s women's magazines were at the height of their cultural power. Never before or since have they been such important disseminators of mass culture.[19]

The circulation figures for the popular women's magazines of the post-World War II era showed a significantly greater popularity than the most popular magazines today. The magazine people knew that **"Only one market really mattered: housewives"**[20] (bold added).

Moskowitz asks and answers an important question about the therapeutic gospel:

But how could they reach into the home? How could they convince ordinary Americans that family life could be improved and solidified by applying psychological principles? The answer was women's magazines, which were read by the very people the mental-health establishment most wanted to reach: housewives. **The content of these magazines also dovetailed perfectly with mental-health professionals' message**.... Psychological professionals could not have created a better vehicle for disseminating the therapeutic gospel.[21] (Bold added.)

She notes:

Rather than presenting relentlessly upbeat images of women, the magazines often portrayed women as profoundly unhappy. Rather than dissuading women from considering their psychological condition, the magazines actively encouraged it.... Instead of ignoring the housewife's discontent, they devoted a great deal of attention to it. In fact, **women's magazines were in the forefront of a new campaign to raise women's consciousness about their psyches.**[22] (Bold added.)

She describes how women's magazines gave women a whole new psychological vocabulary:

The women's magazines also provided women with an entirely new language for expressing their feelings of dissatisfaction, terms such as unconscious, ego, inferiority complex, psychosomatic, defensive reaction, and self-esteem. The use of these terms legitimatized women's psychological inquiries and complaints.[23]

Moskowitz further reveals:

The women's magazines suggested that the real danger was not having problems but *ignoring* them. **For the first time, millions of women were told that they needed to understand psychology in order to understand their feelings and behavior.**[24] (Italics in original; bold added.)

And what was the main message of these magazines according to Moskowitz?

The main message was quite simple: *women had the right to be happy*. Never before had this proposition been spelled out so clearly. This message was particularly evident in the marriage-advice columns, which emphasized that a woman, like a man, was entitled to judge the adequacy of her marriage based on whether it made her happy.[25] (Italics in original.)

The magazines' message was extremely influential and "introduced the reader to the cardinal principle of the therapeutic gospel: that unhappiness was a condition that could be—and *should* be—treated" (italics in original).[26]

Carl Rogers' Influence in Transparency and Exposure

Psychologist Carl Rogers, the most popular psychologist of the last century, led the stampede from private lives becoming public by his exaltation of personal transparency in group therapy, which rapidly ran pandemic throughout America and much of the church. In 1960 Rogers completed his book *On Becoming a Person*. In it he promoted his view of self-actualization. Joyce Milton, in her book *The Road to Malpsychia*, describes what Rogers was promoting in his book. She says:

Rogers outlined a process of self-exploration by which the individual strips away the "false fronts" that he has used to present himself to the world and becomes "the self which one truly is." Anticipating the day when non-fiction would be dominated by personal narratives, he began with a chapter entitled "This Is Me." The remainder of the volume equated "personhood" with the discovery of one's inner, pre-socialized "me." The search for truth, Rogers wrote, must begin and end with identifying one's true feelings.[27]

Milton then quotes Rogers as saying, "Neither the Bible nor the prophets—neither Freud nor research—neither the revelations of God nor man—can take precedence over my own direct experience."[28]

A national survey of psychotherapists, conducted in 2006 as a research project for the National Institute of Mental Health, asked the following question: "Over the last 25 years, which figures have most influenced your practice?" The *Psychotherapy Networker* (*PN*), a journal for psychotherapists, reports:

> Perhaps the most surprising single finding was that in both the 1982 and the 2006 survey the single most influential psychotherapist—by a landslide—was Carl Rogers. In other words, the therapist who became famous for his leisurely, nondirective, open-ended, soft-focus form of therapy 50 years ago remains a major role model today.[29]

The journal adds:

> Virtually *all* therapists today are "Rogerian" in style, no matter what their clinical or theoretical orientation, or what they think of Carl Rogers. Does any clinician not subscribe, at least in part, to the holy trinity of Rogers's psychotherapeutic method: "unconditional

positive regard" or full acceptance of clients as they are; complete empathic understanding of clients, clearly communicated to them; and "congruence," or being authentic, genuine, and transparently "real" with clients?[30]

The *PN* quotes historian Christopher Lasch, who wrote *The Culture of Narcissism*, as saying: "As the founding father of humanistic psychology, the human potential movement, and the encounter group, Carl Rogers has a lot to answer for." The *PN* goes on to say:

> Lasch and other critics essentially accused Rogers of fomenting a runaway, nationwide cult of narcissism and irresponsible individualism, inventing and leading encounter groups that promoted sexual free-for-alls, undermining marriage and morality, and even causing nuns and priests—attending church-sponsored group sessions—to betray their vows (particularly celibacy) and flee the church in droves.[31]

Transparency in Groups

The 1960s saw the rise of the encounter movement based on theories and techniques of group dynamics. The encounter movement was a huge leap from private and personal unveilings in the confidentiality of the counselor's office to public undressings in front of as many others as happen to be in the group with questionable confidentiality. Many Christians participated in the encounter movement at the time and learned the various techniques that can be used to influence individuals and groups. The encounter movement encompasses many forms of group therapies and approaches, including but not limited to T-groups, awareness groups, sensitivity training, and Gestalt. These kinds of groups have general characteristics, activities, and individual variations, depending on the person promoting and leading the activities. Some groups, like the early encounter groups, glorify the dynamic present experience; others emphasize sharing both past and present weaknesses and hurts. These group movements find their roots in social psychology, psychological personality theories, psychotherapy, and other forms of counseling. While their popularity has appeared to rise and fall during the last fifty years and while many are called by different names, the beliefs and practices of group encounter continue to spread their leaven throughout counseling as they entice vulnerable individuals through explicit and implicit promises of personal benefits through expressing private thoughts and inner lives to others.

One of the basic assumptions of most encounter groups is that it is emotionally beneficial to be totally transparent and open. In other words, "let it all hang out," meaning to be completely candid and straightforward, saying whatever you want and condemning whomever you wish without any need to prove anything. Self-exposure has become a therapeutic absolute in the encounter movement and influences all that is said and done. If a person in an encounter group is opposed to or resistant to acting out and speaking out, the group pressures her "to go all the way." If she resists too much, she is rejected as up-tight, unreal, rigid, phony, and plastic.

Transparency leads to deceptive feelings of intimacy, especially when the sharing majors on personal struggles with temptations and behaviors the Bible would label as sin. Such exposure can be very enticing with its focus on self. It is like a big story-telling session about me, myself, and I and everyone else involved in my life. Experience and sharing biased stories engender emotional involvement in the group. And, in some groups sharing personal sins and the "sins" of others becomes a badge of membership.

Sharing personal struggles, hurts, and pain, typically received from others, brings acceptance, makes connection in the group very personal, and binds the group together on the basis of shared secrets. Group cohesiveness depends on the shared experience of "transparency" with accompanying emotions. As personal secrets are exposed, members become bound to one another in the kind of bondage whereby it would be difficult for someone to leave the group after having shared so much with so many.

Group transparency in sharing usually leads people to say personal things about other people who are not there to defend themselves. That often involves talebearing—spreading gossip, secrets, and biased impressions about others who are not present without any need to prove what is said. Any sharing that exposes sins, secrets, or private matters of others can usually be considered talebearing. Therefore, when the participants talk about others not present, they often reveal private matters amounting to talebearing, which is condemned in Scripture.

Women in Counseling

Even before the current counseling era and dating back to mesmerism and its mind cures, women were primarily the ones interested and the ones who participated the most. Fuller declares that **"mind cure appealed to women over men by a ratio of almost two to one"** (bold added). He explains, "Middle-class women in the late nineteenth century had much more leisure time and far fewer constructive outlets for their energies than did their male counterparts." Thus, according to Fuller, many women:

> … found themselves incapacitated by psychosomatic ailments. Mind cure provided a new outlet for their involuted energies. It got them out of their homes and

in touch with people who would listen sympatheti-
cally and then coax them into discovering interesting
new things about themselves.[32]

As we shall explain in chapters Four and Five, there are
significant, meaningful personal differences between women
and men. **Because of these personal differences, counseling is a female-friendly environment in which women
easily open themselves up to being transparent and conversational about the most private matters.**

Men in Counseling

Well, what about men? Aren't men to also be blamed for
this blabbing of private lives in the private offices of counselors? Initially the primary psychological theorists, therapists
and counselors were men. **Therefore, men are responsible
for having created this counseling mania, but women are
and have been the primary participants, thus fueling the
system.** Nevertheless, men generally shun being counselees.
Why? **Unless the man is in the role of counselor, counseling is a dysfunctional environment for men. While most
men would naturally avoid being counselees, they are
often compelled to become involved and to open themselves up to being transparent and conversational about
private matters they would not normally divulge in such
a setting.** More about this later.

The Rise of Biblical Counseling

The biblical counseling movement (BCM) began in
1970 with Dr. Jay Adams' book *Competent to Counsel*. We
were part of the BCM for years until we realized the sinful
problem-centered similarity between the BCM and the psychological counseling movement that preceded it. In fact, if
the psychological counseling movement did not exist, it is

doubtful that the BCM would exist in its present form. Many in the BCM have mimicked much of what is in the psychological counseling movement. The problem-centered format of biblical counseling mimics psychological counseling and mandates lifting the personal veil to private lives. **It is the problem-centeredness of both psychological and biblical counseling that is their most common egregious and serious fault as it inevitably involves personal transparency that leads to unbiblical evil speaking about others at the encouragement of the counselors.**

A Western Phenomenon

Problem-centered counseling and its penchant for sinful speaking is a Western phenomenon. Moskowitz reveals the contrast between "Americans' proclivity for the couch" and other contrasting nations world-wide. She says:

> Though we recognize the therapeutic gospel's grip on our culture, we have little idea how we came to this point. Perhaps this is because the therapeutic has snuck up on us. Perhaps it is because we are only dimly aware that America has not always been obsessed with the psyche. But our therapeutic faith is neither timeless nor universal. Our nation has not always been so preoccupied with personal dilemmas and emotional cures, nor are other nations so preoccupied today. The citizens of Asia, Africa, and Europe do not share Americans' proclivity for the couch. There are fewer psychological professionals in China, Israel, and Korea combined, for example, than there are sex and art therapists in America.[33]

Although corrupt-talk counseling is a Western activity, other countries are beginning to adopt it because of Western influence. While it is on the increase, there has been little of this counseling and public "undressing" in East Asian countries. One major reason it is almost non-existent there is because East Asians have typically **not** been **self-oriented**. They have typically been **we-oriented**, while Westerners are typically **me-centered**. Also, the culture and tradition of East Asians has been to regard the family as sacred. Therefore one would not blame family or parents for one's present life.

One specialist writing on "psychotherapy in Japan" refers to the "family's sacrosanct character" and the reluctance to blame "a parent or parent's role in a patient's neurosis or, especially, the ways in which a maternal figure may not be all-loving and good." The article says, "A Japanese, instead of investigating his past, romanticizes it: Instead of analyzing his early childhood, he creates fictions about it." The contrast to Western individualism is seen in the following: "Even for [Japanese] adults, expressions of individuality are often considered signs of selfish immaturity."[34]

This is changing for two major reasons. First, many East Asians attend American universities and learn about clinical psychology and psychotherapy, change their major, get their degree in it, and then go back to their own countries to teach in higher education institutions or go into private counseling practice. Second, American missionaries who are indoctrinated through their schooling or mission agencies promote the counseling mindset and the "American way" of communicating personal transparency about one's private life.

Many Latin American cultures also represent a contrast to the Western "me" culture. While there are some regional differences, Latin American cultures are generally "we" cultures. Mexican writer Octavio Paz describes this tendency:

> I am another when I am, my actions are more mine if they are also everyone's. So that I can exist I must

be the other, I must leave myself to look for myself among the others, those who would not exist if I did not, those who give me my own existence. I am not, there is no I, **always it is we**.[35] (Bold added.)

In comparing the aspect of collectivism/individualism between Spanish Speaking South Americans (SSSAs) and English Speaking North Americans (ESNAs), Skye Stephenson says that for SSSAs, "the opinions of others are often given significant weight in evaluating personal behavior and deciding upon appropriate actions" and that the "focus on others' opinions, especially for self-evaluation, is encouraged in most SSSAs from a very young age" and is shown in the way children are scolded.[36] **SSSAs are encouraged not to shame the group, while, in contrast, ESNAs are encouraged to follow their own personal beliefs.**

Geert and Gert Jan Hofdsted describe collectivism, in contrast to individualism, as "societies in which people from birth onward are integrated into strong, cohesive in-groups, which throughout people's lifetimes continue to protect them in exchange for unquestioning loyalty."[37] They say that "in a collectivist environment" family and group ties are very strong, "it is immoral *not* to treat one's in-group members better than others," and shaming is used to correct bad behavior because it makes the family or group look bad (italics theirs).[38] So we see a similarity to East Asian culture in many Latin American cultures where the group and family are sacred and where focusing on the self and condemning the group or family are discouraged. Without North American influence, such Latin American cultures are not naturally fertile territory for psychotherapy and counseling.

The Age of Show and Tell

There was a time in America during which private lives were private and public talk did not reveal the underbelly of human living. That time was prior to World War II. Since that time, counseling conversations, in which private lives are made semi-public (shared with a counselor who is to keep it all confidential), have been paralleled by the rising transparency of private lives becoming open to all, both personally and publicly. This public purging to purportedly purify a person was absent a little over sixty years ago and is not even found today in some segments of American society or in many other cultures as we have just shown. The therapeutic gospel was the catalyst that catapulted private lives into public display.

Showtime Silliness

In his book *Amusing Ourselves to Death: Public Discourse in the Age of Show Business*, author Neil Postman contrasts George Orwell's view of the future in *1984* with Aldous Huxley's *Brave New World*. In describing the current situation in America, Postman says that, rather than Orwells's prediction of Newspeak, where one thing is said in the guise of its opposite, what we are actually experiencing is Huxley's idea that, instead of misrepresenting lies as truth and visa versa, "All that has happened is that the public has adjusted to incoherence and been amused into indifference." Postman says of Huxley:

> He believed that it is far more likely that the Western democracies will dance and dream themselves into oblivion than march into it, single file and manacled. Huxley grasped, as Orwell did not, that it is not necessary to conceal anything from a public insensible to contradiction and narcoticized by technological

diversions. Although Huxley did not specify that television would be our main line to the drug, he would have no difficulty accepting Robert MacNeil's observation that "Television is the soma of Aldous Huxley's *Brave New World*." Big Brother [warned about by Orwell] turns out to be Howdy Doody.[39]

In other words, Huxley was right and Orwell was wrong in their predictions.

Postman also contrasts Orwell's view of a "Ministry of Truth" and "Big Brother" with Huxley's view and says:

> As Huxley more accurately foretold it, nothing so crude as all that is required. Seemingly benign technologies devoted to providing the populace with a politics of image, instancy and therapy may disappear history just as effectively, perhaps more permanently, and without objection. We ought also to look to Huxley, not Orwell, to understand the threat that television and other forms of imagery pose to the foundation of liberal democracy—namely, to freedom of information.[40]

In describing the historical evolution of reading and viewing, Postman says, "For countless Americans, seeing, not reading, became the basis for believing."[41]

How did America arrive at the post World War II psychological pandering to the show-time silliness and sinfulness of "baring one's bottom" in public? How did America move from the privacy of private lives to the attention-getting public proclamation of what used to be inviolate personal territory? How did America move from a legitimate journalism mentality to a tabloid journalism mindset that concentrates on sensational and lurid news, in which "the devil is in the details"?

The Age of Oprah

The prototype for the public purging of private personas was played out first through individuals in the confines of the counselor's office, then into group counseling, and finally into the public arena. There are many additional avenues one can pursue to answer the above questions. However, the most fertile area is that of the media and primarily television. In 1967 Phil Donahue moved his Dayton, Ohio, radio call-in show to local TV. *The Phil Donahue Show* "laid the foundation" for the tabloid television talk shows that would follow.[42] University professor Janice Peck describes the rise of this genre of tabloid talk show in her book *Age of Oprah*:

> Donahue made political and social issues a focus of his program. Bringing the studio and home audience into the discussion, he laid the foundation for a new genre of talk TV that violated convention by tackling political topics with a **primarily female audience** when it was widely assumed in the television industry that women had no interest in politics…. In 1973 Donahue moved to Chicago and went national. Blending his passion for politics, his **focus on female viewers' concerns**, and his instincts as an entertainer, he won a large, loyal audience and a reputation for being sympathetic to feminism.[43] (Bold added.)

Peck describes Oprah Winfrey's arrival on the scene by saying:

> When Winfrey was hired in 1984 to host *A.M. Chicago*, a half-hour program airing opposite Donahue's show, he was the undisputed ruler of daytime talk TV. Although Winfrey was initially nervous about competing head-to-head with the "titan of talk," her fears were quickly dispelled as she proceeded

to beat Donahue in the Chicago market within three months.[44]

Peck adds:

> In 1987, upon receiving the first of what would become many Emmy awards, she credited [Donahue] with demonstrating that "women have an interest in things that affect their lives, and not just how to stuff cabbage." Without his example, she said, "my show wouldn't be possible" (Adler 1997, 52). From the beginning, however, Winfrey differentiated herself from Donahue. In contrast to his more intellectual, journalistic, issues-oriented approach, she emphasized emotional intimacy, self-revelation, and her ability to identify with her female viewers' experiences.[45]

Peck further declares, "If Donahue was the architect of the fusion of public issues and private problems that came to define the genre, it was Winfrey who moved it fully into **therapeutic** territory" (bold added).[46]

Others followed Winfrey to the point that Vicki Abt, a researcher from Pennsylvania State University, declares:

> TV talk shows offer us a world of blurred boundaries. Cultural distinctions between public and private, credible and incredible witnesses, truth and falseness, good and evil, sickness and irresponsibility, normal and abnormal, therapy and exploitation, intimate and stranger, fragmentation and community are manipulated and erased for our distraction and entertainment.[47]

Just as counselors think that private details are necessary to help people, talk show hosts think they must bring out such sordid details to truly help both the guests and the audience. Abt says that the "need to educate and inform the audience is the voiced rationale for getting the so-called guests to give ever more titillating details of their misdeeds, or of the misdeeds done to them by family or friends (often not on the show)."[48]

Peck notes that guests "often find themselves revealing things they would not imagine telling anyone, much less a national TV audience. It is the talk show as group-therapy session."[49] Abt reveals one reason why guests on the shows are so willing and eager to reveal so much private information about their lives. She says:

> The underlying assumption—that most social pathology is the result of a medical problem beyond the control of the so-called "victim"— encourages, at least indirectly, people to come on to these shows confessing outrageous stories of anti-social behavior to millions of strangers. Rather than being mortified, ashamed, or trying to hide their stigma, "guests" willingly and eagerly discuss their child molesting, sexual quirks, and criminal records in an effort to seek "understanding" for their particular disease.[50]

It is revealing to see how what really goes on in psychotherapy and counseling is exposed on these talk shows. While these may look exaggerated on TV and less dramatic in the counseling room, the same undressing of private lives goes on with its talebearing about others and its varied exoneration of the one who bares it all. The prying and exposing on these shows are a reflection of the counseling room, and, depending on the types of counseling and the counselor, the reflection may not be too distorted after all. Add to this the following: "In the 'therapy talk show,' topics are cast in psychological terms, the majority of guest experts hail from some sector of the mental health industry, and solutions are framed within a self-help ethos."[51]

Moskowitz describes the extent to which Oprah promoted the therapeutic gospel by saying:

> With the help of representatives from the mental-health industry, Oprah preaches the therapeutic gospel. The show establishes the virtues of revelation and the sins of keeping secrets. Not only is talk cathartic but it cleanses the soul.[52]

Just as counseling and group therapy opened the door to therapy-style talk shows, the openness and public exposure of the talk shows further encourages people to think it's right and good to spill it all out and reveal whatever—the more bazaar, the better.

In her chapter "The Therapeutic Enterprise and the Quest for Women's Hearts and Minds," Peck reveals the popularity of the therapeutic mentality among women and how eagerly women are willing to bare their hearts and souls publicly and to open themselves up like Pandora's Box. This is quite pathetic. From the beginnings of psychotherapy and counseling, led by men, women were not only placed in an inferior, weak position, but were enticed to reveal themselves fully. After all, men were the primary psychological theorists and therapists and women were the primary clients from the very beginning. Peck says: "Assumptions about the natural basis of male power and independence and female dependence and weakness were firmly entrenched in the therapeutic professions by the mid-twentieth century." She further says:

> This obsession with women's psychological deficiencies was organized along two interrelated axes: women were charged with producing weak, dependent male offspring who grew into feminized men and, conversely, with valuing their own indepen-

dence over their family obligations and becoming masculinized women. [53]

She notes that the therapeutic enterprise has "progressively claimed a powerful grip on the hearts, minds, and bodies of women" and that "women are diagnosed as depressed by a rate of two to one over men." She adds:

> In the early 1980s, women comprised nearly two-thirds of adult clients of community mental health facilities, psychiatric hospitals, and outpatient clinics, and **an estimated 84 percent of private psychotherapy patients were female.** [54] (Bold added.)

Peck further notes that, from its inception and into the 1990s, "Winfrey's program was organized around the 'dysfunctional self' associated with the 'recovery movement,'" [55] with women assuming the imposed role of codependent enablers, struggling to change themselves and the members of their family and to find answers to their unhappiness. It's no wonder that women felt desperate and grateful to Winfrey for bringing their private lives out into the open. They believed her when she said such things as, "I ask this question not to pry in your business but to educate parents in our audience." [56] And, of course the more women saw this on their favorite daytime TV talk shows, the more acceptable it seemed for them to turn their lives into public exhibitions and to expose themselves and others in the counselor's office.

Excuse the mixed metaphor, but this historical and even hysterical transformation from privacy to personal publicity is like the proverbial "frog in the kettle" that ends up "cooking someone's goose." Gradually and unnoticeably the frog gets fried in the kettle and ends up "cooking" or ruining someone's hope for real help. In other words the gradualism from no talk to trash talk evolved slowly, but once it arrived

it countermanded the very hope for help that people originally had and the fallout affected the lives of those who were
verbally trashed.

Interestingly, Winfrey herself got out of the trash-talk
business and into a mix of New Age spirituality before
several well-known government leaders "joined forces
in their 'Empower America' campaign to rid the airwaves
of the 'cultural rot' of talk shows, which they charged had
'mainstreamed trashy behavior.'"[57] In fact in 1995, a year
after she began distancing herself from the "trash talk" TV,
Winfrey told *Redbook* magazine, "I cannot listen to other
people blaming their mothers for another year."[58] Nevertheless, counselors continue to listen to these kinds of things
as counselees shell out the money and expose whatever the
counselor seems to be looking for in hopes of solving problems, finding happiness, and gaining self-understanding.

All of this is done in the context of unrestrained self-
revelation while publicly and verbally trashing others. Both
verbal self-flagellation and feisty flogging of others by
guests egged on by the media moguls became sucked up by
the primarily female audiences, eager to see a fleshly verbal
fist fight, like spectators at a modern day coliseum gladia-
tor-like "duel to the death" with evil speaking participants.
Likewise, in the private counselor's office everything said
about self and others can be brutal and requires no proof.
The public proclamation of television tabloid talk about others likewise became the standard to such an extent that the
group of popular media productions majoring in this miserable miasma became known as the "trash pack." These two
concomitant movements in America, counseling and TV talk
shows that expose private lives, have succeeded and been
popular primarily because of women. **While women are not
entirely to blame for the rise of trash talk, they have certainly led the way and thus are primarily responsible**

Publicizing Private Lives Online

Publicizing one's own private life is now open to every person who has access to a computer. Search mechanisms such as Google and Yahoo enable people to search and find almost anything they want publicly displayed for anyone to see. Not only can people find nearly everything; they themselves can post nearly whatever they want by creating their own web pages, developing blogs, and using sites such as Twitter and any of the various social networking sites like Facebook and MySpace. All one has to do is sign up on a social networking site, present oneself exactly as one pleases through photos and self-descriptions, and publicize one's own private thoughts, activities, and emotions. To further the possibilities of publicizing their private lives, individuals can post videos for public consumption on such sites as YouTube, which is very popular with an estimated ten percent of all Internet traffic going to that site.

Various sites provide opportunities for everyone to be the center of attention and the star of their own show through written messages and shared photos. People may choose to what extent they want to reveal themselves and within their self-revelation may come sinful communication about other people who may be problems in their life. For some people, the social networking sites are simply used for "Friends" (people who have permission to interact on a person's page) to keep in touch. For others these sites serve the therapeutic gospel as people openly share their problems in such a way as to appear to be the innocent victims while casting a bad light on the deeds of others who are not Friends in the network. They obtain sympathy and support from any number of Friends. However, if any criticism is posted, the owner of the page may quickly erase it and cast aspersion on the Friend who did not act like a "Friend." In fact, when people do not conform to the expectations of others they can be

"defriended." Or individuals may no longer want to participate on someone's Facebook page because of what is posted
and end up doing the defriending. As one person describes
the process, "On Facebook, that person you barely know or
no longer can put up with is there, all the time, taking up
space on your home page, filling you in on all the mindless
minutiae."[59] Worse than that would be talebearing and evil
speaking about others on the site. Unfortunately, for some
people being defriended can be very emotionally upsetting
as if they themselves have been rejected rather than just their
Facebook page.

People can post or withhold whatever personal information desired, and, although the companies providing these
social networks have staff to monitor the content, some
obscene verbal and visual material comes through. However, some people may not realize just how public their own
private space may be on the Internet. Even when they use
what is called an "avatar," which is the "incarnation of one's
personality in the digital world," or some other form of anonymity by using screen names (other than their own legal
names) and personal passwords, they may be "unmasked by
tracing IP addresses and other identifiers through the Internet."[60] In fact, because of such public exposure of personal
privacy, Dr. Kent Norman of the University of Maryland
says:

> It is recommended that cyberspace designers con-
> vey a greater sense that one is in a public space, that
> one's behavior is in full view of the whole world, and
> that one should take personal responsibility for one's
> words and actions.[61]

It has been reported that many divorce petitions referred to
Facebook, especially when spouses found out about a part-

ner's flirty messages, explicit sexual chats, and badmouthing them to others.[62]

In a society that is "becoming increasingly exhibitionistic…the Internet has witnessed, under the cloak of anonymity, a flood of episodes of self-exposure and public confession in blogs and vlogs" (video logs such as YouTube).[63] **Thus the Internet provides the penultimate of the publicizing of private lives and serves as an ever expanding setting for expressions of the Jeremiah 17:9 syndrome (described in the next chapter) with an audience which may be far beyond the environs of one's own networking circle.**

Conclusion

We have now sketched two tandem and complementary streams of events having to do **first** with the rise of psychotherapy in America with its private lives openly talked about in a private office with a counselor and **second** with the public confession of private lives to whomever, whatever, and whenever. **The publicizing of private lives is umbilically tied to the psychologizing of the American public and began primarily by corrupting the strengths and virtues of women as a conduit through which private lives became publicly exposed and emotively displayed.** Peck says:

> Epstein and Steinberg suggest that therapy, as a "language of self and interpersonal relationships, and even as a way of life," had become so pervasive in late-twentieth-century American culture "that it is virtually impossible to live in the United States without being interpellated into the therapeutic experience in some way."[64]

These kinds of talk shows should be renamed as "therapy talk shows" because that is what they are. Such talk show conversations, almost regardless of the topic, are framed in the psychotherapeutic ethos of the current culture.

The United States has privately and publicly become a therapeutic society where private and public trash talk, which was first led by men counselors and later mainly by women counselors, was primarily fueled by female inclinations and interests. These new private and public personas for women have overshadowed traditional women's roles. Men are being cajoled or cudgeled into the counselor's office in greater numbers than ever before, and in the process they are being brainwashed to think womanly thoughts and to learn that, to save their marriages and salvage their other relationships, they "have to become a woman."[65] **If women were not in counseling as counselees, the men would not be there and the whole counseling mania would disintegrate.** As to the public puffery of the privacy of personal lives by women, men were later enticed to join the melee of media voices, but to this day the public undressing of private lives is female friendly territory and a dysfunctional environment for traditional men. However, the online era has dramatically expanded such therapeutic interchanges to include men in the social networking and the public exposure of private lives and appears to be the penultimate era prior to the Lord's return. **While these streams of discourse have seriously affected the church, we will primarily pursue the curse of problem-centered counseling and the reasons why it should be stopped.**

2

The Heart Is Deceitful

But we are all as an unclean thing, and all our righteousnesses are as filthy rags; and we all do fade as a leaf; and our iniquities, like the wind, have taken us away.

Isaiah 64:6

The sinfulness of mankind has been an undeniable plague upon the earth from the first bite of the forbidden fruit. Rebellion against the Creator has replicated itself throughout the progeny so that "There is none righteous, no, not one…. For all have sinned, and come short of the glory of God" (Romans 3:10, 23). The verdict is in; the judgment is true. Each and every person is a sinner. The only exception is the Lord Jesus Christ, who came to save mankind from the condemnation, power, and eternal results of this putrid condition. The evil and ugliness of sin are obvious when there is bloodshed, destruction, gross injustice, widespread misery, and wartime horrors. Conversely, sin may not appear utterly sinful in the average "nice" person, but it is there lurking beneath the surface and emerging in thoughts, words, attitudes, and actions.

The reason we emphasize this ugly fact regarding the sinful nature of humans is **because no one in the counseling room is free of this evil**. Whenever two or more people meet together, even for seemingly good purposes, they are sinners in the nature of their being. Yes, they may be saved sinners who have a new life and the imputed righteousness of Christ, but even saved sinners are not free of sin, because sin yet dwells in what the Bible refers to as the "flesh," the very nature of the "the old man, which is corrupt according to the deceitful lusts" (Eph. 4:22). Furthermore, if we deny that we are sinners, we are deceiving ourselves (1 John 1:10). Even though biblical counselors may attempt to remove the "logs" from their own eyes before examining the "mote" in their counselees' eyes (Matt. 7:3), they are nevertheless more vulnerable than they realize to their own sinfulness, especially in the process of listening to and participating in the ensuing sinful communication endemic in problem-centered counseling.

Sin is within every individual and therefore it behooves each one of us to recognize this menace, even in its most seemingly benign, form—just a little selfishness here, just a bit of anger there, just a touch of malice, a bit of resentment, or a streak of bitterness nagging away at the soul (Eph. 4:31). Not only must we recognize our sin to repent and turn to God; we must understand how rebellious we are when we operate according to the old ways of the flesh wherein "the carnal mind is enmity against God" (Romans 8:7). In the counseling room much of the conversation has to do with the alleged sins of people who are not there. Even when counselees talk about their own faults and sins, there always seem to be extenuating circumstances to explain away or relieve the guilt. While counseling may appear helpful, it is often superficial and unhelpful. Talking about problems with a counselor may not only be superficial; it is often downright sinful.

The Deceitful Heart

People have learned throughout this counseling era that the counselee is free to say all sorts of evil things about other people. (See Chapter One.) Jesus was very clear about the source of sinful communication. It is the heart, the inner man.

> But those things which proceed out of the mouth come forth from the heart; and they defile the man. For out of the heart proceed evil thoughts, murders, adulteries, fornications, thefts, false witness, blasphemies: These are the things which defile a man: but to eat with unwashen hands defileth not a man (Matt. 15:18-20).

The heart is the issue. The heart (the inner person) is the source of evil thoughts that lead to evil actions and words. It is so deceitful that only God truly knows anyone's heart. He alone is able to reveal the contents of one's own heart through the Holy Spirit and the Word.

> The heart is deceitful above all things, and desperately wicked: who can know it? I the LORD search the heart, I try the reins, even to give every man according to his ways, and according to the fruit of his doings (Jeremiah 17:9-10).

Matthew Poole in his commentary says that the deceitful heart is "unsearchable by others, *deceitful* with reference to ourselves, and abominably wicked so that neither can a man know his own heart, neither can any other know our hearts" (italics his; bold added). [1] Regarding the Lord searching the heart, Poole says:

Lest these hypocrites should pretend that their hearts were not departed from God, or should say, Who then can judge us if none knoweth the Heart? saith God, **Though no creature knoweth the heart of another fellow creature**, yet I know the hearts of all creatures, I search the secret thoughts and counsels and designs of all my creatures; for I will judge them according to their thoughts and the secret motions and affections of their souls, according to all their ways, and the fruit of their doings. You cannot therefore mock me, and tell me your hearts are not departed from me.[2] (Bold added.)

Poole's exegesis of these two verses is consistent with all the commentators we read.

The Deceitful Heart
and the Christian in Counseling

But what about a person who has been born again and has been given new life in Christ? Can a Christian have a deceitful heart? Indeed, every true believer in Christ has been given new life and has the indwelling Holy Spirit. However, there is an ongoing, relentless spiritual battle raging between the flesh and the Spirit, between the old order of the natural man under the ruler of darkness (Eph. 2:2-3) and the new man in Christ with the power of the Holy Spirit and the Word of God. Galatians 5:17 tells us that "the flesh lusteth against the Spirit, and the Spirit against the flesh: and these are contrary the one to the other." Since the deceitful heart resides in the natural man, it continues on and becomes active as soon as one begins thinking or acting according to the flesh rather than the Spirit. In fact, as soon as a believer entertains sinful thoughts, the deceptive heart has already become active. Thus, **one can see that the deceptive heart is very active**

during counseling conversations as counselees describe situations, speak evil of others, and justify self, and as counselors enable such talk in an effort to help their counselees. The deceptive heart is active in both psychological counseling and in what is called "biblical counseling"; it is active in the counselors as well as in the counselees; and it becomes active in Christians because of the very nature of problem-centered counseling. Thus, even while attempting to fix the inner man through counseling, the deceptive heart is activated and deceives both counselor and counselee. The more the deceptive heart is given free rein, the more the flesh is empowered.

Jeremiah 17:9-10 and many other Scripture verses give the reasons why we are against problem-centered counseling. What we reveal in this chapter alone should be a wakeup call to those who counsel. Those who minister to fellow believers should not cross biblical lines set down by God in Scripture in their efforts to help those with problems of living. The fleshly, unbiblical activity involved in problem-centered counseling cannot be justified, no matter the amount of Scripture used.

The Jeremiah 17:9 Syndrome

The dictionary defines a *syndrome* as "a predictable, characteristic pattern of behavior, action, etc., that tends to occur under certain circumstances."[3] What we call the "Jeremiah 17:9 syndrome" is a pattern of behavior found in the circumstances of counseling. **The Jeremiah 17:9 syndrome functions much like a kangaroo court** (trial), which is described as follows:

> The colloquial phrase "kangaroo court" is used to describe judicial proceedings that deny due process rights in the name of expediency. Such rights include

the right to summon witnesses, the right of cross-examination, the right not to incriminate oneself, the right not to be tried on secret evidence, the right to control one's own defense, the right to exclude evidence that is improperly obtained, irrelevant or inherently inadmissible, e.g., hearsay, the right to exclude judges or jurors on the grounds of partiality or conflict of interest, and the right of appeal.[4]

For example, in a regular courtroom there is what is called the "hearsay rule." *Hearsay* is defined as "unverified, unofficial information gained or acquired from another and not part of one's direct knowledge … an item of idle or unverified information or gossip; rumor."[5] *Rule* is defined as "a principle or regulation governing conduct, action, procedure, arrangement, etc."[6] The *hearsay rule* is "the rule making hearsay evidence inadmissible."[7]

In most cases, because the counselee appears by herself, the others to whom she refers are not present to contradict or disagree with what is said. While the counselee may at times have direct knowledge of which she speaks, at other times it is indirect and unverified information, making it hearsay. Moreover, as a counselee describes people and situations, the counselor generally receives and believes what is said about others without cross-examination or proof.

Self-Love

The Jeremiah 17:9 syndrome expressed in sinful self-love is described in the last days' phenomena. The apostle Paul describes evidences of the last days in stark terms, which actually describe the deceptive heart in action:

> This know also, that in the last days perilous times shall come. For men shall be lovers of their own selves, covetous, boasters, proud, blasphemers, dis-

obedient to parents, unthankful, unholy, without natural affection, trucebreakers, false accusers, incontinent, fierce, despisers of those that are good, traitors, heady, highminded, lovers of pleasures more than lovers of God; having a form of godliness, but denying the power thereof: from such turn away. For of this sort are they which creep into houses, and lead captive silly women laden with sins, led away with divers lusts, ever learning, and never able to come to the knowledge of the truth (2 Tim. 3:1-7).

Ever since the fall, mankind has naturally loved, worshipped, and served self more than God and others, but in these last days self-love is amplified.

The following is excerpted from *Matthew Henry's Commentary on the Whole Bible* regarding 2 Timothy3:1-7:

Observe, Self-love brings in a long train of sins and mischiefs. When men are lovers of themselves, no good can be expected from them, as all good may be expected from those who love God with all their hearts. When covetousness generally prevails, when every man is for what he can get and for keeping what he has, this makes men dangerous to one another, and obliges every man to stand on his guard against his neighbor…. When children are disobedient to their parents, and break through the obligations which they lie under to them both in duty and gratitude ... they make the times perilous; for what wickedness will those stick at who will be abusive to their own parents and rebel against them?... And those who will not be bound by natural affection, no marvel that they will not be bound by the most solemn leagues and covenants.... Men may be very bad and wicked under a profession of religion; they may be lovers of themselves, etc., yet have a form of godliness.[8]

The full brunt of Paul's description of the natural man with a deceptive heart can be seen in counseling since problem-centered counseling is fertile territory for self-love to be expressed with all of its sinful possibilities. Because the focus is on the counselees and their problems, the very practice of counseling both stimulates and appeals to the flesh where unbiblical **ingratitude and complaining** are common fare (2 Tim. 3:2; Jude 1:16). As counselees describe personal problems, feelings, and private matters and as the counselors glean as much information as possible, the deceptive heart of both will be activated.

Evil Speaking

The Jeremiah 17:9 syndrome is expressed in evil speaking as counselees engage in talebearing, speaking ill of others, dishonoring parents as they complain about them, revealing confidences, speaking despairingly of people, telling unsubstantiated stories (gossip), and making rude and disparaging comments. Ephesians 4:31 says: "Let all bitterness, and wrath, and anger, and clamour, and **evil speaking**, be put away from you, with all malice." Notice how evil speaking is connected with bitterness, wrath, anger, and malice, which are all conditions of an evil and deceptive heart. Problem-centered counseling involves evil thinking and speaking. which begin in the heart and mind, are further expressed in counseling, and are further magnified in the thinking. As soon as someone says something evil about someone else, that person justifies having done so by remembering and even exaggerating the other person's faults. Such sinful communication is contrary to the Word of God and further damages relationships.

Evil speaking as a major component of counseling violates Scripture. In his commentary on Ephesians, Francis Foulkes says, "Evil speaking translates the Greek *blasphēmia*, a word often used in the Bible for speaking against God, but also common for slanderous or abusive speaking against one's fellow men."[9] Gordon Clark concurs by saying that "the Greek word *blasphēmia* means speaking evil of anyone."[10] Other commentaries refer to evil speaking as: "slander, backbiting, angry expressions, tale-bearing, reproaches, etc."[11]; "blasphemy, that is, injurious speaking—words which tend to hurt those of whom or against whom they are spoken"[12]; "insulting language, slander, abusive speech."[13] Also the term translated "blasphemy" in the New Testament refers to speaking evil about God **and speaking in such a way as to devalue another person** (see 1 Cor. 10:30 in reference to Paul being evil spoken of). Evil speaking is sinful speaking and includes talebearing (Proverbs 11:13; 18:8; 26:20; 1 Tim. 5:13). The dictionary defines a talebearer as "a person who spreads gossip, secrets, etc., that may cause trouble or harm."[14]

Evil speaking is especially egregious when talking about one's spouse or parents. **Speaking ill of one's spouse** is evil communication where the husband is not loving the wife as himself and the wife is not honoring the husband (Eph. 5:22-33; Col. 3:18-19). **Dishonoring parents** includes speaking ill of parents behind their backs (Eph. 6:1-2; Ex. 20:12). This includes **blaming the past**, which we discuss later and has become standard fare in counseling. Much of this originated with Freud, who taught that the first five years of a person's life determines the rest of the life through a powerful, hidden realm that he identified as the "unconscious." This includes blaming parents by seeing one's upbringing as the reason for present problems.

We must further add that, in addition to each person having a deceitful heart when remembering past incidents, the further back into the past one goes, the more untrustworthy the memory, and even the most trustworthy memory is subject to later interpretation. Certain memories may seem more significant when a person is older. Research on memory has revealed that each time a person remembers an event one tends to fill in details that are missing. Furthermore, external circumstances and intervening events may further distort the memory. In fact, some regressive counseling has led to horrific pseudo memories created through both external suggestion and internal imagination. This kind of counseling has created a most horrible form of the kangaroo court where family members have been accused of all sorts of abuse that never happened. As a result families have been torn apart, hearts have been broken, and lives shattered.

Mote and Beam

The Jeremiah 17:9 syndrome expressed in self-bias is at work in the counseling office as people minimize their own culpability and cast blame on others, contrary to Jesus' warnings about the mote and the beam. Whether one comes alone or as a couple, this is a prime environment for judging others and exonerating self:

> Judge not, that ye be not judged. For with what judgment ye judge, ye shall be judged: and with what measure ye mete, it shall be measured to you again. And why beholdest thou the mote that is in thy brother's eye, but considerest not the beam that is in thine own eye? Or how wilt thou say to thy brother, Let me pull out the mote out of thine eye; and, behold, a beam *is* in thine own eye? Thou hypocrite, first cast out the beam out of thine own eye; and then shalt thou see

clearly to cast out the mote out of thy brother's eye (Matt. 7:1-5; see also Luke 6:41-42).

The Jeremiah 17:9 syndrome leaves a wide open field in counseling for exercising the tendency to blame others and protect and justify self. There is a natural failure to recognize one's own sinful heart for what it is—like a "beam" rather than just a "mote" at most.

Victim Mentality

The Jeremiah 17:9 syndrome also shows itself in a victim mentality as the deceptive heart has opportunities to say things that magnify what others have done wrong and minimize or ignore ones' own sinful thoughts, words, and actions. Quite often counseling will support a victim stance even though biblical counselors will sometimes be confrontational regarding what they suppose might be the problem. People play the victim because of a **failure to admit and confess one's own sins** and sinful condition (Isaiah 53:5-6; Matt. 15:17-20; Romans 3:10, 23; Rom. 7:5; Eph. 4:22). **Blaming circumstances and others** began in the Garden of Eden and continues on through problem-centered counseling. Even though biblical counselors speak out against "blame shifting," they nevertheless allow blaming in the form of "reasons why" or reasons behind a particular behavior (Gen. 3:12-13; 1 Sam. 15:14-15; 2 Tim. 3:3).

The self-made victim mentality is allowed and even supported as the counselor asks for more details and as the person tells the story from a victimhood stance, shifting blame from self to others. Dr. Tana Dineen, a licensed psychological counselor who is critical of her profession, has written an entire book showing how psychological counseling actually manufactures victims. She titled her book *Manufacturing Victims: What the Psychology Industry Is Doing to People.*

Because so much of what is called biblical counseling is a reflection of psychological problem-centered counseling, the biblical counseling movement also manufactures victims. When people are encouraged to talk sinfully about their problems they easily assume a victim mentality. When counselees see themselves as victims rather than sinners, they act as hypocrites, complaining about the other person's "beam" and excusing and minimizing their poor little "mote." As we have said in our other writings, there are true victims, but even they do themselves a disservice when they take on a victim mentality and live accordingly.

"A Mind of Its Own"

We have six college degrees, including a doctorate, between the two of us and have read tons of research from psychology and sociology. We have found that unbiased science will unbiasedly support and illustrate, but not add to the truth of Scripture. In that vein we often reveal the scientific research that reflects what Scripture already says. Any truly scientific enquiry into the human heart, even by atheists, will find that it is "deceitful above all things, and desperately wicked." A number of research studies about the mind and behavior give evidence of the general condition of the heart of man as does Scripture. Even though these researchers may identify the inner person as the "brain/mind," one can see that they are describing what Scripture calls the "deceitful heart." Their description of the "brain/mind" is an apt illustration of the Jeremiah 17:9 syndrome.

Our first such offering is from Dr. Cordelia Fine's book *A Mind of Its Own; How Your Brain Distorts and Deceives*, which is described as "a delightfully unsparing look into what your brain is doing behind your back." If you simply substitute the words "deceptive heart" for "brain" and "mind" in the following description of the book, you will see exactly what goes on during counseling conversations:

> Exposing the mind's deceptions and exploring how the mind defends and glorifies the ego, Dr. Fine illustrates the brain's tendency toward self-delusion. Unbeknownst to us, our brain … pushes, pulls, twists, and warps our perceptions. Whether it be hindsight bias, wishful thinking, unrealistic optimism, or moral excuse-making, each of us has a slew of mind-bugs and ordinary prejudices that prevent us from seeing the truth about the world, the people around us, and ourselves. With fascinating studies to support her arguments, Dr. Fine takes us on an insightful, rip-roaringly funny tour through the brain you never knew you had.[15]

Fine offers scientific research and the book is generously footnoted to the original sources of her references. In her understanding of the inner man, Fine attributes all of this deception to the brain, rather than what Scripture calls the "heart." However, her descriptions truly fit the deceitful heart of "the old man, which is corrupt according to the deceitful lusts" (Eph. 4:22). She says in her introduction:

> But the truth of the matter—as revealed by the quite extraordinary and fascinating research described in this book—is that your unscrupulous brain is entirely undeserving of your confidence. It has some shifty habits that leave the truth distorted and dis-guised. Your brain is vainglorious. It's emotional and immoral. It deludes you. It is pigheaded, secretive, and weak-willed. Oh, and it's also a bigot. This is more than a minor inconvenience. That fleshy walnut inside your skull is all you have to know yourself and to know the world. Yet, thanks to the masquerading

of an untrustworthy brain with a mind of its own, much of what you think you know is not quite as it seems.[16]

In her first chapter titled "The Vain Brain," Fine talks about:

The vain brain that excuses your faults and failures, or simply rewrites them out of history. The vain brain that sets you up on a pedestal above your peers. The vain brain that misguidedly thinks you invincible, invulnerable, and omnipotent.[17]

Fine reveals other failings and foibles of the mind such as the "self-serving bias"[18] and says, "Failure is perhaps the greatest enemy of the ego."[19] She refers to "retroactive pessimism" which "makes failure easier to digest." Fine explains how, "In self-handicapping, the brain makes sure that it has a nonthreatening excuse for failure, should it occur."[20]

Based upon the research, Fine says, "Memory is one of the ego's greatest allies."[21] She makes several comments with respect to memory as follows: "It seems that it is easier for a camel to pass through the eye of a needle than for negative feedback to enter the kingdom of memory" and "Not only does memory collude with the brain in the information that it lets in but, as you might begin to fear, it also controls the information it lets out."[22]

In spite of Fine blaming the brain, she certainly describes the multi-faceted inner man, the heart, which is "deceitful above all things, and desperately wicked" (Jeremiah 17:9). As we have shown above, one of the major errors of problem-centered counseling is that it activates this deceptive heart. Counselees describe everything from their own biased, self-protective, self-justifying, and self-excusing perspective. Counselors, in the role of so-called experts, hear and respond to what is said from their own biased, self-serving, self-enhancing, self-excusing, self-aggrandizing, and even self-protective perspective. **When a counselor and counselee meet together to talk about the counselee's problems there are plenty of opportunities for deceptive hearts to take over.** The deceptive heart of counselees very easily equates with the "vain brain that excuses your faults and failures, or simply rewrites them out of history," and the deceptive heart of counselors very easily equates to the "vain brain that sets you up on a pedestal above your peers."

Self Justification

Mistakes Were Made (but not by me): Why We Justify Foolish Beliefs, Bad Decisions, and Hurtful Acts, a secular book authored by Dr. Carol Tavris and Dr. Elliot Aronson, illustrates how evil and desperately wicked the heart is with respect to self justification for even the most evil acts and to how people practice "**confirmational bias.**"[23] Confirmational bias occurs when people seek evidence that confirms their opinions or supports the decisions they make, while ignoring other contradictory information. Confirmational bias is often further strengthened when one's viewpoint is threatened. Because of confirmational bias, evidence to the contrary of one's viewpoint often causes individuals to hang on to their own perspective, position, or belief more vigorously and more emotionally. This is called "belief polarization" or "attitude polarization." One study from Stanford University states:

> People who hold strong opinions on complex social issues are likely to examine relevant empirical evidence in a biased manner. They are apt to accept "confirming" evidence at face value while subjecting "discontinuing" evidence to critical evaluation, and as a result to draw undue support for their initial

positions from mixed or random empirical findings. Thus, the result of exposing contending factions in a social dispute to an identical body of relevant empirical evidence may be not a narrowing of disagreement but rather an increase in polarization.[24]

At the conclusion of the study, the authors say:

> As predicted, both proponents and opponents of capital punishment rated those results and procedures that confirmed their own beliefs to be the more convincing and probative ones, and they reported corresponding shifts in their beliefs as the various results and procedures were presented. The net effect of such evaluations and opinion shifts was the postulated increase in attitude polarization.[25]

Confirmational bias accompanied by belief or attitude polarization is one reason why even the most cogent arguments and quiet logic fail when individuals are emotionally attached to their point of view. It is also the reason why marriage counseling often moves spouses further from one another rather than bringing them to a point of confession, forgiveness, and reconciliation. Read the cases in counseling books and you will see how the Jeremiah 17:9 syndrome plays out. **It is rare to find a person who will take responsibility for the problem without any confirmational bias or attitude-belief polarization, which comes from the flesh.** This is one more reason not to be involved in counseling.

Mistakes Were Made begins with a quote from George Orwell:

> We are all capable of believing things which we know to be untrue, and then, when we are finally proved wrong, impudently twisting the facts so as to show that we were right. Intellectually, it is possible to

carry on this process for an indefinite time: the only check on it is that sooner or later a false belief bumps up against solid reality, usually on a battlefield.[26]

According to the jacket cover, *Mistakes Were Made* is "backed by years of research." It is heavily footnoted to the writings and research of those upon whom the conclusions of the book are based. The authors are both distinguished researchers and writers. They begin their book by saying:

> As fallible human beings, all of us share the impulse to justify ourselves and avoid taking responsibility for any actions that turn out to be harmful, immoral, or stupid…. **Most people, when directly confronted by evidence that they are wrong, do not change their point of view or course of action but justify it even more tenaciously. Even irrefutable evidence is rarely enough to pierce the mental armor of self-justification.**[27] (Bold added.)

They also say:

> Self-justification is more powerful and more dangerous than the explicit lie. It allows people to convince themselves that what they did was the best thing they could have done. In fact, come to think of it, it was the right thing.[28]

In explaining self-justification the authors say:

> The engine that drives self-justification, the energy that produces the need to justify our actions and decisions—especially the wrong ones—is an unpleasant feeling that [Leon] Festinger called "cognitive dissonance." Cognitive dissonance is a state of tension that occurs whenever a person holds two cognitions (ideas, attitudes, beliefs, opinions) that are psychologically inconsistent…. Dissonance is disquieting

because to hold two ideas that contradict each other is to flirt with absurdity.[29]

The authors add:

Dissonance is uncomfortable enough when two cognitions conflict, but it is most painful when an important element of the self-concept is threatened: for example, when information challenges how we see ourselves, challenges a central belief (religious, political, or intellectual), or questions a memory or story we use to explain our lives.[30]

In their book they explain:

So powerful is the need for consonance that when people are forced to look at disconfirming evidence, they will find a way to criticize, distort, or dismiss it so that they can maintain or even strengthen their existing belief. This mental contortion is called the "confirmation bias."[31]

Elsewhere the authors explain "conformational bias" as "the fact that we tend to notice and remember information that confirms what we believe and ignore or forget information that disconfirms it.... Another central bias is the belief that we aren't biased, everyone else is."[32] They also discuss how there is a self-serving bias even in one's memory. They say:

Now, between the conscious lie to fool others and unconscious self-justification to fool ourselves lies a fascinating gray area, patrolled by that unreliable, self-serving historian—memory. Memories are often pruned and shaped by an ego-enhancing bias that blurs the edges of past events, softens culpability, and distorts what really happened.[33]

While Tavris and Aronson are not condemning psychotherapy, they do say:

> Moreover, by its very nature, psychotherapy is a pri-
> vate transaction between the therapist and the client.
> No one is looking over the therapist's shoulder in the
> intimacy of the consulting room, eager to pounce if
> he or she does something wrong. Yet the inherent
> privacy of the transaction means that therapists who
> lack training in science and skepticism have no inter-
> nal corrections to the self-protecting cognitive biases
> that afflict us all. What these therapists see confirms
> what they believe, and what they believe shapes what
> they see. It's a closed loop. Did my client improve?
> Excellent; what I did was effective. Did my client
> remain unchanged or get worse? That's unfortunate,
> but she *is* resistant to therapy and deeply troubled;
> besides, sometimes the client has to get worse before
> she can get better.[34] (Emphasis theirs.)

While Tavris and Aronson are describing secular counseling,
the very same thing happens in biblical counseling. And, no
matter who conducts the therapy, "lack of training in science
and skepticism" will **not** prevent "the self-protecting cognitive biases that afflict us all."

Conclusion

Counselees sometimes feel better after counseling
because they have expressed their thoughts and feelings with
a person who is sympathetic and supportive, especially when
they come alone. Quite often people will say that it is good
for people to express themselves, "to get it off their chest," so
to speak. (See Chapter Four to the contrary.) However, when
people do this they are actually telling a carefully edited
story, leaving out parts that may present quite a different per-

spective and emphasizing their own good efforts. They may actually be justifying themselves, minimizing their own sinful words and actions, and casting blame on others (directly or indirectly) in order to relieve themselves from uncomfortable guilt feelings. Then, when counselors listen with rapt attention to every detail and ask questions along the way, the counselees feel that they have been heard and that their story is worthy of a hearing. Counselors do not find out "the rest of the story." In fact, in all the cases with which we are familiar over the years, we cannot point to one where this has happened. And, even if a biblical counselor confronts sin in a counselee, there will have been enough conversation during the course of counseling to provide enough excuse, reason, or justification to alleviate full culpability.

As we will demonstrate in the next chapter, problem-centered biblical counseling generally involves the Jeremiah 17:9 syndrome, which includes functioning like a kangaroo court with the hearsay "evidence," self love expressed through what is said, mote and beam responses in regard to relationships, and a victimhood mentality. **At least one of the following occurs through the Jeremiah 17:9 syndrome: skewing the story through self-bias, excusing and justifying self, complaining and being unthankful, speaking ill of others, blaming the past, dishonoring parents and/or spouse, and playing the victim, each of which is sinful.** Since sinful thoughts, words, and actions indicate that the deceitful heart is at work, a great deal of deception goes on in counseling.

People may undergo months of counseling and even feel that they are improving simply because the sympathy and support appeals to their deceptive heart. Counselors may counsel on and on and think they are helping people simply because their own deceptive heart tells them so. While counselors may truly desire to be helpful and may not be creeping into houses (2 Tim. 3:6), they may indeed be leading captive women (the prime counselees) astray through problem-centered counseling. Furthermore, as they talk sinfully about problems, both the counselor and the counselee may be "ever learning, and never able to come to the knowledge of the truth" (2 Tim. 3:7). As long as the counseling is problem-centered, the flesh will exert itself and the participants will be further deceived. As long as counseling fosters the Jeremiah 17:9 syndrome and its results, it will rob believers of opportunities for true spiritual growth. **Since the counselors are doing the counseling, they are responsible for fostering the Jeremiah 17:9 syndrome and its results.**

3

Problem-Centered Biblical Counseling

And the tongue is a fire, a world of iniquity: so is the tongue among our members, that it defileth the whole body, and setteth on fire the course of nature; and it is set on fire of hell. **James 3:6.**

The Jeremiah 17:9 syndrome contaminates problem-centered counseling. It is a myth that problem-centered biblical counseling does not violate Scripture. The counselee has free rein to talk about the sins of others not present, including unsubstantiated talebearing and hearsay, without being contradicted. Counselees inevitably skew their stories from their self-protective perspective, which is generally filled with much hearsay, gossip, and self-bias revealing a deceptive heart. In addition, the counselor's flesh can also be activated in a number of ways, particularly in the area of pride.

Because of the problem-centered nature of most counseling, the counselor will ask questions to find out what the problems are and then ask further questions for clarification and detail. **Considering that the counselor is directing**

the conversation through his questions, he is truly the instigator and enabler of the sinful communication. That does not excuse the participating counselees who are ready and eager to speak their minds (generally filled with sinful thoughts when one considers what is said). **Counselors precipitate the sinful expressions of the Jeremiah 17:9 syndrome as they lead counselees into sinning with their tongues.**

The three popular approaches about which we know the most are represented by the National Association of Nouthetic Counselors (NANC), the Christian Counseling and Educational Foundation (CCEF), and the Biblical Counseling Foundation (BCF). To show how the Jeremiah 17:9 syndrome plays out, we will quote from a video of a contrived counseling session, which has been enacted **to demonstrate how nouthetic counseling should ideally work.** Following this we will show how the Jeremiah 17:9 syndrome works in the idols-of-the-heart counseling, which is characteristic of those at CCEF. Thirdly we will reveal how those at BCF function. **We will show how the counselor precipitates the evil speaking, how he probes the counselees, how he expects them to speak the way they do, and how they cooperate.**

Nouthetic Counseling (NANC)

The NANC counseling session is conducted by Randy Patten, who has been a biblical counselor for over 30 years and who is the executive director of the National Association of Nouthetic Counselors.[1] The two persons portraying Trey and Deb "are ministry staff members" who are well acquainted with the kinds of problems and conversations that go on in counseling. Even though they attempt a "realistic portrayal," the session is not reality. It is improvisational play acting **designed to present a perfect example of nouthetic counseling** with a predictable set of problems, questions, and responses. The participants all know the NANC routine. Therefore, even though this is a contrived counseling session, it does reveal what really goes on in biblical counseling. Since the content and progress of the biblical counseling video is controlled by three individuals thoroughly familiar with what ideal nouthetic counseling should look like, **the sessions are nouthetic counseling presented at its very best**. However, we will demonstrate that nouthetic counseling presented at its best has become an accepted venue for sinful communication freely expressing the Jeremiah 17:9 syndrome. **To do this we will discuss the videos as if the counseling sessions are for real.**

Gathering Data

At the beginning of the video, Patten describes the main things he tries to accomplish in the first session: "gather data," "discern the problems," "gain involvement" (e.g., establish rapport so that they will talk about their problems and then be open to the counselor's advice), "give hope," teach, and assign homework. He also said that he used the Personal Data Inventory Sheet, which asks counselees to list the main problem, what they have already done about it, what they expect from their counseling, how they view themselves, and what other information the counselor should know. With the PDI in hand, Patten begins the session and tells Trey and Deb that he "always starts out with Proverbs 18:13" ("He that answereth a matter before he heareth it, it is folly and shame unto him"). This verse sets the stage for Patten to ask questions and for Trey and Deb to tell all without holding anything back. However, in order to honestly and accurately hear the matter, all parties involved should really be heard and that includes those not present, such as spouses, parents, in-laws, other family members, friends, coworkers, etc.

Patten says that he needs to "understand completely what's going on in your life" before giving any advice so that he won't be "a fool in God's eyes" or give them "lousy advice." However, to "**understand completely**," Patten and all counselors would need to hear from all the people their counselees talk about behind their backs. He has not done this. Counselors do not check out the details of the stories they have been told. It is impractical and almost impossible to do so. Thus counseling is rife with kangaroo court proceedings. Counselors believe their counselees, even though research demonstrates that counselees lie to their counselors and will obviously distort the truth to their own advantage. One psychotherapist with a sense of humor once said, "Ten percent of the time clients lie to their therapists and the other 90 percent of the time they distort the truth to make themselves look good." Of course, we're human beings! Nevertheless, the Bible advises getting the facts before believing tales: "He that is first in his own cause seemeth just; but his neighbor cometh and searcheth him" (Prov. 18:17). Patten and other biblical counselors probably never discuss this verse with their counselees in reference to what they say about others.

With the PDI in hand, already loaded with some amount of sinful expression, Patten proceeds to ask his prying, probing questions that precipitate sinful communication on the part of the counselees. He asks for a "brief life history" beginning from when they were "born and raised." Because most people who enter counseling know that they are supposed to talk about problems, the negative aspects will emerge. Trey dishonors his parents by talking about their personal relationship with each other, which included "a lot of fighting." Even though later in the conversation Deb expresses a real fondness for her parents and even hesitates to criticize them, she nevertheless dishonors them by saying, "It's probably not a great marriage." Here is the context of those words:

> My parents spent a lot of time focused on us, their children. I didn't really see them communicate with each other that much…. It's probably not a great marriage…. Sometimes my mom will say things about my dad, but they really don't spend a lot of time talking to each other.

Notice that Deb seemed to be grasping for something wrong and may have thought she should see something wrong in her parents' marriage to help the counselor analyze how that may have affected hers. Thus she is enticed into giving an unkind evaluation of her parents in this kangaroo court counseling session.

Pressing for More Issues and Details

The subject of Trey and Deb's fighting leads Patten to ask them for details about the conflict in their own marriage, how they fight, and how often. While men are usually reluctant to share in counseling, Trey seems to do most of the talking here, probably because the person playing the part of Trey knows the scenario so well and because he is not really talking personally about himself in the video, but rather about the husband he is portraying. Trey again talks about his parents' fighting and says that he and Deb do it nearly every day. When Patten asks, "Do you throw things?" Trey fails to protect his wife and tattles on her instead, by saying. "I don't, but Deb does."

As the questions and conversation continue, sinful speaking spews forth as Trey accuses Deb's family of being "a big problem in our marriage" and goes on to describe how close Deb is to her family and how she is constantly visiting them.

He then plays the victim and complains, "I don't feel like I have the ability to be a leader in my own home. I feel like I am constantly living in the shadow of Deb's mom and dad and primarily her dad." Deb just sits there while Trey dishonors her parents.

Patten then asks Deb, "Are you surprised by what he said?"

Deb answers, "Well, his family lives so far away," and Trey adds that they only live about 3 hours away.

At this point most people would not see anything wrong with the way this counseling is going. They would assume that the counselor needs all of this information. However, as they are sharing their experiences with the counselor, Trey is sinning against Deb by exposing her sinful behavior to a third party. In addition to failing to love Deb as Christ loves the church, as he says hurtful things about her parents, he also dishonors and accuses them by insinuating that they are a major reason for their problems. As we will show later on, this kind of sinful talk is not necessary for help to be given.

As Patten moves on to another issue, one can see that he is simply gathering as much data as possible. He asks Deb "What's another issue?" She says, "Finances." Patten then says, "Explain that to me." So again Trey and Deb complain about each other. This is open season for Trey not to love his wife as Christ loves the church or even as he loves himself, as he complains about how she spends money; and it is open season for Deb to express disrespect for her husband in front of a third party when she says he gets upset when she buys something. The Jeremiah 17:9 syndrome is active as both speak sinfully about each other.

Patten then turns again to the PDI and reads what Deb wrote: "We fight a lot. It seems like we don't like each other that much anymore." He then asks for more details, what might be the contributing factors. Deb is very general in her answer: "I don't know. It seems to be all the stupid little things—big things, yes, but little things."

As Patten continues to ask for other issues, they bring up the following ones: when to begin a family, how they handle finances, conflicts regarding holidays and in-laws, all of which involve sinful communication, primarily dishonoring each other and their parents. Throughout, Trey and Deb unnecessarily and detrimentally describe a whole host of issues, all the while complaining about others and each other and violating Scriptures that speak of how we are to treat one another in our conversation (Eph. 4:29, 31; 5:33; 1 Cor. 13:4-7).

Prying into Private Matters

In response to Patten asking for another issue, Trey says, "I don't know how much you want to get into this, but I'm very dissatisfied with our sex life." Right on cue Patten says, "Describe." Patten's word "describe" is a command for more details. This reveals how deeply worldly this counseling is and the extent to which psychological problem-centered counseling has been emulated and embraced by the church. As much as prying for details is expected and practiced in biblical counseling, details about a couple's intimacy should not be shared with a third party in counseling. Nevertheless problem-centered counseling depends on such details even in these intimate areas. More on this later regarding how one can minister without this kind of exposure and sinful communication.

Trey tells Patten that their sex life is "nonexistent." When asked how long, Trey complains, "For a couple of years. I mean we're lucky if it's once a month. I think there was one point in the last couple of years we didn't have—we had sex once in three months. And that's very frustrating." Here Trey is playing the victim while exposing his wife.

When asked if she agreed, Deb responds, "Yeah." So
Patten asks, "Is it because you're not interested in her or
you're not interested in him or is one being unresponsive to
the other?"

Trey responds, "I would say she is never interested in
sex."

Deb counters, "It's hard to be emotionally intimate with
somebody and that's what matters for sex for me. I mean it's
no—I just don't flip a switch and it's on."

The marriage bed is holy and for Trey to expose his wife
the way he does is sinful. This kind of talk would surely
make a woman feel she has been betrayed. Notice that when
Deb tries to bring in the idea of intimacy and how fighting
harms the intimacy, she is not as rude and crude as Trey. As
Trey and Deb expose each other in this area of intimacy, Patten treats it merely as data, information for future sessions.

Trey and Deb continue to blame the other and justify self.
Of course Patten wants even more details. After about an
hour of questions precipitating evil speaking, further expressions of the Jeremiah 17:9 syndrome, and some teaching,
Patten says, "Based upon what you said today, I estimate that
I will want to meet with you 9, maybe 11 or 13 times." He
asks them to keep a log of the topics they argue about during the week. This initial counseling session had the following evidence of the Jeremiah 17:9 syndrome: kangaroo court
regarding parents, expressions of self-love, evil speaking,
mote and beam self-bias, and a victim mentality. Consider
how much more there will be in Patten's proposed "9, maybe
11 or 13" additional counseling sessions.

Confronting and Commanding

During the video of a later contrived session, the counseling includes a discussion of Trey's TV habits. Trey had
not followed through with his Bible reading homework.

When Patten asks Trey to describe his evening activities, he notes how much time Trey had spent watching TV. The aggressiveness of the interrogation would shame a real counselee. Patten, in one of his several direct, one-up, authoritative stances, issues the command, "No Bible, no TV." Trey shamefacedly commits himself to follow Patten's order. Evidently this kind of treatment is not only permissible, but it is presented as an example of how counselors should treat their counselees in nouthetic counseling.

Patten throughout this counseling enactment usurps and undermines Trey's spiritual headship. Instead of building Trey's spiritual headship he is tearing it down by demeaning him in the presence of his wife who is to "see that she reverence her husband" (Eph. 5:33). Here Patten treats Trey as a one-down inferior to whom he barks an order. His treatment of Trey is one of numerous reasons why men do not want to be in counseling.[3] One of many reasons why traditional men do not want to be in counseling is that they are treated in unmanly ways. Patten's "No Bible, no TV" is a perfect example of undermining the husband in front of his wife. This is reason enough why the real Treys of the world do not return for counseling. Moreover, **the sinful communication expected and promoted in problem-centered counseling is reason enough for no one to be involved.**

Idols-of-the-Heart Counseling (CCEF)

Paul David Tripp is a very popular speaker and writer, particularly among those who are interested in what is called "biblical counseling" and "discipleship." Although he may sound biblical, much of what he is teaching, promoting, and popularizing is the problem-centered, idols-of-the-heart counseling methodology, which has been recycled from psychological insight-oriented counseling methodology and integrated with the Bible by the Christian Counseling and Educational Foundation (CCEF). While David Powlison appears to be the godfather of this latter day mania, **Tripp's writings are an excellent example of idols-of-the-heart counseling recycled from insight-oriented psychotherapy.** The way he connects the heart with the motives and endeavors to cause the person to gain insight into his own heart is very similar to a psychoanalytic therapist's attempt to expose the hidden regions of the unconscious with its so-called unconscious determinants of behavior. Psychoanalytic methods of insight and interpretation lead to much subjective guessing as the therapist analyzes what the counselee reveals about herself. Nevertheless insight-oriented therapists and idols-of-the-heart counselors truly believe that, as they listen to what the person says, they will be able to know and reveal to their counselee's their inner core and what drives them.

After studying biblical counseling at Westminster Theological Seminary, Tripp became a faculty member of CCEF and served as a lecturer in biblical counseling at Westminster. He is a pastor at Tenth Presbyterian Church in Philadelphia, and in 2006 he started Paul Tripp Ministries. From this base he is a much sought-out speaker on biblical counseling.[2] His articles and books reveal his problem-centered, idols-of-the-heart counseling approach.

Distorting Doctrines

Typical of CCEF books and articles, Paul Tripp's book *Instruments in the Redeemer's Hands*[3] includes some good teaching. Tripp emphasizes the heart, the inner man, and teaches some truth about the war between the flesh and the Spirit and about how human beings are in rebellion against their creator and end up serving and worshipping self. Therefore, one will find much to agree with. However, **these truths make the book more dangerous**, because of the way he engages the readers with truth, but is ever so subtly leading them into his problem-centered and thus self-centered, insight-oriented counseling methodology, which assumes that mere humans can know another person's heart if they are especially trained in the elitist idols-of-the-heart counseling methodology. **Tripp's book, written to help counselors see and expose deceitful hearts, is itself a masterpiece of deception as it weaves biblical teachings with recycled insight-oriented psychotherapy.** Scripture is treated as if it must be aided by the counselor's insight to be effective, as if it must be insight infused in addition to being God breathed.

Delving, Digging, and Evil Speaking

The process of getting to know another person and what idols are controlling the person's life involves much digging, delving, and evil speaking about other people who may or not be present to defend themselves in this kangaroo court proceeding. Tripp reveals what kind of information he is looking for in his attempt to know another person's heart in a section titled "Now For Some Good Questions."[4] In the first item Tripp advises, "Always ask open-ended questions that cannot be answered with a 'yes' or 'no.'"[5] Following this he gives over 25 questions as examples. Here are several of his questions:

- What things in your marriage make you sad?
- How would you characterize your communication with your husband?
- Describe how you as a couple resolve conflicts.
- What do you see as the weaknesses of your marriage?
- What could your spouse do to greatly change your marriage?

• Pick one area of your marriage where you think
you have problems. Describe what is wrong and
what each of you has done to solve it.[6]

One has to wonder how these might differ from secular
marriage counseling. They are problem-loaded and will roil
up the troubled waters with the couple complaining, speaking ill of one another, and airing their dissatisfaction with the
marriage and with one another with an attentive listener who
is eager to know more about what's wrong. With this type of
problem-centered counseling, filled with the Jeremiah 17:9
syndrome, it is understandable that some counseling goes on
for over a year and/or ends in divorce.

Counseling that relies on talking about problems and
asking these kinds of questions will often lead counselees
into violating Leviticus 19:16: "Thou shalt not go up and
down *as* a talebearer among thy people: neither shalt thou
stand against the blood of thy neighbour: I am the LORD."
The amount of talebearing in counseling is excessive. In fact,
**without such talebearing this kind of counseling would
cease to exist**, since it inevitably depends upon talebearing
and speaking evil of others.

In his book, Tripp tells about Mike and Marsha who
come to him for help. He says:

> Mike began to tell the most confusing family story I
> had ever heard. They had both been married before
> and had blended two families, each with four older
> children. Marsha occasionally jumped in with details
> that only added to my confusion. I don't think I took
> as many notes in my theology classes at seminary as
> I did that afternoon! Their story was full of plots and
> sub-plots. Their attempts to solve problems invari-
> ably made them worse. It seemed that their children

had made all the wrong decisions as well. It *was* a mess![7] (Italics his.)

Such details provide for much evil speaking about other people. These problem-centered counselors thrive on hearing the "plots and sub-plots" and the messes in the lives of their counselees and therefore take many notes for future problem-centered counseling appointments.

Confessing the Sins of Others
The cases Tripp discusses are filled with information that he could only have gleaned through eliciting gossip, complaints about others, and evil speaking about parents, spouse, and others. He appears to be blind to the fact that much of what he seeks to hear from the counselee is filled with gossip, since he himself clearly speaks out against gossip when he says:

> Gossip doesn't lead a person to make humble confession before God or others. **When I gossip, I confess the sin of another person to someone who is not involved. Gossip doesn't restrain sin, it encourages it.** It doesn't build someone's character; it destroys his reputation. Gossip doesn't lead a person to humble insight; it produces anger and defensiveness.[8] (Bold added.)

We certainly agree with much of what he says here about gossip! However, he obviously allows such gossiping during counseling. Evidently, because he is in the role of counselor, he must see himself as someone who **is** involved, rather than "someone who **is not** involved." This short phrase seemingly makes the counselor privy to all kinds of confessing the sins of others without calling it "gossip." Through the questions he asks and by the information he has gleaned during hours of counseling with individuals, he depends on lots of what would ordinarily be called "gossip" (talebearing) and evil speaking about others in his quest to know the hearts of his counselees. In his attempt to identify a person's so-called motivating idols of the heart, Tripp elicits self-disclosure, but what he is looking for will generally be contaminated with much talebearing and evil speaking about others. Here are some of his scenarios that include information he got from his counselees "confess[ing] the sin of another person" to him in the special role of "counselor."

In the following case, Tripp has figured out that Joe craves respect from others.

> Joe was the kind of guy who lived for the respect of other people. The way he sought to get it at home was by establishing a violent autocracy (though what he got was more fear than respect). Outside the home Joe was known as a real servant, a guy who would give you the shirt off his back. People at Joe and Sarah's church found it hard to believe that he could be capable of the things Sarah said he was doing with her and the children.[9]

Here is an example of a kangaroo court and judging another person's heart. Generally in such situations there is some truth and some exaggeration. Tripp does not give enough information to support his assumption that Joe craved respect, and, even if he had lots of information that may seem to lead in that direction, Tripp is still guessing. Only God knows! While sin comes from within, it is also stimulated by different environments. Joe may have received cooperation in the church environment and resistance at home. Nevertheless in any situation such as this, one does not need to listen to evil speaking about a spouse in order to help a couple move into the direction of a godly marriage. More on this later.

Tripp uses the next case for "organizing data biblically."[10] He says:

> Imagine that Greta, a woman from church, asks to talk to you. She is concerned about her husband John, who has an increasingly short fuse. He yells at her and the children at the drop of a hat. He is critical and demanding. He is spending more time at work, and most of his home time is spent on the computers. When she asks John what is wrong, he says that life stinks. Greta says that John's dad was a negative guy who thought that people were out to get him. John was not like that when she married him, but Greta is afraid he is turning into his father. When Greta asks John how she can help him, all he says is, "Just give me a little space so I can breathe."[11]

There is no acknowledgment that Greta's complaining about her husband is dishonoring to her husband and to her father-in-law, or that this is a kangaroo court proceeding, or that this is biased gossip, even if there is some truth in what she said. However, this is a case ripe for digging and delving. Therefore, Tripp uses it to show how to organize data, as if he is dealing with factual information rather than a one-sided, distorted, exaggerated, and/or incendiary description. Interestingly in this illustration **the questions all have to do with the husband who is not there**. The question "What is going on?" is where Tripp puts "the information that describes the person's world (his circumstances), both past and present." Here is where he records information about John from what Greta has said about him, "raised by a negative, cynical father." The next question having to do with the person's response again has to do with the person that is being talked about behind his back rather than with the one who is seeking help. The question, "What does the person think about

what is going on?'" draws the answer: "All we know about
John so far in this category is that his wife reports that he
says, 'Life stinks.'" Now for the "motives": "This includes
what you know about the person's desires, goals, treasures,
motives, values, and idols." Tripp admits that so far he does
not know what John "means by 'a little space' or why he
wants it."[12] However, if the couple is enticed into this kind
of counseling, John will have plenty of opportunities to provide more data, which will likely contain much evil speaking
about his wife, parents, children, and people at work. Tripp
is the expert here. He is the evaluator and the judge. What a
place for the temptation for pride to come in without anyone
noticing.

In one of Tripp's possible scenarios, "Dan comes to you
concerned that Jim is doing things that are unbecoming of
a Christian." After Dan reveals personal information about
Jim, we find that "Dan has also been hurt that Jim has vio-
lated his confidence when he has shared personal things."[13]
What is the difference between Dan sharing personal things
about Jim and Jim having shared personal things about Dan
to the counselor? The difference must be that a "counselor"
is the recipient of the sharing of "personal things" about
another person, rather than just any old person. Counseling
truly opens the door to all kinds of confidences being vio-
lated, as well as gossip and other forms of sinful communication.

Deceptive Dependence on Counselee's Self-Disclosure

Tripp insists that personal things, including private information about others (which may or may not be accurate),
must be disclosed. He says: "We learn to ask questions that
cannot be answered without self-disclosure." He supposes
that through the counselees' self-disclosure he will be able
to know them better than they know themselves—as if he

will know them inside and out. While he will **not** know them better than they know themselves, knowing private information about other people puts him in a power position. Furthermore, people will trust what he says because of his claim to be able to recognize aspects of their inner person. While Tripp becomes dependent on their self-disclosure, his counselees become dependent on him.

Tripp claims to "filter everything we learn about people through the grid of Scripture," because the goal is "not only to know others biblically, but to help them know themselves in the same way."[14] As demonstrated here and in our newsletter, Tripp does not filter everything he learns about people through the grid of Scripture.[15] Can one individual truly know another individual biblically by supposing that he can know the contents of another person's heart? **This is utter self deception. Moreover, this is God's territory! Humans can only guess, surmise, and draw subjective conclusions.**

One gets the strong impression from Tripp's writings that believers who are indwelt by the Holy Spirit cannot know themselves without an expert such as Tripp to reveal their inner heart to them. One also gets the impression that if believers are to minister to each other they must know Tripp's special methods of gaining insight by eliciting a great deal of sinful communication (thereby leading fellow believers into sin) so that the one believer can supposedly know what idols of the heart might be ruling another believer. **Needless to say, one who follows the idols-of-the-heart counseling methodology will be deceived into thinking that he can know what only the Holy Spirit knows. This is a dizzying height for humans to think they can know the hearts of others when they don't even know how deceptive their own hearts are in the very process. This is fertile ground for Jeremiah 17:9 to be operating.**

Self-Confrontation (BCF)

The Biblical Counseling Foundation (BCF) was originally formed by John C. Broger, who developed a Biblical Counseling Training Program and wrote the original *Self-Confrontation Syllabus: Biblical Counseling Training – Course One* (1978). The syllabus has been revised several times and we have been told that the 1991 edition, published by BCF, is still in use.[16] However, a 1994 edition was published for the general public by Thomas Nelson, Inc. under the title *Self-Confrontation: a manual for in-depth discipleship*, since BCF uses the terms *counseling* and *discipleship* as synonyms.[17] With many verses and 105 principles to learn, one is likely to become overwhelmed and intimidated to the point that these instructions and tools can become shackles of legalism and bondage.

Nevertheless, numerous people have trudged through the manuals, done all the homework, and attended the courses because they want to be counselors. **The appeal to be a counselor may not only be to help others, but to be part of an elite society within the church, where the counselor is often put on a higher level than a pastor or Bible teacher.** Additional BCF manuals and guides are directly related to the BCF counseling courses, which are extensive, ponderous, and unnecessary for ministering to others. As with other biblical counseling approaches, there is a voluminous amount of material, but a total absence of literal counseling, with only two instances of contrived cases, one of Mary and one of Peter.[18] BCF, like other BCM approaches, is problem-centered, and unbiblical communication is clearly involved in the counseling itself, as shown in the case study of "Mary's Husband Has Left Her." **The problem-centered approach inadvertently appeals to self-effort, superficial**

change, and even strengthening the flesh rather than growing spiritually.

"Mary's Husband Has Left Her"

The case of Mary is, of course, a contrived case presented as a teaching tool to show others how this counseling is to be done. The following is the description of Mary, after saying that her husband, Tom, had just left her: "She was in a highly emotional state (weeping, frantic in her tone of voice, disheveled) ... she and her husband had been arguing all night." Mary said that "she has been a good wife and can't understand how this could have happened to her," that "she cannot understand how her husband can be so insensitive," and that "she is now bitter towards her husband and threatened to get even with him for walking out on her."[19] This brief description is loaded with the kind of information that could only have been gleaned through Mary speaking sinfully as she presents her case (kangaroo court) from her perspective and much evil speaking about her husband and much mote-and-beam self-justification. Dialogue in the following sessions includes expressions of the Jeremiah 17:9 syndrome.

At the beginning of Mary's first session of counseling with the counselor and a whole cadre of "assistant counselors," the counselor asks her about her conversion. Mary replies:

> I accepted the Lord at a Christian summer camp when I was 16. I had real joy in the Lord. I regularly attended church and Sunday school for a couple of years after that. I also had plenty of Christian friends. (Pause) In college I started down a spiral. I met Tom who was not interested in the Christian life.[20]

Mary then proceeds to complain about her husband. After Mary states a few more complaints about Tom, the counselor asks, "When did the problems first start between you and your husband, Tom?"[21] The counselors are evidently satisfied with Mary's testimony. However, one might well wonder whether Mary really heard the Gospel at the camp or if she simply had an emotional response to an emotional appeal. From what Mary says during the dialogue, there is no evidence of repentance for sin or genuine conversion (beyond attending church and having some Christian friends for two years) or of any sense of her own sinfulness as she continues to complain about her husband and berate him.

Platform for Evil Speaking

There is a great need to establish Mary's position in Christ. Instead, the counselor proceeds with questions about the problems with the husband, when her spiritual life should have been the first direction of the counsel. Rather than pursuing the genuineness of Mary's faith, the counselors give Mary a platform for talking about her husband behind his back. In response to the question about when the problems started, Mary says that she felt let down when he stopped writing her love notes and giving her flowers and expected her to get up and fix his breakfast every morning. When the counselor asks about her response to that, Mary says, "I told him to fix his own.… On top of that, he's so irresponsible: he leaves his dirty clothes just laying [sic] around. It really irritates me. He knows it irritates me."[22] Here is an example of counseling being a kangaroo court as she bad-mouths her husband to the counselor. Mary is presenting herself as a victim and just the counselor listening in a care-giving manner will support her stance.

The counselor then gives Mary another opportunity to speak evil of her husband behind his back by asking about

other "specific problems." Mary says "The finances are a
mess because he doesn't balance the check book or stick to
the budget…. I remember several times he wrote checks that
bounced and I had to go to the bank to straighten it out…. I
was so embarrassed!" The counselor further enables Mary
to continue her evil speaking by asking if there is anything
else, to which Mary replies, "He never takes an interest in
disciplining the kids. I always feel like I have to do it. We
fight about that the most…. I tell the kids that it will be all
their father's fault if they turn out rotten … just like he is!"[23]
Here Mary is given a platform to further dishonor her husband (Eph. 5:23), who is not present to defend himself in this
kangaroo court called counseling.

Focusing on Problems
Of course this is fodder for much counseling. The contrived dialogue reveals the kind of talk that is accepted,
encouraged, and depended on in counseling. Counselors
are looking for problems they can address with the counselee. They depend upon this sinful speaking to work on the
problems. When she claims that Tom is not willing to make
the marriage work and that she has "done so much for that
man!" the counselor will use this to teach Mary biblical principles, **which could easily be taught without all the prior
evil speaking!** However, if Mary has not been born again,
teaching her biblical principles may just go as far as tuning
up what the Bible calls her "flesh."

Rather than teaching Mary about the new life in Christ,
the counselor points out that Mary's "most serious problem
is that she is not loving God."[24] But, Mary is incapable of
loving God if she does not have new life in Christ. Nowhere
has it been established that she has been truly converted.
Then, in the next session, Mary sounds as bad as or worse
than at the first session.

Since the counseling room allows and enables the Jeremiah 17:9 syndrome with all sorts of evil speaking, Mary feels perfectly free to say: "Even though my husband has remained at home [he evidently never left, after all], he only takes care of himself. He doesn't care about anyone else!" Then she complains about all she has to do to take care of the children while he is at work. She says, "Tom is never around to help! He doesn't appreciate me and all that I do! My children don't appreciate me either. I get tired; I do all the work and nobody cares. They treat me like a doormat. I'm sick of being everyone's victim."[25] This list of complaints includes the kangaroo court, hearsay, self-love, sinful speaking, the mote and beam, and the victim mentality. From start to finish it is the Jeremiah 17:9 syndrome at work, naturally enabled and expected in the counseling environment.

So many of Mary's complaints sound trivial in this contrived counseling dialogue, which reveal Mary's faults to set the stage for teaching. Nevertheless the counseling emphasis for Mary is not about her new life in Christ, who is the believer's very source for godly living and behavior, and there is no warning about sinful communication or evil speaking or the other aspects of the Jeremiah 17:9 syndrome, which are tolerated and even enabled in this counseling. Even though the complaints are trivial, the manner of complaining about spouse and others is exactly what goes on in counseling, and the counsel given is characteristic of those in the biblical counseling movement.

While this case may be based on a real one, it sounds phony, probably because the authors are trying to squeeze in what they want to teach and leave out most of the conversation that would have occurred. In fact, at the very next session Mary has suddenly changed. Little change was revealed in the previous sessions. But here, glowing things are said about her being quite transformed, so much so that her husband, Tom, is now coming to the counseling session with Mary. The assumption is that her change is due to spiritual growth. Evidently the counselors were satisfied with her shallow testimony, because one counselor tells Tom that Mary has changed "because of her commitment to please the Lord and be obedient to God's Word, which began with her spiritual new birth."[26] These contrived cases always have happy endings. Nevertheless, they are vile mixtures of the Jeremiah 17:9 syndrome and some good teaching, but quite often given in a prescribed, legalistic mode. While BCF claims to be biblical, the way they handle this contrived (ideal) case violates many biblical standards and reveals how sinful they are in practice.

Self-Deception

The *Self-Confrontation* manual is prescriptive about what questions to ask and how to proceed to gather enough information. Supplement One at the end of both the manual and the syllabus says: "In counseling that is true to God's Word, **a biblical counselor will collect enough information to enable him to recognize and understand the problem in order to formulate the biblical solution." But, one cannot assume that data gathering will necessarily enable anyone to "recognize and understand" someone else's "problem in order to formulate the biblical solution."** The counselor's own bias, as well as her own shortcoming and self-deception, may drastically contaminate her evaluation and understanding. Moreover, throughout all this there will be much unnecessary unbiblical talk and many opportunities for both the counselee and the counselor to operate according to the Jeremiah 17:9 syndrome. (For a more thorough critique of *Self-Confrontation: a manual for in-depth discipleship*, see the position paper titled "Confronting the

Biblical Counseling Foundation's *Self-Confrontation* Manual: A PsychoHeresy Awareness Position Paper." [27])

Conclusion

As biblical as biblical counselors desire to be, they are not being biblical, because they conduct problem-centered counseling that evokes expressions of the Jeremiah 17:9 syndrome. There is no place in Scripture where this kind of conversation is presented as an example of how people should help one another. This came from the world of secular counseling and serves as an unbiblical justification for people to verbally lambaste one another, to cast blame on others, to dishonor spouses and parents, to justify self, and play the victim, all in the name of "biblical counseling."

Problem-centered biblical counselors have no idea that they themselves are affected by the Jeremiah 17:9 syndrome even as they are counseling others. Not only are they self-deceived as far as their own importance in the lives of fellow believers, especially in the authoritative, one-up position many of them take, but **they are sinning dreadfully by enabling others to sin.** Counselors not only precipitate sinful communication through their questions; but they provide a place and an ear to hear more evil speaking as they continue to pry and probe. Perhaps they would say that the end justifies the means, but when does God ask us to sin in order to help others grow spiritually? Today counselors are sought out as the ones who are equipped more than anyone else in the church, including the pastor, to enable people to solve personal and relational problems and grow spiritually. One has to ask with the apostle Paul, "What shall we say then? Shall we continue in sin, that grace may abound? God forbid. How shall we, that are dead to sin, live any longer therein?" (Rom. 6:1-2). Rather than abounding in sin to get rid of sin through biblical counseling, it would be far more profitable to get back into the Word of God and look to all that Christ has done and is doing in everyone who is truly born again by His Spirit. More on this later.

4

The Myth of Problem-Centered Counseling

**That your faith should not stand in the
wisdom of men, but in the power of God.
(1 Corinthians 2:5)**

Problem-centered counseling is fueled and sustained by
a myth, which is "an unproved or false collective belief that
is used to justify a social institution."[1] Here we will demonstrate that sinful problem-centered counseling is indeed
being justified by "a false collective belief." There are many
elements in this false collective belief. First and foremost
is the fact that counselors and counselees alike believe that
when individuals, couples, and families have personal and
interpersonal problems it is necessary for the counselees to
talk about them and for the counselors to fish out the details
and fossick about in the problems for understanding in order
to help—as we demonstrated in the past chapters. This is
a myth! We have shown that the pillars of this myth began
with the publicizing of private lives (Chapter One), com-
pounded by the Jeremiah 17:9 syndrome and all its ramifications (Chapters Two and Three).

The Rise of Problem-Centered Counseling

We have written extensively about the history of the rise of psychological and biblical counseling[2] and will only touch on it here. As demonstrated in the academic literature and mentioned earlier, the beginning of modern counseling is attributed to Franz Anton Mesmer (1734-1815). Mesmer's rudimentary original healing approach evolved over a period of time from the use of magnets to **conversation (talk) as the medium of cure and problem-centeredness (problem solving) as the method of cure.**[3] Henri F. Ellenberger, in his book *The Discovery of the Unconscious*, summarizes it well when he says that Mesmer discovered "that a therapeutic effect did not originate from the magnets, but from a magnetic fluid emanating from his own person."[4] In other words, the counselor is the source of the therapeutic effect.

While the format for modern day counseling was established by Mesmer and is practiced in a variety of ways through hypnosis and positive thinking, it also led to the background of modern day psychoanalysis devised by Sigmund Freud (1859-1939), whom many regard as the father of modern psychotherapy and counseling. **It was through the work of Freud that conversation (talk) as the medium of cure and problem-centeredness (problem solving) as the method of cure was popularized.** Psychoanalysis was the first popular, systematized, formalized, licensed, and professionalized counseling with medical doctors as counselors.

Early on Freud and other early counselors, such as Carl Jung and Alfred Adler, were the popular approaches of that era prior to World War II. However, because these counseling approaches were very intensive, involving visits three to five times a week, and were very expensive, involving a highly paid medical doctor, they were completely unaffordable to the average person and therefore the number of counselees was small.

Free association is the main ingredient in the psycho-analytic conversation. However, free association is a special kind of conversation. One text describes it in the follow-ing way: "In free association, patients say everything that comes to mind without any censoring, regardless of whether they believe the thought to be unacceptable, unimportant, or embarrassing."[5] If psychoanalytic psychotherapy were all that would be available today, the counseling industry would be very small indeed.

As we indicated in Chapter One, in psychoanalysis, in present-day psychotherapies, and throughout most of our society there this assumption that expressing one's feelings is beneficial and that repressing them, in the ordinary sense of the word, is harmful. However, in spite of the almost uni-versal acceptance of this idea as a basis for counseling, it is questionable, based upon research. Using the ordinary (non-Freudian) meaning of the word *repress*, it has been found that "**A growing body of evidence suggests that repressing one's feelings may have greater psychological benefits than expressing them**."[6] Here are just a few conclusions from the research: "Grief-stricken individuals who express intense negative emotions when discussing their loss appear to do **worse** in the long term, while so-called repressors recover more successfully" (bold added).[7] "Holocaust survi-vors who have been induced to 'talk it out' fare significantly **worse** than repressors" (bold added).[8] And, from a group of "middle aged men and women who had lost their spouses," the researchers concluded:

> The inhibition of negative emotion did not have a cumulative cost; rather, it might be an undervalued coping skill. For that reason, laughter, optimism, and

inappropriate-seeming positive emotions should not be simply stigmatized as "denial."[9]

This belief that talking about troubles and expressing one's negative feelings are beneficial undergirds all kinds of counseling. Nevertheless the research simply does not support that idea. We know that considerable research dealing with what is called "Post-Traumatic Stress Disorder" (PTSD) indicates that those who receive treatment "do no better than those who don't and that a significant number of people treated . . . do even worse than those who didn't receive treatment." Reporting on the extensive research, the writer says:

> This negative reaction seems to emerge because, for some people, the very act of focusing on their negative feelings . . . increases their distress and leads to more difficulties, such as flashbacks, nightmares, and anxiety attacks.[10]

While most problem-centered counseling does not deal with PTSD, most counseling does involve "the very act of focusing on ... negative feelings." This research conclusion about PTSD should by extension raise serious questions about problem-centered counseling. This evidence regarding PTSD definitely relates to the negative aspects of talking about problems, as in problem-centered counseling. Such emphasis and emotional expression have been shown to be detrimental to those who seek relief by rehearsing, rehashing, reliving, and regurgitating their problems. Such emphasis on problems and negative emotional expression not only bode badly for the individual, but pose potential harm to relationships with others. We believe that the rapid rise of marriage counseling since World War II, with the focus on problems, negative feelings, and "tell it all" milieu, has been one major contributor to the rising divorce rate that affects believers as well as others. Too many individuals, including believers, have been drastically deceived by the Siren call to express all, in spite of the many biblical admonitions to the contrary.

It was not until the post World War II era that licensed counseling began with its sinful problem-centeredness. Shortly thereafter the biblical counseling movement followed along with the same sinful problem-centered format, as we demonstrated earlier. As we document in Chapter One, **women were primarily responsible for going public with their private lives both in and out of the counseling office**. The therapeutic gospel after World War II included the publicizing of personal lives, only with a new and expanded psychological vocabulary and a willing and eager audience—women.

The real surge of problem-centered counseling called psychotherapy was when (after World War II) the federal government poured large sums of money into clinical psychology programs at universities to train counselors. *The Practice of Psychology* says that the Veteran's Administration,

> …as an agency of the federal government became a major source of funding for the training of psychologists and psychiatrists. In short order, psychology training programs at the college and university level (which had previously suffered from a severe lack of financial support and student interest) now found an abundance of both.[11]

It was out of these clinical psychology departments that professional counselors began to be trained.

The new conversational approaches to counseling that are less expensive (no medical doctor needed) and less intensive (usually once per week) ushered in the new era. While

these initially came in through clinical psychology departments at universities, they expanded into a multiplicity of
types of conversations through a variety of sources, including seminars and self-help books. From this small beginning
there was a slow, at first, and then a burgeoning growth of
such programs during the 1970s. However, even as late as
1970, George Albee, PhD, then president of the American
Psychological Association "was quoted in *Psychology Today*
as predicting the death of clinical psychology in his presi-
dential address," titled "The Short Unhappy Life of Clinical
Psychology: Rest in Peace."[12] Excuse the pun, but he was
dead wrong. It was during the 1970s that clinical psychology
programs greatly expanded with numerous students becoming intensively interested in the exploding new psychological counseling field, which promised self-knowledge and a
means of making a living.

Charles Sykes, a senior research fellow at a think tank in
America, describes the situation well. He says:

> The triumph of the therapeutic mentality…which
> insisted upon seeing the immemorial questions of
> human life as **problems** that required solutions…. The
> therapists transformed age-old human dilemmas into
> psychological **problems** and claimed that they (and
> they alone) had the treatment.[13] (Bold added.)

During the last half of the 20th century the practice of
psychological counseling accelerated rapidly. Ellen Herman,
in her book *The Romance of American Psychology*, contrasts
pre and post World War II by saying, "Before World War II,
professional healers and counselors were few; most individuals allied with psychology did work unrelated to "helping."
In contrast, she declares: **"Throughout the entire postwar
era, the United States has trained and employed more
psychological experts, per capita, than any other country**

in the world"[14] (bold added). Herman also says, "Psychology may have seeped into virtually every facet of existence, but that does not mean that it has always been there or that what experts say has always mattered as much as it matters today."[15]

Shift in Confidence

During the past fifty years there has been a dramatic shift in confidence on the part of Christians—away from the sufficiency of God's Word for problems of living and towards man's wisdom. After World War II, materialism and affluence led to selfism and a breakdown of the nuclear family. This rising affluence with its accompanying narcissism, as prophesied in 2 Timothy 3, provided fertile ground for the problem-centered counselors and their openness to sinful speaking. Early on, the mental health associations began sponsoring meetings for dialog between local psychological counselors and pastors. These counseling psychologists convinced pastors that they were not qualified to handle the hard cases and that they needed to be referred out to professional counselors.

With the field of psychological counseling exploding and pastors beginning to refer their flocks to professional counselors came the great "psychological awakening" of evangelical Christianity. If pastors must send their flocks to professional counselors, then there was a crying need for Christians to become trained in psychology. After all, pastors did not want to send their people to "godless" counselors who might not appreciate Christianity. Thus began the era of so-called "Christian psychology." At the same time Christian students were going to state colleges and universities and learning about clinical psychology, which was just rising in popularity with the influx of government monies. These Christian students changed their majors to clinical psychology for purposes of employment and some also prepared themselves for the new market place of people in need. After graduation, these same students filtered into teaching at Christian colleges and universities and eventually into Bible colleges and seminaries, or they became licensed counselors. Soon the doors were wide open, both in public and private educational institutions, for those Christians who fell for this craze.

One of the godfathers of the integration of psychology and the Bible was Clyde Narramore. His book *The Psychology of Counseling* was published in 1960. He was one of the first to promote the wedding of secular psychology with the Scriptures. Narramore's message demeaned the role of pastors, supposedly limited to Scripture in the understanding of the human condition. He promoted the psychological understanding of man in addition to Scripture but downplayed some of the humanistic and psychoanalytic teachings. Narramore's integrationist teaching, along with his Foundation, was a seed bed of the numerous similar teachings that followed. Many of the early integrationists, such as James Dobson, were directly and greatly influenced by Narramore. And, of course Narramore and those that followed him swallowed whole the sinful problem-centered psychological format.

A little over fifty years ago there were no state licenses for counselors; now all fifty states have licensing requirements. At that time there were no insurance reimbursements for counseling; now most insurance companies provide at least minimal reimbursement and the new equity for counseling federal law expands that availability. At that time there were no Bible college, Christian university, or seminary programs providing psychology majors; now there are many with psychology being one of the most popular majors.[16] At that time there were no uniform graduate programs leading to licensing for counseling; now all major state universities, as well as many private universities and even Bible colleges and seminaries, provide such programs. **Fifty years ago evangelical Christianity was almost totally devoid of what we call psychoheresy; now it is predominantly embraced by Christian schools at all levels, mission agencies, denominations, and Christians of all persuasions.**

Few people realize how America moved from no problem-centered counseling, as we know it today, prior to World War II to its current popularity. This all occurred primarily through the political efforts of fourteen men who referred to themselves as "The Dirty Dozen" and they even admitted how money became the determining factor through what they called the "devil's deal." The Dirty Dozen's work has been documented in the book *The Practice of Psychology*, which cites the high compliments paid to those men on the part of various professional organizations for their outstanding work. One such citation says: "Once scorned, and confronted by seemingly insurmountable odds, the following fourteen professional psychologists, affectionately called The Dirty Dozen, changed for all times the face of the American Psychological Association."[17]

In Chapter Six we reveal facts about psychotherapy, some of which applies to all problem-centered counseling. Some of what we reveal includes the fact that counseling as we know it today was not a scientific breakthrough or a new field of science, but rather a promotion of a pseudoscientific activity through the politicking of "The Dirty Dozen" and the financial incentives of the "devil's deals." Moreover, on average psychotherapy only provides mild to moderate relief. Also, it has never been proven that professionals do better than amateurs at counseling, and there are potential detrimental effects in all counseling with certain counseling approaches being quite odious.

Biblical Counseling Movement

As we noted in Chapter One, the biblical counseling movement (BCM) is not that old. It started with Dr. Jay Adams' book *Competent to Counsel* in 1970. In it Adams set forth his methodology of counseling. Adams later wrote: "Over the past 12 years I have worked assiduously to produce a body of Literature in a field that, prior to that time, **virtually did not exist**: the field of biblical counseling"[18] (bold added). Since Adams began the BCM it has grown phenomenally. Fifty years ago there were no formalized biblical counseling programs and no formalized biblical counseling movement; now there is a burgeoning biblical counseling movement with numerous and varied biblical counselors offering their services to Christians spread throughout much of the church with its sinful problem-centered copycatting of the psychological counseling movement's sinful problem-centeredness.

Over the years we have been adamantly opposed to all the intimidation of mature Christians by those in the biblical counseling movement (BCM) with all their problem-centered mentality leading to training programs, certificates, degrees, and numerous books that one must read to become an adequate biblical counselor according to those in the BCM. We are opposed to all that for one major reason and that is because the BCM is sinfully problem-centered to the core. Piggy-backing on the rise of the "psychological experts," came those who claimed to be "biblical experts"; however the so-called biblical experts swallowed whole the sinful problem-centeredness of the psychological experts and foisted it upon their naïve and willing counselees with a similar prospect of happiness here and now. It is amazing that Christians who are so biblically knowledgeable could be so ignorant of the biblical violations of the biblical counseling provided to individuals with problems of living.

"So Sorry, One Mistake"

"So sorry, one mistake" is the punch line of a series of similar stories we've heard over the years. The story begins by telling about some great feat or accomplishment, often on the part of a very brave individual, that is entirely undone and, worse, ends in a disaster because of "one mistake." In reading various teachings in books and hearing various messages on the computer or on CD's we think about the expression, "So sorry, one mistake." Why? Because at times we hear such great biblical teachings that are undone by "one mistake" that seriously damages an otherwise excellent teaching.

In our writings we expose numerous examples of "So sorry, one mistake." The biblical counseling movement (BCM) is one example. In reading various books on biblical counseling and hearing various counseling DVDs and CDs, we see and hear quite excellent teachings at times, but we are forced to add the punch line, "So sorry, one mistake." In the case of the BCM, the one big mistake is the sinful problem-centeredness of the movement in which counselors inevitably elicit evil speaking. Whatever excellent teaching that may occur in the BCM is undone by its sinful-speaking problem-centeredness. The counselees come in with a problem and are encouraged to describe and discuss the problem along with its cast of characters. This inevitably violates biblical admonitions about talebearing, honoring father and mother, playing the victim, violating the one flesh in marriage, blaming the past for present problems, and so on. These and other biblical violations occur in the process of problem-centered counseling with its evil speaking and other characteristics of the Jeremiah 17:9 syndrome described in Chapter Two. **This**

one mistake on the part of the counselors is the undoing of the entire BCM. The great attraction of the BCM is that it provides an alternative to the psychological counseling movement. The added attraction is the good teaching that may occur during the counseling. But, **in spite of how biblical a counselor may be, after all is said and done we have to say, "So sorry, one mistake," because of the evil speaking problem-centeredness of the BCM. Sinful speaking is a two-way street.** The counselee comes in with a problem primed by the current culture with a "no-holds-barred" attitude about what is said; and, the counselor comes in with an inherited-from-the-psychological-counseling-movement agenda for problem understanding, amplification through questions, and resolutions after opening Pandora's Box with its evil contents spilling out in expressions of the Jeremiah 17:9 syndrome.

Those who counsel are not responsible for what the counselee may say, but they are responsible for how they respond to what is said. And that is what marks the difference between counseling and ministry. We have given many examples in this book and former writings of counseling, which inevitably leads to evil speaking, and ministry, which avoids problem-oriented questions by the counselor and problem pursuits by the counselee. More of what can be done comes in later chapters.

Linchpin for Sinful Communication

Typical of the biblical counseling movement (BCM) is the use of Scripture verses, not only for some of the biblical concepts that they teach, but also for justifying the sinful communication that they encourage. They consistently and repeatedly use Proverbs 18:13 to justify the sinful communication they elicit: "He that answereth a matter before he heareth it, it is folly and shame unto him."[19] Proverbs 18:13 is the linchpin of sinful problem-centered biblical counseling, which supposedly permits evil speaking. This verse is consistently used in Nouthetic Counseling (NANC) where the counselor makes a point of quoting the verse at the beginning of counseling an individual or couple to explain how the counselor needs as much information as the counselees can give so that they can be helped. This serves as an encouragement for counselees to tell all. Because they are problem-centered, these counselors contend that they must find out as much about the problems as possible even when such investigation includes the elements of the Jeremiah 17:9 syndrome discussed in Chapter Two. The Biblical Counseling Foundation uses Proverbs 18:13 to support their statement: "Understanding the problem requires that biblical inquiry be made."[20] However, this "biblical inquiry" ends up being unbiblical in that it draws forth evil speaking. **Whether or not other biblical counselors use Proverbs 18:13 directly, they definitely practice the implications of it to the degree that Proverbs 18:13 is the linchpin of sinful communication in the BCM.**

A Lopsided Linchpin

However, these counselors generally use Proverbs 18:13 in a lopsided manner, because they do not investigate all the facts regarding what is said about other people behind their backs. This would be like a kangaroo court (see Chapter Two), listening to all the complaints and making a decision without full investigation of all parties involved. Counseling is a specialized environment where counselors enable and encourage their counselees to express their feelings and air their complaints about other people. For instance, where is the outside investigation made regarding parents who are bad-mouthed by their adult children, as in the cases discussed in Chapter Three? If these counselors cannot help the person without hearing all the dirt, they had better find out the truth behind the dirt. In other words, they should use Proverbs 18:13 in its biblical sense, that is, hearing the **entire** matter from all parties involved. We have never found this to be done, in spite of the fact that the Bible itself would require one to do so if a judgment is to be made.

Just four verses after Proverbs 18:13 is Proverbs 18:17, which says, "He that is first in his own cause seemeth just, but his neighbour cometh and searcheth him." The following are remarks from Matthew Henry (with other commentaries saying similarly):

> This verse shows that one tale is good till another is told. He that speaks first will be sure to tell a story so that his cause shall appear good, whether it really be so or no. The defendant should be heard and perhaps may make the matter appear quite otherwise than it did. We must therefore remember that we have two ears, to hear both sides before we give judgment.[21]

While Proverbs 18:13 is prolifically, but partially practiced among biblical counselors, Proverbs 18:17 is regularly ignored. **If Proverbs 18:17 were practiced it would disable the biblical counseling movement and its problem-centered counselors.**

Legitimate Use of Proverbs 18:13

If a fellow Christian asks advice about a particular matter, such as what to do in a particular situation, such as whether to seek a different position at work or to ask for a sabbatical, and some details are needed for the decision, Proverbs 18:13 would apply. Questions would need to be asked in order to give some advice. However, this kind of seeking advice would not involve ongoing meetings devoted to talking sinfully about others. There are times when believers need to seek advice from fellow believers where direct advice from one's knowledge of Scripture may be given and where encouragement may be extended. However, when the advice sought has to do with ongoing interpersonal conflict, another direction of ministry must be taken, where the believer would be encouraged to focus on Christ, walk daily according to the Spirit, and thereby be equipped to handle the conflict in Christ rather than according to the natural means of the sinful nature. (See later chapters.)

Another legitimate use of Proverbs 18:13 is when a judgment is to be made by the elders regarding the report of a fellow believer's sinful behavior, such as involvement in adultery. If a judgment is to be made, there must be some investigation to gain factual information. However, in counseling there is no true investigation. What counselees say about others is generally not questioned, so there is no true investigation. As mentioned earlier, the information gleaned is generally biased opinions and hearsay.

Counselor Playing Judge

Actually one reason people go to marriage counseling is for the counselor to judge the other person and bring about correction. A wife will complain about her husband and he will complain about his wife. Why? Simply to air their griefs and "tell on" each other? Partly yes, but in these situations they want the counselor to fix the situation by making the spouse change. Quite often the counselor becomes the judge as the two wrangle in their attempt to convince the counselor which of them really needs to change. And, while the counselor may attempt to be unbiased and even sound impartial, the counselor is making judgments all the time, and these judgments may have more to do with the counselor's own personal biases than with the matter at hand.

Problem-centered counseling is not designed to be like courts of law to determine the guilty party and set forth the due punishment. Counselors using Proverbs 18:13 to elicit information generally fail to gain accurate information, because counselees do not have to prove their case and can say whatever they want about others who are not present. Thus counselors are left with the counselee's biased perspective. Counselors are bound to fail in their information gathering because they are satisfied with much misinformation. Unless they call in every person who has been discussed in counseling and unless they can gain substantial proof of everything that has been said, they cannot answer a matter in the way they apparently think they can. Furthermore, as mentioned earlier, counselees themselves often withhold essential information.

The Five Blind Men and the Elephant

Counselors who think they are able to understand the person and the problem and to bring about the correct diagnosis and treatment are very much like the five blind men and the elephant. In fact, they are worse off than the blind men who knew they were blind. While investigating all that is available to them with their probing questions and the detailed stories of their counselees, counselors are left with even less than each blind man touching a different part of the elephant. At least the five blind men were able to feel an actual entity, whereas the counselor must sift through the counselee's biased, self-serving self-disclosure, unconfirmed stories of people not present, and numerous descriptions of problems, feelings, and circumstances. In addition to selective speaking on the part of the counselee, there will inevitably be selective listening on the part of the counselor. That is, the counselor will be listening for certain things according to his life experience and counseling training and may overlook the most important information. Even after hours of gathering "data," even if these hours extend through months of once-per-week, fifty-minute conversations, the counselor has only a snippet of the person's life. He cannot see the person's soul. He cannot see the true landscape of the person's life or even the entire landscape of the person's problems. Counselees are individuals with multifaceted personalities whose lives are interconnected with a wide array of other multifaceted personalities within vast and varied circumstances. Counselors are also individuals with multifaceted personalities whose lives are interconnected with a wide array of other multifaceted counselee personalities within vast and varied circumstances that that will color everything that is said and heard in the counseling room. Add to this the multiplicity of counselees seen each week by the counselor and the subjective mix becomes even more contaminated, especially when case A seems similar to case B. Counselors who think they will truly be able to know and understand their counselees and their problems appear to be as deceived as the five blind men. In contrast, the Lord knows each person through and through. Nevertheless, counselors often compare what they do with what medical doctors do in finding out all the details to diagnose and treat a person. But that is a false analogy, because medical doctors are dealing with a physical body that can be examined and treated, but counselors are dealing with the unseen realm of the soul. That is why we want to direct all to God. He is the one who knows every detail and uses all circumstances to conform each of His children into the image of Christ.

We are not necessarily recommending what follows, but what if prior to beginning the first counseling or ministry session one were to read Psalm 19:14? "Let the words of my mouth, and the meditation of my heart, be acceptable in thy sight, O LORD, my strength, and my redeemer." And what if one then were to read Matthew12:36-37? "But I say unto you, That every idle word that men shall speak, they shall give account thereof in the day of judgment. For by thy words thou shalt be justified, and by thy words thou shalt be condemned." What if the one counseling or ministering were to comment that by extension, "These words apply to all of us," and then read James 3:2? "For in many things we offend all. If any man offend not in word, the same is a perfect man, and able also to bridle the whole body." Then what if words were added about the control of one's tongue being a barometer of the spiritual maturity of a person? Other verses could be read and further instruction about the tongue could be given. Such an introduction would never be given by a problem-centered counselor! Whether or not these verses and principles are verbalized, they should be kept in mind by the one who ministers mutual care, since individuals in need of help tend to follow the usual sinful problem-centered obsession and soon need to be brought to a biblical bridling of the tongue.

Problems do not always need to be discussed for one believer to minister Christ to another believer. However, because of the problem-centered nature of present-day counseling, the assumption is that one cannot help other people until all details of their stories have been aired and heard. However, what one really needs to know about is a person's walk with the Lord. In other words, **we want to hear how His Story (the truth of Jesus) has impacted their story.** Much greater progress can be made when the purpose is for the fellow believer to grow in knowing and trusting Christ than when the plan is problem-solving through ongoing conversations filled with the Jeremiah 17:9 syndrome. Problems are opportunities for spiritual growth and mutual care among believers. Problems can be used to motivate believers to turn to the Lord Jesus Christ and remember all He has given them: salvation through His death, burial, and resurrection; identification with Him in His death and resurrection; new life in Him; and all they possess in Him to deal with their own problems of living. Our desire is that believers will realize and remember that they are equipped in Christ to live His life and to gain victory in the midst of problems through Him.

Onerous Ones

Those who say they are being biblical practice the same sinful problem-centeredness that inevitably leads to sinful speaking and the same "onerous ones" we have written about elsewhere. We have often referred to the "onerous ones," which many in the biblical counseling movement use and which are similar to what happens in the psychological counseling movement. Many in the biblical counseling movement have regular offices and follow these onerous ones: one-to-one (most of the time there is one counselor and one counselee, except in marriage counseling); one day a week (while this is the standard, some counselors meet more often with their counselees); one hour (the 50-minute hour is the standard); one week after another (for some it goes on weekly month after month and even year after year); one fixed price (many charge or encourage a donation for biblical counseling); one right after another (counselees often follow other counselees in the counseling lineup); one up/ one down (the counselor is up as the expert and therefore the counselee is down). **There is no biblical precedence for this!** Those who function in this way are merely following those in the psychological counseling movement. In fact, **if the psychological counseling movement did not exist, the biblical counseling movement would not have followed** in its footsteps in the vocabulary and format in which it currently exists.[22]

A Paid Friend?

We've all heard the expression that a psychotherapist is a paid friend. We disagree with that definition! Yes, they are paid, but true friends they are not!!! As a matter of fact, we consider "paid friend" to be an oxymoron, i.e., a contradiction in terms. Prior to 60 years ago there were no such "friends" who had a license to counsel anyone about problems of living and therefore there were no such "paid friends" in existence. Everyone knew then, as we should all know now, that true friends do not charge for conversations about personal and often painful matters.

We served at a church as unpaid "part-time" workers, which expanded to nearly full-time, still unpaid, in which we ministered to those in need regarding difficult issues of life. In addition, we trained others to do likewise. None of us would ever think of charging! At no time was anyone in need charged and it was made clear that no gifts were to be given, as they would not be accepted. In contrast to the paid faux-friend counselors, many of us ministered to those in need in areas beyond conversation—needs such as home repair, moving, baby sitting, food, clothing, money, etc., and availability 24/7 for emergencies. Yes, we all, on occasion, received calls in the middle of the night to which we responded.

Only in the narrowest possible sense is the paid psychological or biblical counselor a friend, and that is in the confines of the 50-minute hour and only in the office. Paid counselors do not have lunch or fellowship with their counselees or visit one another as real friends do. As one typical counselor, when invited to lunch, instructed her counselee,

"I am your counselor, not your friend." We have never found paid counselors who did what often happens biblically in true Christian fellowships.

We have often wondered how many of these "paid friends" would still be friends if they were not paid. We mean friends in the true sense of the word, where there is no pay and no material rewards, just the blessings that come from serving the Lord: "It is more blessed to give than to receive" (Acts 20:35), and with "unfeigned love of the brethren, see that ye love one another with a pure heart fervently" (1 Peter 1:22).

Sadly, biblical and psychological counselors are highly esteemed inside and outside of the church, even though there was no "gift" called "counselor" given to the New Testament church (Eph. 4:11). Remove the pay, remove the special office, and remove the mistaken notion that the psychotherapists have gleaned superior-to-the-Bible knowledge through their training and that biblical counselors have gained a superior biblical understanding of people and their problems. Remove the mythology, their professional status, and external accoutrements and have these counselors minister broadly, as we did, and then watch the special prestige evaporate, leaving paid counselors on an even plain with all who minister mutual care in the body of Christ.

Not Like the Real World

Jacqueline Olds and Richard Schwartz discuss one of the serious realities of counseling in their book *The Lonely American*. This serious reality exists because of the problem-centered nature of counseling. They first mention "a curious set of rules" that exist in counseling and say, "the rules are quite different from the rules for ordinary relationships. The most striking difference is that the **usual expectation of**

reciprocity disappears" (bold added).[23] All the drama and narrative dialogue are about the counselee and her issues and problems. The counselee gets to talk about herself and her litany of personal problems and the counselor does not get to talk about herself and her litany of personal problems, except for something brief that might be said to establish rapport. The expectation is that the focus of the counseling will be on the counselee's "problems and life and words."[24] The counselor does not get equal time for her own issues. Dr. Thomas Szasz describes counseling simply as "rhetoric" and refers to counseling as "conversation." Szasz asks, "In plain language, what do [the counselee] and [counselor] actually do?" He answers, "They speak and listen to each other." Szasz asks and answers, "What do they speak about? Narrowly put, the [counselee] speaks about himself, and the [counselor] speaks about the [counselee]."[25] The spotlight during the counseling hour is on the counselee.

The counselor/counselee relationship is diametrically different from normal relationships where there is reciprocity. Turn-taking occurs in normal relationships. One person speaks and another listens, but the listener gets to speak as well. The focus of attention is shared between one another's "problems and life and words." In normal conversation there is close to equal time given to and taken by both parties. The down side of the counseling relationship is that it is not the normal way conversations are carried on in the real world.

While "there are no reliable statistics" on what is called "self-disclosure," it is considered to be unprofessional for a counselor to disclose her own personal issues to a counselee whether the time is paid for or not.[26] Imagine a counselor talking about her own marriage problems or her own relational or (if paid) her own professional issues, saying for example, "My husband and I do not see eye to eye lately on a lot of matters," etc., or "This has been a tough month. Some of my counselees have not returned and I have expenses to cover and my own personal income needs." When such self-disclosure occurs, it is typically the end of the counseling. Why? Because the counselee is there to talk about her own problems and not to listen to the counselor's problems, especially if she is paying for the counseling time.

Regardless of how dull and boring the counselee may be, the counselor has the responsibility to listen thoughtfully and often to hang on every word the counselee utters in an effort to obtain an accurate understanding of the problem and to respond appropriately. Normal friends will seem mundane after a therapeutic love-in that can occur in counseling. Olds and Schwartz aptly describe such skewed relationships:

> The special partnership that allows a therapist to earn a good living and a patient to focus on neglected aspects of his life and experience would be a disaster outside of the office. Used as a template for other intimate relationships, it is selfish and self-absorbed. Other than therapists, only an occasional very self-sacrificing parent or a spouse who aspires to martyrdom is likely to sign on for that long term. A problem with psychotherapy is that it can make all other relationships look like they fall short when it comes to sustained, attentive caring and leave the patient circling back to therapy as the only relationship that is good enough.[27]

If one replaces the word "therapist' with "biblical counselor" and "psychotherapy" with "biblical counseling" the application would be the same.

Women in Counseling

At the beginning of the contemporary counseling era men were primarily the counselors, but women were primar-

ily the willing and even eager victims of this male dominated psychic search that fossicked about in the regions of
the mind. The men are the ones responsible for formulating
and peddling the forbidden fruit of counseling to their hapless women victims, who, in turn, are fertile territory for spe-
lunking into the hidden mysteries of the mind. As counseling
moved from an almost sole preoccupation with the unconscious through psychoanalysis and its contemporary counseling variations to a greater focus on the conscious mind
through the behavioristic, humanistic, and transpersonal
streams of counseling psychology, women were the primary
objects and subjects. And, they continue to be a ready market for pandering the prolifically expanding available psychotherapies.

From the very beginning of the talk therapy movement
after World War II, the statistics always favored the prepon-
derance of women over men as counselees. While more men
are now entering counseling as counselees, the latest figures stand at two-thirds women and one-third men. Women
enter counseling as counselees because they are attracted to
it as a means of solving problems. Thus, problem-centered
conversations come naturally to them. Professional therapists in America are now predominantly women. Members
of the National Association of Marriage and Family Therapists are at least two-thirds women and the percentage of
women clinical psychologists is catching up. Psychology
ads for training counselors and ads for needed counseling or
recovery are aimed primarily at women. Women's pictures
are in almost all the ads. So often it ends up being woman-
to-woman counseling with reciprocal possibilities to expand
the problem-centeredness with its sinful speaking about others.

Although such statistics are hard to come by, one survey by the American Psychological Association (APA)

concluded: "For the clinical hour they were surveyed for, 78% of the psychologists saw a single person in session for therapy or counseling."[28] The figures received from the American Association of Marriage and Family Therapists (AAMFT) seemed to indicate a 62% figure for a marriage or family therapist seeing a single person in session for therapy or counseling.[29] Granted that the APA and the AAMFT are not the only two professional organizations for counselors, they nonetheless represent a large enough sample to make an estimate. **We conclude from prior research and the above information that the typical counselee is a woman who comes in by herself and sees a woman counselor, except for biblical counseling where the counselors are still predominantly men.**

Men in Counseling

Counselors typically usurp the man's spiritual headship by giving answers to questions men are not asking and by corralling them into strange touchy-feely pastures not of their liking. Notice in Chapter Three how the counselor is in charge and the one up/one down ("expert/dummy") relationship exalts the counselor and diminishes the man's spiritual headship.

The *Psychotherapy Networker* (*PN*), a journal for psychotherapists, devoted an entire issue to "The Secret World of Men: What Therapists Need to Know." One *PN* therapist confirmed that:

> Men usually get therapy only because someone else has insisted on it. When I ask men in an initial therapy session, "What are you doing here?" the answer I hear is "My wife told me I needed to be here." Other times, it may be their boss or their grandmother or their doctor, or even a probation officer.[30]

Another *PN* therapist affirmed the same fact by saying, "Men more often came into therapy under pressure from someone else, frequently an unhappy spouse."[31] Also, the psychotherapist writers for *PN* would **all** no doubt agree with one of them who bluntly says that "even with men who know they need help is the very idea of sitting in a room, talking *out loud* about all this touchy-feely stuff; it creeps them out" (italics in original).[32]

Men in counseling are often caught between the proverbial "rock and a hard place." They are yanked out of their reluctance to express the very feelings that women demand and are then criticized for expressing them. They often go into counseling wary and come out wimps. Men on the whole are either not that interested or they are repelled by the whole idea of going to counseling. *Psychology Today* discussed this topic in an article titled "Man's Last Stand: What Does It Take to Get a Guy into Therapy?" Regarding men seeking counseling, the article says:

> More often than not, the impetus is a woman. A typical male patient has been sent—usually by his wife, girlfriend or children, sometimes by his employer. Behind the command performance is a threat: "You change, or it's all over."[33]

One author-therapist, Terrence Real, refers to these as "wife mandated referrals." He says, "The average man is as likely to ask for help with a psychological problem as he is to ask for directions." Real gives the reason: men do not consider counseling to be "manly."[34] This is doubly true among Christian men who are biblically knowledgeable and by common sense know they should not be there.

Of the total of those in counseling, the men who enter **voluntarily** are small in number. Gary Brooks, in his book *A New Psychotherapy for Traditional Men*, says, "Traditional men hate psychotherapy and will do most anything to avoid a therapist's office." He continues, "In fact, I believe that men's aversion to therapy is so powerful that it's wise to assume that most male clients, at some level, don't want to be there."[35] The *Psychology Today* article adds another factor:

> Then there's the matter of stigma. More than one in five men in the Therapy in America survey said they didn't trust therapists and wouldn't want to be associated with the type of person who receives therapy."[36]

Thus men are encouraged, intimidated, or brow-beaten into it by this culturally sanctioned phenomenon of counseling.

In *Psychotherapy Networker* one therapist reveals through humor the situation of men in counseling. He says:

> You've heard the jokes. Every couples therapist has skid marks at the front door from husbands being dragged into the office. Or this one: A man is convicted of tax evasion, claiming that he had to do it because his wife spent too much. The sentencing judge gives him a choice: "Do you want to go to federal prison or marriage counseling" The guy asks, "Could I have a private cell?"[37]

This therapist further adds:

> The vast majority of the couples I see are therapy veterans, whose former therapists have thrown up their hands in defeat and referred them to me. When these couples come to my office, the women are exhausted, or bitter or both; the men cynically describe what they've learned in their previous therapy: "To save my marriage, I have to become a woman."[38]

The encouraged-by-the-counselor transparency and intimacy for men is dangerous in cross-gender counseling. More about this later.

Many cultural factors intimidate men into being open to sharing as a means of dealing with personal problems. These include feminism, the confusion of male roles, and the exaggerated claims by promoters of the counseling mentality and model. In a self-focused society, these cultural phenomena have eclipsed the biblical roles for men.

As much as men are not attracted to counseling, virtually all avenues in and out of the church force them into it. Again, counseling is a female-friendly activity, which obtains male clients mostly through intimidation, exaggerated claims, expectations of others, or coercion. Behind most men in psychotherapy or in biblical counseling is a woman, a court, an employer, a church denomination, or, as we have demonstrated elsewhere, a mission agency.

The fact of a man often being coerced into counseling is not to suggest that a woman is the sole reason for it, but rather to say that she is a major reason. We conclude that, absent a woman behind getting a man into counseling, the counseling movement would be seriously damaged, since up to one-third of the counselees (men) could disappear. Moreover, if the other personal, cultural, promotional, and legal incentives and mandates towards counseling were removed, men, on their own, would avoid it all together.

Conclusion

In conclusion and based upon our past and current writings, we repeat a challenge we have issued to biblical counselors. Prior to stating our challenge, we review several things to clarify our challenge. **When we use the word *problem* we are referring to those problems normally talked about**

with a psychotherapist or a biblical counselor. They are the mental-emotional-behavioral problems for which people seek counseling help. When we use the word *counseling* we are using it in the sense that those in the BCM use it. Those in the BCM use it to mean problem-centered counseling, since that is what they primarily do. Problems are presented by the counselee and pursued and discussed by the counselor in an effort to know all the details and thereby give the solutions, and **that is where the sinful talk arises.**

We repeatedly say in our book: **Problem-centered counseling inevitably leads to sinful counseling. No matter how biblical one claims to be, so-called biblical counseling is defaulted by its counselor-led problem-centeredness with its sinful communication.** Problem-centered counseling done in the BCM involves many violations of numerous Bible verses warning against such talk.

With the thousands of individuals claiming to do biblical counseling and the Bible colleges and seminaries that teach it, one should be able to find a biblical counseling session (or a series of sessions) in writing or on audio or video that is truly biblical and therefore without evil speaking. We have searched thoroughly and found none.

We challenge biblical counselors to provide a word-for-word counseling session or a detailed description of one to demonstrate that they are truly biblical. To date no biblical counselor has met the challenge and all of the available biblical counseling sessions and numerous case descriptions we have examined have failed the test!

It is perplexing to us that, after combing the biblical counseling literature for so many years, there are almost no real biblical counseling sessions on CD or DVD or in writing, and that includes none from the American Association of Christian Counselors, the Association for Clinical Pastoral Education, the Biblical Counseling Foundation, the

Christian Counseling and Educational Foundation, and the National Association of Nouthetic Counselors. Yes, there are contrived cases, as we have discussed here and in our other writings, but almost no real cases with real counselors with real-time counseling, and what exists does not meet the acid test of being biblical.

Finally, those who promote, educate, refer out to or practice biblical counseling are promoting sinful talk. That includes those in the biblical counseling movement, whether as institutions or organizations that provide counseling degrees, certificates or training or those who actually do the biblical counseling or those pastors and others who send these counselors people in need of help.

5

Cross-Gender Counseling

For all that is in the world, the lust of the flesh, and the lust of the eyes, and the pride of life, is not of the Father, but is of the world.   1 John 2:16

Because of the evil speaking that will occur, our first hope is that counselors will stop their problem-centered counseling and start ministering biblically. We also hope that, as a result of reading this book, those who claim to be biblical in their counseling will **stop cross-gender counseling**. Cross-gender counseling occurs prolifically with men counseling women, women counseling men, and a man or a woman counseling a couple. The bigger offender of the two is the male counselor because at least two-thirds of the counselees are women. And, while licensed psychological counselors are mostly women, biblical counselors are still mostly men.[1] Unfortunately a male counselor with a female counselee is standard practice among many biblical counselors. **In this chapter we indicate both biblical and practical reasons why all cross-gender counseling should cease.**

No Biblical Examples

We look to the Bible to see what Scripture reveals. As we repeatedly say, Scripture presents no example of what is called biblical counseling as it is practiced today. Also, nowhere in Scripture is there a hint or example of a man counseling a woman as currently practiced in biblical counseling, and nowhere in the Bible is there an example of a woman counseling a man as currently practiced in some biblical counseling circles. There are numerous teachings and admonitions throughout Scripture about life, living, and the issues of life, but there is no example in all of these of any cross-gender counseling.

Women and Men in Counseling

There are great similarities between men and women; however, there are some significant differences which affect cross-gender counseling. It seems trivial and almost unnecessary to say, but men and women are different from one another and these differences enter into the counseling setting. In addition to biblical differences between men and women, there are biological, behavioral, hormonal, and functional differences.

Differences between men and women begin before birth and continue throughout life. *Science News* reports:

> The reason boys like trucks and girls like dolls relates to fetal differences in brain development, explains Heather Patisaul, a neuroendrocrinologist at North Carolina State University in Raleigh. Males develop differently from females—physically and behaviorally—largely through programming by androgens (male sex hormones such as testosterone).[2]

The *Scientific American Mind* reports in "The Neural Roots of Intelligence" on the differences in the neural networks of intelligence in men and women. They say:

> The specific areas in this network are different in men and women, suggesting there are at least two different brain architectures that produce equivalent performance on IQ tests. In general, we found that in women more gray and white matter in frontal brain areas, especially those associated with language, was correlated with IQ scores; in men IQ scores correlated with gray matter in frontal areas and, especially, in posterior areas that integrate sensory information.[3]

Of course there are similarities between the brains of men and women. However, *Scientific American Mind* says, "It turns out that male and female brains differ quite a bit in architecture and activity."[4] The journal also says that "over the past decade investigators have documented an astonishing array of structural, chemical and functional variations in the brains of males and females."[5] The *Scientific American Mind* produced a special issue devoted to "Male vs. Female Brains" with the words "His Brain, Her Brain, How we're different" on the cover.[6] While this special issue does speak of similarities between the sexes, it is primarily about the differences. One writer sums it up by saying: "There is ample evidence that men and women think, express themselves and even experience emotions differently."[7] Linguist Deborah Tannen explains "Genderspeak" as follows: "Men's talk tends to focus on hierarchy—competition for relative power—whereas women's tends to focus on connection—relative closeness or distance."[8] The differences in the brains of men and women influence how they perceive and act. **These differences are played out in cross-gender counsel-**

ing. There are many other gender differences, but we offer only a few more in the following paragraphs.

Medical doctor Louann Brizendine, in her book *The Female Brain*, describes a woman as "a person whose reality dictated that communication, connection, emotional sensitivity, and responsiveness were the primary values."[9] Brizendine's theme throughout the book is that women are different because they have different brains, and, as a result, women are deeply sensitive to emotions and form strong relationships. One group of researches reveals the following:

> Beauty is in the brain of the beholder. Go to any museum and there will be men and women admiring paintings and sculpture. But it turns out they are thinking about the sight differently. Men process beauty on the right side of their brains, while women use their whole brain to do the job, researchers report in Tuesday's electronic edition of Proceedings of the National Academy of Science. They even explain it differently....
>
> Researchers were surprised by the finding. "It is well known that there are differences between brain activity in women and men in cognitive tasks," said researcher Camilo J. Cela-Conde of the University of Baleares in Palma de Mallorca, Spain. "However, why should this kind of difference appear in the case of appreciation of beauty?" The answer seems to be that when women consider a visual object they link it to language while men concentrate on the spatial aspects of the object.[10]

Dr. James W. Pennebaker of the University of Texas at Austin and his colleagues have "developed a computer program that analyzes texts called Linguistic Inquiry and Word Count (LIWC, pronounced 'Luke')."[11] Through the use of

LIWC, Pennebaker et al reveal by statistical analysis that "the way we write and speak can reveal volumes about our identity and character." They say, "In general, women tend to use more pronouns and references to other people. Men are more likely to use articles, prepositions and big words."[12] This certainly affects conversations in cross-gender counseling.

According to some theories, men in general are "better at systemizing" and "women are better at empathizing."[13] Here, too, these differences affect conversations in cross-gender counseling. Counselors encourage women to do what they do so well—being verbal, nurturing, and relational. Women tend to share and converse. Communication, as it occurs and is encouraged in problem-centered counseling, comes naturally to women and can result in miscommunication in cross-gender counseling. In the manner in which they function, counselors appeal to women to come for help. The counselors offer an environment for relationship and for exploring and expressing emotions in a conversational, female-friendly setting that suits women's feeling-oriented inclination to share. Problem-centered counseling provides an environment in which these female feelings and thoughts can easily be misunderstood or not understood at all in cross-gender counseling. Moreover, an understanding male counselor may stimulate romantic feelings in a woman as he listens to her every word with rapt attention. She may romanticize about their relationship and even believe that he has feelings for her as well. At the least this male counselor/female counselee intimacy may well make a married woman's husband appear second-rate in comparison.

The primary reason men should not be in counseling is because their spiritual headship is generally corrupted. It is bad enough when the man's spiritual headship is corrupted by another man; it is doubly bad when it is corrupted by a women counselor. In summary, cross-gender counseling is detrimental for both men and women. **The spiritual headship of men and women's relational virtues are often and easily corrupted in problem-centered counseling.** Oftentimes in counseling what the counselees talk about can be classified under "the lust of the flesh, and the lust of the eyes, and the pride of life" (1 John 2:16) and the world, the flesh, and the devil. These sinful areas are discussed, elaborated, and questioned during the counseling process. In cross-gender counseling men and women regard these areas differently, respond to them differently, and usually speak about them differently. Therefore cross-gender counseling is detrimental to honest and clear communication and can lead to much confusion and misunderstanding. He talks as a male counselee and she responds as a female counselor or she talks as female counselee and he responds as a male counselor. **The speaking, listening, and responding are all affected by inherent gender differences in cross-gender counseling.** The above represent only a small fraction of the support for the existence of differences between men and women that can play a significant role in cross-gender counseling.

"Gender Bias Is Ubiquitous"

Biblical counselors will claim that they preach, teach, and evangelize in the counseling room and use that as a reason for cross-gender counseling. If that were all they did we would rejoice. However, that is not all they do; they do have problem-centered conversations that inevitably involve evil speaking. The evil of evil speaking is magnified in cross-gender counseling, because, in addition to being indwelt by the Holy Spirit, Christians are also living in the flesh, which is particularly vulnerable in the context of modern-

day counseling. The counselors are men and women living in the flesh, man as man and woman as woman. **Both
counselors and counselees are individuals to whom the
Jeremiah 17:9 syndrome applies.** Because of this fleshly
gender orientation, men who counsel will carry male biases
into counseling and women who counsel will carry female
biases into counseling, which will affect what is said. (See
Chapter Two.)

One prolific writer and university counseling professor
notes "how much more comfortable a therapist (or anyone)
feels working with people who are most similar to her in
terms of religion, race, socioeconomic background, and core
values."[14] This is very true, and gender identity, male to male
and female to female, is also an added strong factor in being
"most similar." This is a fleshly factor that also affects biblical counseling.

One academic text on counseling reveals what should
be obvious to a believer about a fleshly orientation in cross-
gender counseling. Regarding cross-gender counseling, it
says, **"Gender bias is ubiquitous."**[15] Research shows that
male counselors counsel according to the "male norm."
Imagine a male counselee who is involved in pornography
speaking to a female counselor whose **flesh** could not relate
to it or not have a clue about that kind of lust; and imagine a female counselee who is heart sick over her romantic
fantasies about some man and speaking to a male counselor
whose **flesh** could totally misunderstand her or not be able
to relate to this kind of response. The flesh of both counselors would no doubt be involved in the counseling. **Hope-
fully no one is naïve enough to think that their flesh is
not involved in their counseling.** Those who would say that
this does not happen in Christian counseling are overlooking
Jeremiah 17:9 and other verses referring to the flesh and self-
deception as we reveal in Chapter Two.

While the apostle Paul would give wise counsel to men on an individual basis, such as with his missionary partners along the way and with fellow workers regarding ministry and conduct, most of what we see in his teachings to women, as individuals and as wives, come through his ministry of preaching and teaching to groups of individuals and through his letters to both churches and individuals. Examples of such teachings about living the Christian life are given throughout the New Testament, and Paul's teachings about the marriage relationship in Ephesians 5:21-25 are clear and very Christ-centered. Notice how often he points to Christ and His relationship to the church and how the marriage is to be a picture of that relationship.

Paul certainly did not waste his time or theirs talking about such trivial matters as husbands not picking up their socks and wives not cooking meals the husband likes, et cetera, ad nauseam. He was well aware of the problems that Christians were facing, but he taught and wrote to all in such a way that Christ was central and with the understanding that the Holy Spirit would make applications in each life. We note one exception in that the apostle John wrote a letter to "the elect lady and her children," but this was not a private counseling session and simply had to do with walking faithfully with the Lord and guarding against deception. This was a far cry from any private conversation resembling today's counseling. **Those who do cross-gender counseling cannot point to the apostle Paul or any biblical example of any cross-gender counseling occurring in Scripture!**

Rapport and Bonding in Counseling

In his monumental book *The Discovery of the Unconscious: The History and Evolution of Dynamic Psychiatry*, Henri F. Ellenberger gives a detailed history of the background and emergence of psychotherapy. He says, "Whatever the psychotherapeutic procedure, it showed the same common basic feature: the presence and utilization of the **rapport**"[16] (bold added). If one is to best assist the counselee, rapport is both a necessary ingredient and a common factor in all counseling and psychotherapy. Through rapport a bonding occurs between the one in need and the one who desires to help.

Rapport is often described as a harmonious or sympathetic relationship as can occur in counseling. Some describe it as sharing a world view between counselor and counselee. Others describe it variously as the magic, glue, sympathy, warmth, acceptance, and encouragement that exist in the relationship. Whatever terms are used to describe *rapport*, they are terms of intimacy, which the dictionary defines as "a close, familiar, and usually affectionate or loving personal relationship with another person."[17] And, no matter how rapport is described, for the counselor it is regarded as the most important ingredient for success in counseling, as we will demonstrate in Chapter Six. The counselors' responsibility is to strive for the highest level of rapport in their quest for success.

Everyday relationships in the family or with close friends or others generally include some element of rapport. However, the counseling relationship, because it involves a greater emotional intensity due to personal issues, usually requires a deeper rapport in order for trust and confidence in the counselor to be established for therapeutic success. It is at this needed-for-success deeper level of rapport that one can enter the danger zone in cross-gender counseling.

Think about cross-gender counseling with a man counseling a woman or a woman counseling a man where there is deep rapport with a harmonious or sympathetic relationship, including a shared world view, between a warm, accepting, empathetic and encouraging counselor and an expectant, trusting counselee. This type of relationship is intimate and close and is often entered into with a complete stranger or with one not formerly intimately known by the counselee.

Another term that is used to describe the ideal in counseling is *bonding*. There are various definitions for *bonding*; however, we define it here as a close relationship that is achieved in counseling as a result of intense experiences described by the counselee and one in which the counselee and counselor can become emotionally attached to one another. It is one with inherent dangers that common sense would dictate be avoided between the sexes. The end result of such deep rapport and bonding is seen in various studies regarding such close counselor/counselee relationships. One professional journal says, "Research suggests that therapists have a long half-life and remain inside their clients for years."[18] That same journal reports on two professional journal articles on this phenomenon. The first is the *Psychiatric Times*, where:

> Psychiatrist Barbara Young reported on her personal project asking former clients how they'd internalized their therapy. A client from 20 years before, who told Young that she checks in daily with God about her decisions and feelings, suddenly looked at Young and exclaimed, "He talks to me just like you used to!"[19]

The second is from *Psychotherapy Theory, Research, Practice, Training*, where:

> James Mosher of Miami University reported on a study about how former clients who've been in therapy for varying periods internalized their therapists over time. One client, who'd had eight sessions, described her therapist as a protective shell. "It was

like being on *Who Wants to be a Millionaire* and using a lifeline," said another short-term client. After a while, however, clients experienced the therapist's presence as being inside. Therapy, said one longer-term client, became "something that was deepening in me."[20]

The biblical blueprint for an intimately personal male/female relationship is the godly marriage as described in Scripture where spiritual headship with all its responsibilities and privileges is the man's and where spiritual submission with all its responsibilities and privileges is the woman's (Eph. 5:22-33). Granted that the extent of the intimate relationship in counseling is not the same as in the marriage relationship, it certainly strives for the type of intimacy that occurs through rapport and bonding, which can have serious possible consequences as we describe later in the section titled "Sex and the Counselor."

Should a female counselor strive for rapport and bonding, which would lead to an intimate relationship with a male counselee who is not her husband? Should a male counselor strive for rapport and bonding, which would lead to an intimate relationship with a female counselee who is not his wife? **The obvious answer is no!** Based upon the absence of any biblical example or exhortation regarding such a relationship, it follows that no such male-female counseling relationship should exist among God's people. Can you imagine the Apostle Paul recommending, endorsing, or utilizing this kind of rapport and bonding in cross-gender counseling?!

"Transference" and "Countertransference"

There are certain common occurrences in counseling that have been observed, named, and described.[21] One of these is when counselees tend to transfer into the relationship with the counselor the sometimes intense feelings experienced with other significant figures in their life. These are very "often manifested as an erotic attraction towards a therapist, but can be seen in many other forms."[22] This is referred to in the literature as "transference." Another, which is related, is called "countertransference," which is when the counselor experiences the total range of feelings, positive and/or negative, towards a counselee.

In his book *On Being a Therapist*, Professor Jeffrey Kottler says:

> Several researchers have urged clinicians to examine their fantasies with clients as a clue to how counter-transference may be operating. Whether these fantasies are primarily rescue oriented, sexual, or expressive of rage, frustration, and anger, **most therapists entertain fantasies and daydream about many of their clients.**[23] (Bold added.)

Because of the problem-centered nature of biblical counseling, these same fantasies are possible with a biblical counselor as well.

While a high level of rapport and bonding are what the counselor desires to achieve, they can lead to transference and countertransference, with its problems and difficulties, which a counselor would want to avoid. These occurrences commonly happen in both psychological and biblical counseling, but are unlikely to occur in the ministry of mutual care. While one may disagree with using these terms and explanations, we know that there are intense feelings, both positive and negative, that a counselee can experience towards a counselor and vice versa. Regardless of the explanation for these intense feeling that occur and are labeled "transference" and "countertransference," they nonetheless do occur and need to be considered, especially in cross-gender counseling.

Because we know such intense emotions can exist in counseling between the counselee and the counselor and because they do occur, we point out that cross-gender counseling involving cross-gender intense feelings should be avoided. Here again common sense alone should dictate that, outside the marriage and appropriate family relationships, these types of intense feelings should be avoided between the sexes, especially in the counseling setting. Counselors often have multiple counseling appointments during each day and throughout the week, with up to 40 counselees being seen during the week. It is amazing that they can keep the details of the multiple appointments clear in their minds **while juggling each unique form of rapport and bonding needed for each individual along with the fallout of transference and countertransference that can occur**. We repeat, all of this occurs in most cases between a counselor and counselee who are usually strangers to one another outside the counseling office.

Sex and the Counselor

Within the "Lord's Prayer" is the expression "and lead us not into temptation, but deliver us from evil" (Matt. 6:13). Matthew Poole says:

> The term *temptation* in the general signifieth a trial, and is sometimes used to express God's trials of his people's faith and obedience, but most ordinarily to express Satan's trials of us, by motions to sin; which may be from our own lusts, James i.13, 14; or from the devil, who is therefore called the tempter; or from the world. These are the temptations which we are commanded to pray against: not that God leads any

persons into such temptations, unless by the permission of his providence.[24]

The cross-gender environment is rife with "motions to sin; which may be from our own lusts ... or from the devil ... or from the world." William MacDonald adds that "This petition expresses a healthy distrust of one's own ability to resist temptations or to stand up under trial."[25]

An extremely important reason why cross-gender counseling should not be done is because of the sexual attraction that often occurs in both psychological and biblical counseling. Obviously some situations are more vulnerable to this than others. This vulnerability occurs in both psychological and biblical counseling. In a random sample of members of the American Psychological Association, the *Los Angeles Times* reports:

> Of the 585 psychologists who responded, 87% (95% of the men and 76% of the women) reported having been sexually attracted to their clients, at least on occasion. Sixty-three percent felt guilty, anxious or confused about the attraction, and about half of the respondents received no guidance or training on this issue.[26]

The Harvard Mental Health Letter reports:

> Research has shown that sexual contact with patients is common and often injurious. Between 7 and 12 percent of psychotherapists (psychiatrists, psychologists, and social workers) admit sexual relations with patients. Therapists who treat sexually exploited patients report that all of them are harmed.[27]

The Seattle Times, in response to the question, "Who does the most harm?" says, "More registered counselors were disciplined for sexual misconduct than any other health-care practitioners." They add: "Based on the rate per 1,000 licenses, psychologists rank as the top offender."[28] Because these surveys depend upon the honesty of the counselors reporting, many have said that the figures are no doubt much higher.

Although we do not have statistics regarding Christian counselors, we do have a file folder filled with stories about individual Christians who were exposed because of their sexual misconduct. Irrespective of whether there are statistics on Christian counselors and their sexual misconduct or not, the same dynamics exist and provide one more reason why this type of cross-gender counseling should be avoided.

Men and women may be sinfully attracted to one another in the counseling relationship. For men it is usually direct sexual lust; for the woman it is usually romantic lust. A female counselee who has a kind and compassionate male counselor can develop romantic feelings for the counselor and she may think about him lots between appointments. Such tempting thoughts can feed an inordinate desire of a romantic sort—sinful lust. She becomes vulnerable to the male counselor and she may become a snare to him.

A further topic to consider when evaluating cross-gender counseling is the way a woman presents herself in personal manner and appearance. Clearly the Bible teaches modesty (1 Timothy 2:9-10; 1 Peter 3:1-4) and warns against worldliness (1 John 2:15-16). However, even in the church one can see the influence of the world while women adorn themselves according to the latest fashion rather than in "modest apparel." The fashion industry does all it can to woo women into buying clothing that enhances their sexual appeal, and the more provocative the clothing available, the looser the standards become to the extent that even Christian women can be seen wearing low-cut tops, short skirts, and tight clothing. While there is a broad spectrum regarding clothing among Christian women, there are certain modes of dress that would be especially problematic in cross-gender counseling. A woman's apparel may be a snare in cross-gender counseling, whether she is the counselor or the counselee. If she sports the latest fashion she is a temptation and a snare to other women who might follow her example. She is a more dangerous temptation and snare to her male counselees, who may seem to be hanging on her every word while engaging in voyeurism. Such can happen in cross-gender counseling. Further, consider the possible distracting thoughts of a male counselor counseling a female counselee who is wearing clothing that reveals more than should be seen in public and/ or tightly outlines the rest of her body. Under such circumstances he can be tempted to lust and will be unable to give proper attention to what is being discussed. Even if a woman is appropriately dressed, some women's facial expressions and eye contact can come across as sexual, whether or not it is on purpose. A steady eye contact by a woman or man counselor or counselee, which can often occur, may come across as flirtatious or romantic, whether intended or not. Thus, sexual appeal is often magnified in the counseling setting by the manner of dress, mannerisms, and facial expression, including eye contact, during cross-gender counseling and is one more reason to avoid it.

Spiritual Headship

God has clearly established the authority structure of the family and outlined the means by which it is to be followed by Christians. In 1 Corinthians we have the line of authority coming from Christ: "But I would have you know, that the head of every man is Christ; and the head of the woman is the man; and the head of Christ is God" (1 Cor. 11:3). This is further emphasized in Ephesians 5:23: "For the husband is the head of the wife, even as Christ is the head of the church: and he is the saviour of the body." Ephesians 5:22-33 then gives believers the way this is to be worked out in the relationship of marriage with wives to "submit yourselves unto your own husbands, as unto the Lord" and to "see that she reverence her husband" and with the husbands to "love your wives, even as Christ also loved the church, and gave himself for it" and to "love his wife even as himself." Thus God has given the man the headship, which includes both authority and responsibility. This God-given authority has been resisted, misused, and abused by sinful humanity, but those who are in Christ are called and equipped to follow what God has set forth for His glory and their good.

While biblical counselors see themselves as helping couples and families to follow God's ordained authority structure in the family, they themselves violate the man's headship when they counsel a wife or unmarried daughter. Both psychological and biblical counseling are structured to give the counselor a position of authority in the eyes of the person being counseled. Thus it is in error biblically when men counsel women and children who already have a spiritual head. Most of the time an adult woman comes in by herself for counseling and very often she complains about circumstances involving her husband, who is not present during the counseling. In cross-gender counseling she would then be looking to another man rather than to her husband, to whom she is to submit and reverence. If an unmarried daughter is being counseled by a man other than her own father, she is inadvertently placing him in the position of headship. Cross gender counseling diminishes or violates the spiritual headship that God has ordained. It is especially egregious for a woman to counsel a man, who then comes under her authority rather than under Christ. There are times for mutual care in the body of Christ, but here again believers need to remember and respect the man's headship in the family.

A Man Counseling a Woman or a Couple

The counseling of a woman by a man needs to be viewed biblically in the context of spiritual headship. Who is the spiritual head of a woman? As we just indicated, if a woman is married, her husband is her spiritual head (1 Cor. 11:3), Eph. 5:23). An unmarried daughter is under the spiritual authority of her parents (Eph. 6:1-3). In problem-centered counseling, when a man counsels a married woman or couple, there is a danger that he will displace the husband's spiritual headship to some degree, whether or not the husband is present. The types of problems a woman brings to a biblical counselor are often those that should be discussed with her husband; or, if she is not married and at home, discussed with her father, mother or a more mature woman (Titus 2:3-5). **How many biblical counselors even think to ask the husband's consent to counsel his wife or a father's consent to counsel his dependent children?** And, how many biblical counselors know whether the husband or father has agreed to such counseling?

Oftentimes a wife will enter problem-centered counseling without her husband because of his reluctance, but this is also contrary to the headship given to men, because the counselor now functions in place of the husband. In fact, if the counselor is a man, he probably spends more time listening to other men's wives than to his own. What's worse is that the husband of the woman being counseled may be unfairly compared to the male counselor who spends time listening to the husband's wife in a contrived setting, in which he can appear extremely attentive and focused on her. In contrast, the husband may not appear as attentive and focused on her in the midst of their real life situations. Another tragic result of a man counseling a woman is the fact that, absent the reality of the home environment of the woman, the counselor can misdirect the woman's loyalty and submission away from her husband or father, which can result in the counselor usurping the husband's or father's headship. Moreover, too many temptations occur in such counseling circumstances and many divorces have occurred because of them. Also, talking about the husband in his absence (Prov. 18:17) could easily be biased, include talebearing (Prov. 11:13; 18:8; 20:19; 26:20, 22), reveal confidences, and diminish the husband's headship by dishonoring him to a third party. Considering the above concerns, men should **not** be counseling women.

Paul David Tripp, a popular biblical counselor, is a good example of this unbiblical practice of a man counseling a woman. In his book *Broken-Down House* he discusses a marriage counseling situation and says:

> In desperation, she began to seek help for her marriage. She wanted solid advice before she approached Henry again. But it wasn't long before **she was meeting with me alone.** Henry wouldn't come.[29] (Bold added.)

Tripp's meeting alone with a woman counselee has been a regular practice, as he says: "In counseling I have heard countless recitations of men's wrongs against their wives."[30]

Considering all of the writings of the apostle Paul about life and conduct, can you imagine a woman coming to his room for counseling?! And imagine this woman coming to the apostle Paul's room week after week to meet privately, alone with him, to discuss the kinds of matters discussed in biblical counseling. Or, can you imagine the apostle Paul supporting or recommending that a man meet privately with a woman at a specified place and time for lengthy conversations about her and her problems every week, sometimes for months at a time? He would certainly not do such a thing as meet with a woman in such privacy for even a moment, let alone hours and hours, week after week! Such private meetings as occur in biblical counseling would countermand his very teachings about spiritual headship over the woman and other matters, besides the inherent sexual relationship danger and questionable appearance of evil. In spite of this total lack of example in Scripture, many men who do biblical counseling do counsel many women, and these men would probably be horrified to think that their female counselees should not be there.

A Woman Counseling a Man or a Couple

In problem-centered counseling, a woman counseling a man or a couple often erodes the biblical role of the man and reduces or usurps his spiritual headship. It is difficult to counsel someone without having a spiritual headship role in the relationship. Biblical counseling is a spiritual setting; there will be doctrinal teaching and it is easy for a woman to usurp spiritual authority over a man in such a problem-centered environment, where biblical suggestions are made, spiritual directions given, and Bible study homework assigned. It is interesting to see those denominations and churches that would not permit a woman to preach in their pulpits nonetheless refer men to female counselors, who are obviously problem-centered and who, by the very nature of counseling, wield authority in spiritual matters.

Leslie Vernick, a licensed counselor, says she counsels "from a biblical world view."[31] She gives examples in her books of counseling men with and without the man's wife present. The Christian Counseling and Educational Foundation (CCEF) has offered her books and used her at their conferences. Ed Welch, the Director of Counseling at CCEF, wrote an endorsement for one of her books. We know of no biblical counseling organization, including CCEF, that has identified the offenders and made a biblical issue of this practice of women counseling men in such intimate relationships as occur in counseling or of this cross-gender counseling arrangement being detrimental to the God-given spiritual headship of men. In an article for *Psychotherapy Networker* titled "Women Treating Men," the author psychotherapist states what is known throughout professional circles. She says, "With my male clients, I became keenly aware that often I was seen by them as a woman first and a therapist second."[32]

The reverse of a man counseling a woman, as we discussed, can occur where the woman counselor can appear extremely attentive and focused on him. In contrast, the wife may not appear as attentive and focused on him in the midst of their real life situations. Again, too many temptations occur in such counseling circumstances and many divorces have occurred because of them. Also, talking about the wife in her absence (Proverbs 18:17) could easily be biased, include talebearing (Prov. 11:13; 18:8; 20:19; 26:20, 22), reveal confidences, and violate the one-flesh principle. Sadly, while many biblical counselors would be opposed to women counseling men, we know of none of the well-known leaders of the BCM making a public outcry against that practice and naming those in violation.

Conclusion

Cross-gender counseling creates situations that put both men and women at risk and should not be tolerated in the church. Yet it not only exists, but is prolific throughout the church. With all the biblical and practical reasons against cross-gender counseling, it is a wonder that it still exists among Christians. However, this is one additional look-alike from the psychological counseling movement, which never gave a second thought to there being anything negative about cross-gender counseling. **The biblical counseling movement merely continues the cross-gender counseling of the psychological counseling movement and also apparently never gave it a second thought either.** We have not heard one leader of the biblical counseling movement cry out publicly against such an unbiblical and foolish practice or name those individuals and organizations involved. NANC, CCEF, and BCF do not have a written policy regarding or prohibiting a man counseling a women or a woman counseling a man.[33] In fact, we know of no counseling organization that has such a written policy. With no visible opposition to cross-gender counseling within the church, it is no wonder that it still exists. **However, if this one unbiblical and foolish practice were stopped, it would probably decimate both the psychological and biblical counseling movements.**

6

Research
Against Counseling

**O Timothy, keep that which is committed
to thy trust, avoiding profane and vain bab-
blings, and oppositions of science falsely so
called.   1 Timothy 6:20**

This chapter will affirm the ministry that believers grate-
fully used prior to the rise of the counseling mania by exposing the fallacious and foolish wisdom of men called "counseling" with its fabricated fetish of problem-centeredness.
We do this by offering scientific reasons why one should
not trust counseling. The evidence we present should be
an encouragement to those who, regardless of education,
degrees, or training, are equipped with the Sword of the
Spirit to do battle in the ongoing spiritual warfare in this
woefully wayward, wicked world (Eph. 6:10-18).

There is a plethora of scientific research on psychological counseling, also known as psychotherapy. We will briefly
discuss the research findings, which we previously addressed
in our past writings, in which we have given the specific scientific research support for what we have said by thoroughly
footnoting original sources.[1] Here we reveal truths about

psychotherapy that may apply to all similar counseling. Our conclusions about psychotherapy from the research also, by extension, often apply to biblical counseling. **Since both psychological and biblical counseling's central activity is problem-centered conversation, the research results of psychological counseling could possibly apply to biblical counseling.**

Science or Pseudoscience?

Throughout psychotherapy's history we have seen the rise and wane of one therapy after another, one promise of cure after another, one hope of success after another, and one polluted psychological stream after another. The pendulum has swung 180 degrees through four forces of psychotherapy from Freud's rejection of religion as an illusion to new combinations of religion and psychotherapy. Psychotherapy has moved in its various iterations and forms from a dependency upon the natural world as being the sole reality in life to an inclusion of spirituality as a necessity. *Bergin and Garfield's Handbook of Psychotherapy and Behavior Change* (Fifth Edition) is regarded in the field as the most trustworthy volume on outcomes in psychotherapy. They say:

> A clear trend in psychotherapeutic interventions since the mid-1960s has been the proliferation not only of the types of practitioners, but also of the types and numbers of psychotherapies used alone and in combination in day-to-day practice. Garfield (1982) identified 60 forms of psychotherapy in use in the 1960s. In 1975, the Research Task Force of the National Institute of Mental Health estimated that there were 125 different forms. Herink (1980) listed over 200 separate approaches, while Kazdin (1986) noted 400 variants of psychotherapy.[2]

Currently it has been estimated that there are about 500 different psychotherapies, which are obviously not all compatible, and many of them are contradictory of one another. **We begin by bluntly saying that counseling theories, methodologies, and techniques are not science.** We have written much about this[3] and, based on the work of distinguished individuals, have concluded that these constitute pseudoscience, which the dictionary defines as "a system of theories, assumptions, and methods erroneously regarded as scientific."[4] Pseudoscience or pseudoscientism uses the scientific label to protect and promote opinions that are neither provable nor refutable, which is required to qualify as a science. One science writer contends that

> ... there exists in psychology no systematic body of laws or principles, no basic units of analysis, and not even a commonly accepted methodology for investigating behavior from which credible deductions about the unobservable events could be made.[5]

Think about it. What tangible, observable, measureable basic units of the mind are there? Certainly none that have been accepted by the scientific community.

This question of scientific and pseudoscientific theories intrigued Sir Karl Popper, who is considered one of the greatest philosophers of science. As Popper investigated the differences between physical theories, such as Newton's theory of gravity and Einstein's theory of relativity, and theories about human behavior, he began to suspect that the psychologies underlying the psychotherapies could not truly be considered scientific.[6] Although such theories **seem** to be able to explain or interpret behavior, they rely on subjective interpretations. Even the claims of clinical observation cannot be considered objective or scientific, because they are merely interpretations based on the theories familiar to the observer.[7] These theories depend upon confirmation rather than testability. If one is looking for verifications or confirmations, they can be found with every psychotherapeutic theory. But, the person who is trying to test a theory will try to disprove it. Popper says: "Every genuine *test* of a theory is an attempt to falsify it, or to refute it"[8] (italics in original); and, "Confirming evidence should not count *except when it is the result of a genuine test of the theory*"[9] (italics in original). Furthermore, Popper declares that psychological theories formulated by Freud, Adler, and others, "**though posing as sciences, had in fact more in common with primitive myths than with science; that they resembled astrology rather than astronomy**"[10] (bold added). He also says, "These theories describe some facts, but in the manner of myths. They contain most interesting psychological suggestions, but not in a testable form."[11]

Other researchers echo the same conclusions. Jerome Frank refers to psychotherapies as psychotherapeutic myths because "they are not subject to disproof."[12] Research psychiatrist E. Fuller Torrey, in his book *The Mind Game*, says, "The techniques used by Western psychiatrists are, with few exceptions, on exactly the same scientific plane as the techniques used by witchdoctors."[13] Dr. Adolf Grünbaum, a distinguished professor of philosophy and research, levels extensive criticism at *The Foundations of Psychoanalysis*, which is the title of his book. Based on his writings, it is obvious he would condemn the psychological foundations of psychotherapy and would not regard them as scientific theories.[14]

Although counseling does not qualify as a scientific field, it is true that the scientific method can be used to evaluate its claims just as the scientific method can be used to evaluate the claims of other nonscientific activities such as astrology. While the scientific method has been used at times to evaluate some biblical counseling approaches, the research we have seen has been poorly done. Also, such research is often done by those with vested interests. However, the problem with the biblical counseling movement is not its claim to science, but its claim to be biblical. The psychological counseling movement claims that what they do is truly scientific; the biblical counseling movement claims that what they do is truly biblical. **Both are in error and the fundamental and common flaw in both is their subjective problem-centeredness.**

Scientific Research

A number of distinguished researchers disagree with the idea that psychotherapy is at all helpful and believe that either no treatment or sham treatment is equal to treatment. One such individual who makes such a claim is Dr. Hans Eysenck, who is arguably the most cited psychological researcher of the past century.[15] Others claim that the most positive research reveals that, on average, psychotherapy appears to work. **We will pursue the claim that it appears to work.** However, understanding why it purportedly works is necessary for knowing how it works and that is what we will show.

We will present psychotherapy in the most positive light that research permits. Then we will add the research details of the broader picture of the various facets of it. **We will demonstrate that, if one is honest and fair about the research results, one will at minimum question the use of professional psychotherapy, if not reject it altogether.**

A reminder: At one time Freudian psychoanalysis was regarded as the ne plus ultra of the mind cures; now in its pure form it is held in disregard by many. Distinguished researchers Dr. Bruce E. Wampold et al explain the dilemma well in their "Research Forum," published in *The Behavior Therapist.* Please excuse the complexity of the following, but it is the last sentence that is the most important.

> Given the complexity of the therapeutic endeavor, it is not surprising that interpreting the *evidence* is complex—if it were not, the debate surrounding empirically supported treatments (EST) would be inconspicuously absent.… What constitutes evidence is ultimately decided by a confluence of two factors—the phenomenon itself and people (Hacking, 1983; Latout, 1999). The phenomenon, under various environmental conditions, is observed by people (i.e., the scientists), who then draw conclusions about the phenomenon. **The road from observation to conclusion is saturated with social influences on the scientist.**[16] (Italics theirs; bold added.)

There is a great variety of biblical counseling approaches. In varying the preceding conclusion, we say: "The road from observation to conclusion is very saturated with" problem-centered "influences on the" biblical counselor. One's biblical counseling approach is finally confirmed in "the eye of the beholder." **No matter the training, certification, or academic degree of the counselor, the sum of the biblical counselor's background adds up to whatever is received, modified, and applied by the counselor to the counselee in the counseling office.**

"Only Mild to Moderate Relief"

Some years back the American Psychiatric Association (APA) Commission on Psychotherapies published a book titled *Psychotherapy Research: Methodological and Efficacy Issues.* In it the APA stated: "Whether the magnitude of the psychotherapy effect is medium or small remains a moot point; **no one has claimed that it is large**"[17] (bold added). While no researchers would claim that psychotherapy's level of relief is large, many practitioners and popularizers of psychology do.

Many new psychotherapies and research studies have occurred since the APA's findings, but the same conclusion remains. In an interview with Dr. Martin Seligman, past president of the American Psychological Association, he was asked, "As a therapist and researcher who has spent three decades trying to build a bridge between the world of science and the world of everyday practice, are you impressed with the hard evidence of psychotherapy's effectiveness?" After discussing the results of averaging all the therapy outcome studies, Seligman admitted that "by and large, we produce only mild to moderate relief." After "regularly revising a formal textbook about abnormal psychology that has gone through five editions" over the past 25 years, Seligman indicated that not much has changed over the years with respect to his conclusion of "**only mild to moderate relief**" from psychotherapy.[18] Dr, Hans Strupp, a distinguished professor at Vanderbilt University, says, "Psychotherapy is most helpful to those who need it least."[19]

While some individual lives may change dramatically and others may remain the same or become worse, **scientific research on psychological counseling indicates that, on average, counseling probably produces "only mild to moderate relief."** The same would no doubt be true of biblical counseling, since biblical counseling is so much the same as psychological counseling in being problem-centered.

Equal Outcomes Phenomenon

A research group summed up the evidence on psychotherapy's effectiveness by referring to the dodo bird in *Alice in Wonderland.* On one occasion in the story, all the animals were wet and the dodo bird suggested that a "caucus-race" would be the best way to get dry. The dodo bird marked out a race course "in a sort of circle." The animals could start anywhere or stop and start when and where they wanted during the race. A "half hour or so" after the race started, it was obvious that the animals were all dry. Then the dodo bird called out, "The race is over!" The animals then wanted to know who had won the race. After some thought, the dodo bird announced, "*Everybody* has won, and *all* must have prizes."[20]

This anecdote has often been used throughout the psychotherapy literature to illustrate what the research indicates about the effectiveness of psychotherapy.[21] Not all of the approximately 500 approaches to therapy have been tested, but for the many that have, the overwhelming conclusion is "*Everybody* has won, and *all* must have prizes." In other words, all psychotherapies appear to work, even though many contradict each other. With certain exceptions, the research findings add up to the claim that **all psychotherapies work and all seem to work equally well no matter how contrary they are to one another**. This result is known in the research literature as the "**equal outcomes phenomenon**."[22]

The fact that there are about 500 different, often-conflicting psychological counseling approaches and thousands of not-often-compatible techniques with various incompatible underlying psychological theories must raise a huge question mark over **why they all seem to work equally well**. The exception to this conclusion is the fact that there are certain types of psychological therapies, such as regressive therapy, that produce up to forty percent detrimental effects.

This equal-outcomes finding, for which we provide research support elsewhere,[23] is not believed by those with individual therapeutic approaches, such as cognitive behavioral therapy and psychodynamic therapy. **However, the fact of the matter is that no one has been able to demonstrate scientifically that there is a best approach when it comes to psychotherapy or any form of counseling.** If research established that one of the almost 500 approaches to psychotherapy were declared the winner, there would be only one counseling approach agreed to by all. For every research report that declares one of the approaches to be the best there will be other research reports that will discredit that conclusion and claim equal outcomes.

To paraphrase from the psychological counseling research, "All biblical counseling works and all seems to work equally well" if put to the test. The exception to this conclusion is the fact that there are certain types of biblical counseling that are regressive, such as inner healing and Theophostic Prayer Ministry, that will probably produce up to forty percent negative effects, just as their psychological lookalikes. And just as with psychological counseling, certain biblical approaches will seem to be the best. But, with no research to support such claims, it is best to ignore such rhetoric. For example, no research has demonstrated that NANC counseling or CCEF counseling or BCF counseling is better than most others.

Common Factors

The equal outcomes phenomenon (all therapies work and all seem to work equally well) naturally raises the question of what factors are common to all therapies. **What are some common factors that would, on the average, give all therapies and therapists mild to moderate positive results?** Therapy consists of a counselee or client, a counselor or therapist, and the conversation, which is the medium through which counseling methodology moves. Thus, the counselee, counselor, and conversation are the three most obvious factors to investigate to find what might be common to all therapies. Of these three, and far more important than the other two, is the person being counseled. As a matter of fact, it would be quite appropriate to say that **the counselee is not only the most important factor in counseling, but is also the one factor that determines the usefulness of the other two factors.**

Counselee (Client)

There is a variety of research guesses about exactly how important the counselee is in the process of change. However, **there is no question that the counselee is the most important and essential element in change.**

Counselor/Rapport

As we said in Chapter Five, Henri F. Ellenberger gives a detailed history of the background and emergence of psychotherapy in his monumental book *The Discovery of the Unconscious: The History and Evolution of Dynamic Psychiatry.* He says, "Whatever the psychotherapeutic procedure, it showed the same common basic feature: the presence and utilization of the rapport."[24] If a counselor is to best assist the counselee, rapport is both a necessary ingredient and a common factor in all counseling and psychotherapy. Through rapport a bonding occurs between the counselor and the counselee.

As mentioned earlier, these formalized conversations between a person in need and a counselor began with Franz Anton Mesmer. Because Mesmer's theory included the idea of a magnetic fluid, he and those who followed him were known as magnetizers.[25] Mesmer eventually recognized the important element of rapport. In reporting on the origins of psychotherapy through Mesmer, Ellenberger says:

> A magnetizer, Mesmer proclaimed, is the therapeutic agent of his cures: his power lies in himself. To make healing possible, **he must first establish a rapport**, that is a kind of "tuning in," with his patient.[26] (Bold added.)

Ellenberger also says: "Psychotherapy relied mostly upon the use of hypnotism and suggestion, **with special consideration given to the rapport between patient and magnetizer**" (bold added).[27] The rapport necessary was developed through conversation, which Mesmer formalized during his time. **The current research stresses the great importance of rapport for success in counseling and calls it the "therapeutic alliance."** This term and its significance in successful counseling is repeatedly seen in the literature.[28]

A *Psychology Today* article says:

> Researchers who compare the success rates of various schools find that by and large, techniques and methods don't matter. What does matter is the powerful bond between therapist and patient. The strength of this "therapeutic alliance" seems to spell the difference between successful therapy and a washout.[29]

Dr. Bruce E. Wampold, a distinguished psychotherapy researcher, reveals through his meticulous research that the characteristics of the counselee and the counselor and their relationship (therapeutic alliance) had a far greater impact than the treatment approaches. Wampold's research further demonstrates that there are **no differences in outcomes** when bona-fide treatments (i.e., those that have not demonstrated detrimental effects that would disqualify them) are compared.[30]

The *Harvard Mental Health Letter* refers to the therapeutic alliance and says that it is "the working relationship between patient and therapist that is probably the most
important influence on the outcome of therapy."[31] *Psychotherapy Networker* says:

> The incontrovertible evidence is in: studies of the top
> 25 percent of therapists—those whose success rates
> are at least 50 percent better than the average—show
> unequivocally that neither training, experience, per-
> sonality style, theoretical orientation, nor (get this)
> innate talent—has anything much to do with what
> makes the greats better than all the rest.... The thera-
> peutic alliance—the ability to engage a client in ther-
> apy, to forge and maintain a strong, personal connec-
> tion with her, convince her that the two of you are on
> a common path—remains the single most important
> element of all therapy.[32]

**Regardless of the counseling approach (psychological
or biblical), the two most important factors for success
are the personal qualities and circumstances of the one
who comes for help and the rapport that exists between
the counselor and counselee.**

Ingredients for Successful Counseling

One text estimates that the counselee and the rapport
(therapeutic alliance) if established by the counselor would
average about 70 percent of the success with **counselee or
client factors being the greater of the two.**[33] However,
think about it. Who determines whether the **rapport or
therapeutic alliance** is effective? Who decides whether the
counselee/counselor relationship is a warm, empathic, sympathetic one? Answer: **the counselee does.** The counselor
may try to establish rapport through various means, but the

counselee is the one who responds or rejects, and thus the estimated figure of 70 percent of any success really has to do with the counselees and how they view the relationship.

One therapeutic alliance (rapport) researcher says:

> When you're a therapist, you think you know the most important things about your client and therapy; it's the client's perceptions about how things are going that have the greatest predictive value of the outcome of therapy.[34]

After surveying counselees who had recently been in therapy, the authors of the study concluded:

> The most powerful alliance-building behaviors turn out to be basic human courtesies and fundamental relationship skills, which have nothing to do with therapists' techniques or diagnostic abilities. Greeting clients with a smile, making eye contact, sitting still without fidgeting, identifying and reflecting back feelings, making encouraging and positive comments, truthfully sharing negative information, normalizing feelings and experiences, and remembering details from previous sessions turned out to be extremely important factors.[35]

This evidence is seen repeatedly in the research: that the counselees' perceptions of the counselor "have the greatest predictive value of the outcome in therapy" and the personal qualities of the counselor that are rapport building will encourage the counselee to receive whatever counseling is offered. Nevertheless, the effectiveness of the counseling still depends on the counselee receiving it.

One more important factor for success in counseling is the placebo effect, to which the authors give 15 percent. The placebo effect is a sham treatment, in this case a psychological treatment that through belief on the part of the counselee is received and responded to as a valid treatment.[36] In other words, no matter what the psychological treatment by the counselor, the counselee responds positively to it and there is a therapeutic effect. **Notice that it does not matter what the treatment is; the receiving and responding are on the part of the counselee. Thus the resulting estimate should add up to about 85 percent for the counselee.**

Finally, the authors give only 15 percent to the type of conversation or techniques used. However, we remind the reader of the equal outcomes phenomenon, which means that no specific counseling and no specific technique is necessarily the best and thus required for success. **Excluding the counseling that is known to be detrimental, whatever technique or theory is selected has a considerably smaller effect than the counselee/client factors.** However, a small effect can have a major impact on the outcome when it is detrimental and the outcome negative.

Professionals versus Amateurs

We digress to reveal the startling fact that it has not been demonstrated that professional counselors do any better than amateurs. Professionals are those individuals who, through extensive training (usually at least a Master's degree) and licensing, practice counseling, which includes a variety of names, such as psychotherapy. Amateurs are those individuals who do not have the above training and license, but at times are provided with a minimum of training, and who are used to counsel. One dictionary definition of a paraprofessional is "a person inexperienced or unskilled in a particular activity," in this case counseling.

How do professional counselors compare with amateur counselors? As we have revealed elsewhere, according to distinguished researcher Dr. Robyn Dawes, "the training, credentials, and experience of psychotherapists are irrelevant, or at least that is what all the evidence indicates."[37] Dawes also says that "the therapists' credentials—Ph.D., M.D., or no advanced degree—and experience were unrelated to the effectiveness of therapy."[38] It is amazing to us that Christians who have no psychological training and may not ever have gone to college are so reluctant or may be fearful to minister to fellow believers when the research demonstrates the following:

> In a meta-analytic [research] review of studies that address level of training, Berman and Norton concluded that professionally trained therapists had no systematic advantage over nonprofessional therapists in evoking treatment gains.[39]

Dawes says:

> **Evaluating the efficacy [effectiveness] of psychotherapy has led us to conclude that professional psychologists are no better psychotherapists than anyone else with minimal training—sometimes those without any training at all; the professionals are merely more expensive.**[40] (Bold added.)

Numerous other studies could be used to support the effectiveness of nonprofessionals. Dr. Jerome Frank, distinguished professor of psychiatry, once referred to the shocking fact of "the inability of scientific research to demonstrate conclusively that professional psychotherapists produce results sufficiently better than those of nonprofessionals."[41] The conclusion of a recent article in *Perspectives on Psychological Science* regarding the use of paraprofessionals (those with minimal or no training and not licensed) says, "Many clinicians would reject the notion that a trained paraprofessional could deliver psychotherapy effectively. There is little evidence that compels this view, however."[42] In other words, though some would reject this idea, the fact is that paraprofessionals can do effective psychotherapy.

It is important to be aware that most of the recent popular therapeutic approaches, such as Rational Emotive Behavior Therapy, Cognitive Behavioral Therapy, and Dialectical Behavior Therapy can be learned in a one or two day workshop, which is often offered, or by reading a single book absent any other training or background. Thus, most anyone educated, degreed **or not** can learn the basics of psychotherapy in a short period of time and be successful at it. Therefore, the logical conclusion is that most any believer who is mature in the faith, whether educated, degreed, or not, can minister mutual care and be as successful on average as the trained, certificated, and degreed biblical counselors.

Detrimental Effects

Some people think of psychotherapy in a manner similar to the way they think about vitamin supplements: may be helpful, but at least not harmful. This seems to be the prevailing attitude towards psychotherapy: it can be helpful, but at least it can't hurt anyone. **Research reveals that view is false.** In medical literature the word *iatrogenic* refers to unexpected detrimental effects of taking medicine or receiving other medical treatment. For example, a person may come to a medical doctor with an infection, receive antibiotics, and then suffer negative reactions to the antibiotics. This negative effect is called an *iatrogenic effect.* It is an adverse, though unexpected result of treatment. Research shows that a similar effect occurs in psychotherapy. While mild to moderate improvement may occur under treatment, a patient may also get worse or deteriorate as a result. **Psycho-**

therapy may be somewhat helpful to an individual, but it may also be harmful.

As we just demonstrated, the most important factor for success in biblical counseling is the person in need who comes for help. The truth is that many who come for change do not have an earnest desire to change and therefore look into counseling as the answer to their dilemma. **Once the level of desire for change on the part of the counselee reaches the need for change, then change is highly probable.** Change occurs primarily by the personal efforts put forth by the counselee. However, if support and encouragement are needed, any person whose rapport efforts the counselee will receive may be helpful. **Once the level of rapport reaches the level needed by the counselee for change to occur, the greater the probability for change.** This rapport is the counselor's most important contribution to success, far greater than the techniques or methodology used, but it is actually up to the counselee to receive it.

Negative effects average around ten to twenty percent and up to forty percent for some types of therapy![43] When therapy succeeds, the counselor generally takes much of the credit; however when therapy fails, the counselor often blames the counselee. If one considers that the research shows that much of the success is due to counselee/client factors, one might assume that therapy failure is due to the counselee. However, when one looks at the detrimental effects, one can see that to a great extent failure has to do with the counselor and methodology, and the harm rate increases in those therapies that emphasize the past and lead counselees into talking about and even re-experiencing traumatic past events.

The question arises as to how reliable are therapists' judgments of deterioration or detrimental effects (harm) in counseling. A study reported in a professional journal "examined therapists' ability to detect counselee/client deterioration [harm] through the review of therapy progress notes" and concluded that:

> Therapists had considerable difficulty recognizing client deterioration, challenging the assumption that routine clinical judgment is sufficient when attempting to detect client deterioration.[44]

Sharon Begley, a technology and science writer, summed up her criticism of psychotherapy in her *Newsweek* article titled "Get Shrunk at Your Own Risk," by saying, "**What is remarkable about psychotherapies, though, is that few patients have any idea that 'just talking' can be dangerous to their mental health**" (bold added).[45] The very process of therapy designed to empower people and to help them solve their problems often weakens them and causes them to be dependent on counselors and too self-consumed to fulfill their responsibilities in society. (See Chapter Four.)

In their book *One Nation Under Therapy: How the Helping Culture is Eroding Self-Reliance*, Christina Hoff Sommers and Sally Satel, M.D., say, "Therapism tends to regard people as essentially weak, dependent, and never altogether responsible for what they do."[46] They contend that "treating addicts as morally responsible, self-determining human beings free to change their behavior is, in the end, more effective, more respectful, and more compassionate." **They "reject therapism's central doctrine that uninhibited emotional openness is essential to mental health" and say, "Recent findings suggest that reticence and suppression of feelings ... can be healthy and adaptive" and "an excessive focus on introspection and self-disclosure is depressing." They note that "Trauma and grief counselors have erred massively in this direction."[47]**

Marriage counseling is big business in the world and in the church. As more and more people have been going to marriage counseling, more and more have become divorced, and this includes professing Christians, who are divorcing at about the same rate as unbelievers.[48] With all the time and money and the great expectations that counseling will help married couples, it is disconcerting to learn that marriage counseling only helps about half of the time, which is similar to sham treatment. Why are the results so poor? The editor of *Psychotherapy Networker,* a journal for practicing psychotherapists, confesses that "most therapists who actually do marital therapy (about 80 percent of all clinicians) don't really know what they're doing." He says:

> Untrained in and unprepared for work that requires a highly skilled touch and nerves of steel, many therapists blunder ineffectually through sessions until they're fired by their clients or, overwhelmed by a couple's problems, they give up too soon in trying to save a marriage.[49]

But then he admits that skilled, experienced therapists are often unsuccessful as well. One psychotherapist reported in a professional journal article that :

> Controlled outcome studies show that only about half of couples improve with treatment. And even among those who do make progress, a disheartening chunk, 30 to 50 percent, relapse within two years.[50]

Recovered memory therapy is especially dangerous as horrific memories are created, experienced, and re-experienced until the newly created false memory is stronger than real memories. Counselees have ended up accusing their families of abuse that never occurred, cutting themselves off from their families, and needing ever more therapy to recover from the so-called recovered memories. Thankfully some truth has come forth through memory research and through counselees confessing that these memories were created in therapy.[51] Nevertheless, many lives and relationships have been grievously harmed and even destroyed through recovered memory therapy.[52] But even as these things have come to light, many Christians continue to engage in various forms of inner healing, which combine recovered memory therapy with aspects of the Bible plus hearing Jesus say things never recorded in Scripture.[53]

Another dangerous form of therapy that sometimes follows recovered memory therapy is for what used to be called multiple-personality disorder (MPD), but now called Dissociative Identity Disorder (DID). In this therapy, the counselor believes that the counselee has hidden identities or "alters" and therefore seeks to discover these alters and then attempts to help them work together or to merge into one personality. **This idea became popular as a result of the Sybil story, which was later shown to be spurious.** *The Boston Skepticism Examiner* reveals that "The number of diagnosed MPD cases went from about 75 before Sybil to 40,000 after Sybil." The reviewer further reports:

> During the MPD craze, therapists are reported to have often diagnosed patients with symptoms no more outrageous than depression or anxiety with [so-called] repressed memories of childhood sexual abuse. They would then set about seeking the alters they knew to be present in the subject.[54]

Therapists worked hard to get their patients to remember horrible abuse and then convinced them that they had developed alters to deal with the abuse. The reviewer puts the situation more bluntly: "The patients learned to become multiple under the coercion of therapists who would continually ask to speak to the personality that maintained the memory of the trauma."[55] Indeed, through suggestion, hypnosis, and even coercion, this kind of therapy actually creates these so-called alters to begin with, and as the therapy increases, so does the number of alters and the amount of confusion and mental distress.

Another very popular form of counseling given whenever tragedies occur is "stress debriefing" with the idea that if people talk about it right away and express their emotions to a trained counselor they will not succumb to PTSD (post-traumatic stress disorder). However, as mentioned in Chapter Four, just the opposite appears to happen. Research studies indicate that "many of those who undergo stress debriefing develop worse PTSD symptoms than those who deal with the trauma on their own." One possible reason given is that "the intense reliving of the trauma impedes natural recovery."[56] In reporting on research regarding "critical incidence stress debriefing," the *Harvard Mental Health Letter* says, "Not only was it ineffective for preventing PTSD, in some instances it appeared to increase the incidence of psychological distress."[57] The more people focus on the trauma and on the accompanying feelings, the more those feelings of sadness, helplessness, and even depression take over.

Regarding sadness and grief, most people will be surprised to learn that "counseling sometimes prolonged and deepened grief, leaving more depression and anxiety than in those who worked through their loss on their own."[58] In spite of known negative effects, lack of research support for positive effects, a number of exposes demonstrating that prescribing the manner of grieving is unnecessary and can be harmful, many Christians have bought into the method. Moreover, many still insist that those who have suffered loss need grief counseling. This is one more example of how

Christians have turned to the world rather than to the Lord, who is the God of all comfort (2 Cor. 1:3-4).

People need to remember that there is definitely a potential harm rate for every seemingly wonderful idea from the psychological systems of men. While spiritual harm rate cannot be measured, there is potential spiritual decline when the counseling is not fully biblical, because using the psychological wisdom of men may very well lead to strengthening the flesh rather than nurturing the spirit. People also need to remember that psychological ideas can be made to sound biblical so that the counselee may very well be strengthening the flesh even while believing that the counseling is bringing forth spiritual growth.

To paraphrase: biblical counseling may be helpful to an individual, but it may also be harmful, because it is problem-centered. Because so many biblical counseling approaches are similar to psychological approaches, it is possible that similar negative effects apply with the "average around ten to twenty percent and up to forty percent for some types" of counseling, such as Theophostic Prayer Ministry and various forms of inner healing.

In summary, the counselee is the keystone to successful counseling. This fact is the reason for psychotherapies being about equally effective (equal outcomes phenomenon), with the exception of those that produce as much as a 40% harm rate mentioned above. **In other words, the counselees who are motivated to succeed, who engage in the rapport with the counselor (therapeutic alliance), and who believe that they are receiving a valid treatment (placebo effect) will most likely succeed, regardless of the counseling approach and regardless of the counselor being an amateur or professional.** Therefore, counselees who meet these conditions and are given entirely different types and even contradictory therapies tend to have similar mild to moderate success rates. However, those who minister to fellow believers in need should have as their highest goal to encourage their relationship with Jesus rather than to enhance their own therapeutic alliance.

These same factors of counselee, counselor, and counseling occur in biblical counseling, and, since both psychological counseling and biblical counseling are problem-centered, the importance of each of these factors would likely carry over to biblical counseling. Because of the equal outcomes phenomenon, one should not be afraid to minister biblically, because the Bible offers what no counseling outside of it can offer and that is salvation, spiritual growth, and an eternity with Jesus. Ministering biblically would go far beyond the equal outcomes level of mild to moderate change! **We challenge anyone to demonstrate through scientific evidence that there is even one psychological counseling theory, technique, or methodology that can trump the biblical care of souls to the extent that it would, on average, produce a better success rate.**

Syncretism and Psychoheresy

Syncretism is defined as "the combination of different forms of belief or practice." Syncretism is one of Satan's most deceptive and appealing techniques devised to destroy the true faith and undermine the Christian's faith in and dependence on Christ. Syncretism can happen in different ways. One way is accommodating customs and religious beliefs and practices by renaming and redefining them, such as cultures turning native deities into Catholic saints.[59] Another way is using facets of philosophical systems that seem compatible with Christianity, such as assimilating aspects of Greek Stoicism having to do with morality and consolation. Through syncretism, doing penance was added to repentance after confession of sin. While restitution was to be made and certain punishments were meted out for specific sins, we do not see a system of penance in either the Old or New Testaments. However, penance for the purpose of purification was a practice of some of the Eastern religions and later syncretized into Christianity.[60]

Our concern is with the syncretism of psychotherapy and its underlying psychologies with Christianity. As we have demonstrated in our writings, psychotherapy and its underlying psychologies are actually religious in nature and practice.[61] Robert C. Fuller, in his book *Americans and the Unconscious*, states this very clearly:

> Insofar as psychological theories purport to interpret reality and orient individuals within it, they inevitably assume many of the cultural functions traditionally associated with religion. And to the extent that psychological concepts are used to guide individuals toward life's intrinsic values and ultimate mysteries, their religious character becomes prominent.[62]

We call this syncretism *psychoheresy*, which is taking psychological ideas, theories, and practices and mingling them with Christianity.

The euphemism for this kind of syncretism is "integration," which occurs when two or more ideas or systems are able to be combined. However, those who take the psychological counseling theories and attempt to combine them with Scripture **cannot** truly integrate them. They are as different as oil and water! One works with the old man of the flesh (carnal); the other works with the new man in Christ (spiritual). They are at enmity with each other, just as the flesh and the Spirit are contrary to each other (Gal. 5:17) just as the carnal man is at enmity with God (Rom. 8:7). They cannot mix because they are enemies, just as the idols of the nations around Israel were at enmity with God. Thus these so-called Christian psychologists and other mental health professionals are not practicing and promoting ordinary integration, but rather religious syncretism. They are overlaying their psychology with the Bible, which ultimately serves to disguise the psychological religious systems they are using. As we have shown through the years, this psycho-syncretism subverts and subtracts from the faith.

The syncretism of psychology and Christianity appeals to those Christians who believe that what is being discovered about the mind, the will, and the emotions is science, that it is part of God's creation yet to be discovered in the same way as discoveries are made in physics, chemistry, and biology. Since psychology presents itself as a science and psychotherapeutic ideas are organized into theories, many pastors believe that there is no syncretism of religion when adding the models and methods of counseling psychology. This faith in science and belief in a "scientific psychology" goes quite far back. Fuller says:

> Underlying the ability of late nineteenth-century Americans to embrace scientific psychology as a source of spiritual edification was a long tradition of seeing nature as fraught with theological significance. Throughout the first half of the nineteenth century, American Protestants were increasingly fascinated by scientific method.[63]

We realize that this includes the majority of those individuals, churches, denominations, schools, seminaries, mission agencies, and pastors in America! We stress "in America" because the United States is where this sinful psychotherapeutic gospel found its most fertile ground. It is through the psychotherapeutic gospel in America where the Jeremiah 17:9 syndrome found its friendliest friend; where the sinful nature of man is given free reign; and where sinful thinking and sinful behaving are expressed without restriction, questioning, or proof.

There are subtleties and similarities between certain ideas from psychology and Christianity that increase the vulnerability for one to begin thinking and ministering psychologically rather than biblically. That is why Christians need to be spending time in the Word and in prayer rather than in looking for answers to life's dilemmas outside Scripture. Psychotherapy and its underlying psychologies are not science.[64] They are human speculations about the soul with a pseudo-scientific façade.

Each of the approximate 500 different systems of psychotherapy has its own array of speculations, peculiarities, and methods. Most psychotherapists, clinical psychologists, and marriage and family counselors are eclectic. They dip into various systems and use what seems to work for them. In other words, they each have their own array of speculations, peculiarities, and methods. Those who are Christians attempt to accommodate the faith, but this syncretism will activate the flesh rather than minister to the spirit, because what is added comes from the world rather than the Word.

There has been so much searching outside Scripture to find ways to minister to suffering saints that a whole cadre of psychologically trained or at least psychologically tainted professionals and lay counselors are prepared to minister the ways of men and the wisdom of men along with Scriptures that seem to support their practice. This is syncretism. Others who are also guilty of syncretism are: (1) Those Christian schools and seminaries that positively promote the use of counseling psychology and/or prepare individuals to become licensed to practice psychotherapy, especially those Christian schools that have programs accredited by the American Psychological Association (APA), such as Baylor University, Biola University, Fuller Theological Seminary, George Fox University, Regent University, and Wheaton College; (2) Those pastors or others who promote and affirm those psychological ideas and/or refer congregants out to psychotherapists; those authors and organizations that promote a psychological understanding of man; (3) Those professing Christians who are deeply committed to this syncretism, which comes from not believing that Scripture is sufficient for life and godliness (2 Peter 1:3); (4) Those in the biblical counseling movement who add the psychological problem-centered approach to biblical soul care.

Instead of following the ways of the world, Christians need to search the Word to find out how God changes individuals from the inside out without one human being probing into another person's inner man, which only God can know. God does the primary work of change and has clearly set forth what believers are to do for one another: preach, pray, admonish, instruct, help, and encourage one another to seek the Lord daily through praying; worshiping; giving thanks; reading, studying, memorizing, and meditating on Scripture; thinking biblically; walking by faith; loving, serving, and obeying God; and loving and serving one another. This care of souls is to be practiced mutually in the body of Christ so that all may grow and flourish in the "faith which was once delivered unto the saints" (Jude 3). There is no system or program. Instead, it is the very life of Christ in every believer bearing fruit and bringing each to maturity through the Word of God, the work of the Holy Spirit, and the fellowship of the saints.

Conclusion

Come let us reason together and think about the evidence against psychotherapy and for biblical ministry.

A little over 50 years ago personal and interpersonal problems were primarily handled in the family, with close friends, or in the church rather than with strangers.

Psychotherapy is "science falsely so called" (1 Tim. 6:20).

It has not been demonstrated in the plethora of research to date that educated, degreed, licensed psychotherapists do any better at assisting those in need than amateurs.

It has been demonstrated that psychotherapy produces only mild to moderate relief.

No one has proven that psychotherapy, which is so highly regarded in and out of the church, is one whit better at helping individuals in need than the biblical ministry that existed and has been practiced since the inception of the church.

Psychotherapy and counseling psychology are the very wisdom of man about which God has warned His people against (1 Cor. 2, etc.).

Detrimental effects do occur as a result of using psychotherapy to deal with problems of living with some very negative effects occurring with some very popular approaches.

Adding psychotherapy with its underlying psychologies to the Bible is syncretism and contradicts the sufficiency of Scripture.

Finally, a question: Did God leave the church helpless to deal with the issues of life for almost 2000 years before the current psychotherapeutic era? If the answer is "no," then why has the sinful psychotherapeutic gospel trumped the pure biblical Gospel throughout most of the church during the past 50 years?

Fundamental to our charge of psychoheresy against individuals and organizations is the fact that they do not believe in the sufficiency of Scripture for the problems of living normally taken to a psychological counselor rather than being ministered to biblically by a fellow believer. When we name those individuals and organizations that are guilty of an insufficient view of Scripture because of their promoting psychoheresy, many Christians who are blessed to hear these guilty individuals and love these erring organizations become upset with us when they should be upset with them!

In Chapter Four we gave a challenge to those in the biblical counseling movement. **Here we challenge the majority in the church who have compromised on the sufficiency of Scripture for dealing with the issues of life and have turned to the psychological wisdom of man to provide a word-for-word counseling session or a detailed description of one that is truly biblical.** We add that there are no literal psychological counseling cases that we could find after years of looking that are truly biblical. As we indicated in Chapter Four, after calling several Christian counseling organizations we found almost no real cases with real counselors with real-time counseling, and what exists does not meet the acid test of being biblical.

Based on the scientific research, we have maintained for years that psychotherapy has achieved what is called "functional autonomy." **Functional autonomy occurs when a practice or procedure continues after the evidence for its support is gone.** [65] It would have been true of bloodletting had medicine not turned to science. In spite of all the research to the contrary, psychotherapy with its multitude of approaches, educational requirements, licensure, and high fees will continue on with more and more people seeking and obtaining psychological treatment for their problems of living. This is functional autonomy! It keeps on going in spite of its only mild to moderate helpfulness and also in spite of its 10% to 40% harm rate.

With the multitude of biblical counselors of all persuasions and denominations and with all the universities, colleges, seminaries, and schools promoting biblical counseling and with all the well-known and highly respected Christians supporting it, we now declare that **"biblical" counseling has also achieved functional autonomy.** We have demonstrated in our books that the biblical evidence for its support is gone. We repeatedly say that the big, serious mistake made by those in the biblical counseling movement occurred because of its adopting and using the problem-centered approach from psychology. As we have repeatedly shown in our writings, problem-centered "biblical" counseling inevitably leads to evil speaking with the possibility of strengthening the flesh. **In spite of this major biblical flaw, "biblical" counseling, like psychotherapy, will continue on as it has also achieved functional autonomy.**

Finally, in spite of the fact that there are numerous well-known and highly visible Christians who oppose the psychologizing of the faith that we call "psychoheresy," there are almost none who are willing to make a public issue of it by naming individuals and organizations that are promoting it and by publically exposing their biblical errors. While these very visible pastors, teachers, schools, authors, and others who oppose what we call "psychoheresy" would like to be known as defenders of the faith, they have failed to expose this one egregious, popular, and unbiblical practice that has engulfed the church.

7

In Cahoots?

…freely ye have received, freely give.
Matthew 10:8b

In Chapters One through Four we have discredited the biblical counseling movement because of its problem-centered counseling. In addition, we have revealed in Chapter Five the biblical and practical reasons that cross-gender, problem-centered counseling should not occur, and in Chapter Six we gave the research discrediting counseling. In this chapter we discuss two additional activities that discredit many in the biblical counseling movement (BCM). These activities are charging for biblical counseling and operating separated-from-the-church biblical counseling centers. Not all in the BCM charge and not all in the BCM are in separated-from-the-church biblical counseling centers. **However, it appears that all are in cahoots with one another regarding these two practices, as we will explain.**

ABC, AACC, CCEF, NANC & "Filthy Lucre"

An Association of Biblical Counselors (ABC) confer-ence reveals just how unbiblical the biblical counseling

179

movement (BCM) is.[1] In addition to ABC, the following counseling organizations were featured and represented by speakers at the conference: American Association of Christian Counselors (AACC), Christian Counseling and Educational Foundation (CCEF), and the National Association of Nouthetic counselors (NANC). Other counseling organizations were represented as well.

We have indicated in past writings and in Chapters One through Six why these organizations are unbiblical and why Christians should **not** seek counsel from counselors belonging to these organizations. The additional evidence for our conclusion is found in articles and books available free at our ministry web site.[2] One more grossly unbiblical practice, of which all of these organizations are either directly or indirectly guilty, **is charging money for biblical counseling.** Our book *Person to Person Ministry* would be the best single source discrediting the BCM.[3]

Hand Holding Among the Counseling Organizations

The announcement for the ABC conference indicates that their symposium was a "First Time Ever," "Groundbreaking" event. The ABC ad says:

> 4 Different Associations [ABC, AACC, CCEF, NANC]
> 4 Different Counselors [Jeremy Lelek (ABC), Eric Johnson & Bob Kelleman (AACC), David Powlison (CCEF), Steve Viars (NANC)]
> 4 Different Views
> 1 Common Bond
> 1 Common Quest

We always knew that these various counseling organizations were holding hands with one another, either publicly or behind the scenes. Now for the "First Time Ever" all these organizations were holding hands together publicly at the ABC conference. **We will now reveal that these BCM organizations are actively or passively supporting the practice of charging.**

Association of Biblical Counselors (ABC)

We begin with the Association of Biblical Counselors (ABC) that sponsored the conference. The president of the ABC is Jeremy Lelek. The ABC web site says:

> Jeremy Lelek is a Licensed Professional Counselor in the state of Texas. He has earned a Master of Arts degree in Counseling from Amberton University and a Bachelor of Arts degree in Psychology from Liberty University. He is also a Ph.D. Candidate at Regent University where he is earning an advanced doctoral degree in Counseling, Education, and Supervision.[4]

We called Lelek's office and were told that Lelek's fee for biblical counseling ("that's all he does") is $135 per hour. We were told, "If your insurance company covers services from an LPC [Licensed Professional Counselor], we will give you receipts for the counseling which you can then file with your insurance company." We were also told that another counselor in Lelek's office is available for $115 per hour. In addition we were told that there are counseling interns available who are trained but not yet licensed. (We assume they are putting in hours under supervision.) The charge for an intern is $100 per hour.[5] Also, cross-gender counseling is available. Lelek claims the sufficiency of Scripture in his Bio,[6] but contrary to the Bible he charges for his biblical counseling and his hourly rate is at the top of those counseling ministries we have examined. The vice president of ABC is Scott Lowery, who has "a Master's of Education in Marriage and Family

Therapy," so we assume along the way he too has charged for counseling.

American Association of Christian Counselors (AACC)
    AACC is the largest of the Christian counseling groups. AACC's web site says: "Nearly 50,000 members and growing stronger every day." Thousands enroll for their annual World Conference. We have written a number of articles about the AACC indicating that they are the most integrationist (the Bible plus psychology) of all the evangelical counseling organizations. **AACC has a façade of Christianity and often refers to the Bible but is a prime example of psychoheresy at its worst.** It goes without saying that AACC not only has no objection to charging, but also supports the idea that its Christian counselor members have a right to charge. AACC even hypes the amount of money that one can earn after completing some of their programs.
    The fact that AACC was included in a conference for biblical counselors should be a red flag for those who know the unbiblical nature of integrating psychological counseling theories and therapies with the Bible. By including and even featuring AACC, the BCM is showing its true colors. They have already embraced enough integration to join hands with AACC to the degree that there are fewer and fewer differences between professional psychological practitioners who are Christians and those who claim to be biblical counselors. Their similarities range from one end of the continuum to the other, but **they all agree on being problem-centered, doing cross-gender counseling, and being permissive about charging money for biblical counseling**.

Christian Counseling and Educational Foundation (CCEF)

CCEF charges for biblical counseling, as stated on their web site: "Our basic counseling rate is $85.00 per hour. The initial hour costs $90.00 for set-up fees. **All counseling charges are due before each appointment**" (emphasis theirs).[7] While the following is dated (2007), nonetheless CCEF's total annual revenues reported then amount to $2,801,613. This includes all activities of CCEF. However, most of this amount is probably directly or indirectly related to their problem-centered counseling. In 2007 CCEF reported "counseling fees" of $361,375 and the "biblical counseling" amount at $355,366, making a total of $716,741. Add to this the fact that, while for many of those who are charged it is a financial burden to them and their families, Dr. Tim Lane, President of CCEF, was paid $131,450 in 2007, plus fringe benefits. We would guess his salary and fringe benefits are currently higher. **This one serious violation of Scripture and its pharisaical justification should be enough for all to turn away from the "cash, check or credit card" mentality of CCEF.**[8]

The principal speaker for the five ABC conference plenary sessions was Paul Tripp. As we mentioned earlier, he is listed as "President, Paul Tripp Ministries" and "adjunct faculty" at CCEF. We assume that he charges for biblical counseling since he has counseled at CCEF where they charge.

National Association of Nouthetic counselors (NANC)

NANC has no policy prohibiting NANC certified counselors from charging for counseling.[9] However, two of their current board members charge for biblical counseling.

Holding Hands

The "Endorsements" list for ABC contains over thirty individuals. A variety of churches, schools, and ministries are represented. We select only two from this list: John Mac-Arthur (The Master's College and Seminary) and Stuart Scott (Southern Baptist Theological Seminary). These two schools represented by MacArthur and Scott obviously see no biblical problem (serious or otherwise) with charging or endorse the practice or are opposed but are unwilling to make a serious issue of it.

Because the various biblical counseling organizations have joined together for mutual endorsements and conferences, to make an issue of charging would affect the camaraderie among them. Any organization or leader of the biblical counseling movement sounding an alarm would disrupt the unity which they have established for mutual benefit. **The issue of charging has become an untouchable subject in the biblical counseling movement to the detriment of those in need of personal care.**

Another area in which money influences whether or not there is an outcry against a practice that produces money is the proliferation of biblical counseling programs at various Bible colleges and seminaries. Not all professors at Bible colleges and seminaries are happy with the biblical counseling programs at their schools. However, since student enrollment translates into tuition income for their schools, there is a financial incentive for Christian higher education institutions to offer such programs and expand them when possible. The professors in these programs regard them as biblical and beneficial. The professors who might question these programs are colleagues with those who offer them and in many cases they are close friends. Because there is a strong incentive to continue and even expand programs that attract students with the accompanying tuition, little is even said to question their inclusion. Raising an outcry about charging for biblical counseling would dissuade prospective students from enrolling in such programs. However, as we have biblically demonstrated in our book *Person to Person Ministry,* in this present book, and in our other writings, charging for such personal ministry should cease.

The various biblical counseling organizations, schools, and seminaries are holding hands on the subject of charging fees for biblical counseling. Not one leader in this movement of which we are aware has publicly condemned this unbiblical practice and named individuals and organizations that are guilty. **There is much handholding among the leaders of the biblical counseling movement with respect to not exposing this spiritually fraudulent unbiblical practice even among those leaders who privately disagree with the practice of charging!** We have cried out against this practice for all the years that we have been writing and speaking on this subject and even challenged the leaders of the movement and the biblical counseling organizations to do likewise. But so far we cannot identify one leader of the movement or one biblical counseling organization that will do it.

If charging for biblical counseling is in opposition to what the Bible teaches, then it is sinful. Who among the biblical counseling movement leaders who privately oppose charging will say that it is sinful and identify by name those who charge and are therefore sinning? We have been asking that question for years and so far not one BCM leader or president of any Bible college or seminary has cried out in opposition to this practice. Thus, these men who claim the inerrancy and sufficiency of Scripture and who are not willing to speak out against this grossly unbiblical practice are guilty of collaboration by default.

The $75 to $135 per hour prices charged by biblical counselors are often paid by those who cannot truly afford it. In addition to being unbiblical, these fees have been a strain on the living expenses of many who seek help. Biblical counseling is, in most situations, not covered by an insurance policy. In those cases the fees are an out-of-pocket expense. As we have indicated, it is not a small expense, and those who cannot afford it must dig deep in order to pay those fees. Often sacrifices must be made by those who can least afford it. Everyone who charges and who supports the practice, directly or even by default, must share the blame, and this includes both individuals and organizations, such as ABC, AACC, CCEF, NANC, The Master's College and Seminary, and the Southern Baptist Theological Seminary. Think of those who are in need of personal ministry and are referred out to a pay-as-you-go counselor or, as in many cases, to a **pay-before-you-go counselor**. In most cases, these Johnny-come-lately counselors do not realize that their charge for counseling is a recent phenomenon in the church and is actually a spin-off of the psychological counseling movement, which only began after World War II.

With our past writings, recent *Person to Person Ministry* book, and this current book, we are challenging those who claim the Word of God as their touchstone to step up, speak up loudly, and publicly identify the names of leaders, organizations, schools, and colleges who are in violation. This "pay-for-play," price-tag commercialization of counseling needs to be exposed biblically, condemned, and rooted out of the church wherever it exists. Who will be the first leader to step forward on this important issue?

A Profession or a Calling?
Psychological counselors consider themselves to be professionals and therefore charge fees for their counseling. In

fact, they go into the profession as a means of livelihood just as other people may choose a career to make a living. This is a normal practice in the secular world. These people are selling their services and many simply become "paid friends" and confidants. (See Chapter Four.) In contrast, those individuals who are called by God to serve as pastors, teachers, evangelists, elders, bishops, and deacons are in a different category. They are called and equipped by God to serve a body of believers. Depending upon the extent of their duties, they may or may not be financially supported by the congregation, but they must not charge!

There is a world of difference between those who choose a profession to make an income and those who are called by God to serve in local congregations. Financial gain is a very strong consideration when choosing a profession. However, there is no place for financial gain being an incentive for ministry. Scripture is clear about how it is up to believers to support those who minister on a full-time basis. **It is the believers' responsibility to provide maintenance, but Scripture does not support the practice of charging for ministry.** We have covered this subject extensively in articles available at our web site and in *Person to Person Ministry*.[10]

Is Charging for Biblical Counseling Biblically Justifiable?

Many of those who refer to themselves as biblical counselors charge a fee for their services. They attempt to justify charging money for ministry by quoting various verses from Scripture. Therefore we will look at some of the Scriptures they use to determine whether they have a right to charge.

1 Timothy 5:17-18
We often hear "Thou shall not muzzle the ox" as a justification for charging. This phrase is in the context of ruling elders receiving a reward:

> Let the elders that rule well be counted worthy of double honour, especially they who labour in the word and doctrine. For the scripture saith, Thou shalt not muzzle the ox that treadeth out the corn. And, the labourer is worthy of his reward.

This Scripture is clear about the responsibility of a body of believers to provide support for the elders who "rule well" and "who labour in the word and doctrine." In fact they are to be "counted worthy of double honour" if they are faithfully and effectively fulfilling their calling. **Nevertheless, there is no hint of the elders charging a fee for ministry.** The teaching here is that those who receive spiritual help are responsible for giving necessary support to their elders for "the labourer is worthy of his reward." The word translated "reward" can also be translated "hire" or "wages." In other words the person may receive payment, but there is no indication in Scripture that the one who ministers can set the fee and charge those whom he serves. Neither do any of the commentaries we read suggest that a fee may be charged.[11] Therefore this verse cannot be used as a justification for charging a fee for biblical counseling.

Galatians 6:6
Paul sets forth a similar teaching in Galatians regarding the responsibility of the person who receives ministry: "Let him that is taught in the word communicate unto him that teacheth in all good things." This verse is in the context of personal ministry to one who needs spiritual help. Therefore those who charge for biblical counseling may think that this

verse justifies the practice of charging. Here again the admonition is being given to the one who "is taught in the word" to "communicate unto him that teacheth in all good things." The word translated "communicate" can also be translated "distribute," "share." **It cannot be translated "charge money."** The *Believer's Bible Commentary* says:

> Believers are responsible to support their Christian teachers. To share in all good things means to share with them the material things of life, and also to sustain them with prayer and godly interest.[12]

Matthew Henry clearly says, "Christians are here exhorted to be free and liberal in maintaining their ministers."[13] However, this verse says nothing about ministers charging for ministry.

John Gill says that those who receive godly instruction should:

> … impart of their worldly substance to them, for their honourable and comfortable support and maintenance; for since they spend their time, and make use of their talents, gifts, and abilities, for their instruction in spiritual things, it is but reasonable, and no such great matter, that they partake of their carnal things; and especially since it is the will and ordinance of Christ, that they that preach the Gospel should live of it.[14]

Note that this instruction is for those who receive the ministry to share with those who minister. **It is not a command or even permission for those who minister the Word to charge for individual teaching.**

Luke 10:7

Quite often we hear these words used as a justification for charging for biblical counseling: "the labourer is worthy of his hire." Jesus used this analogy in His instructions to the seventy that He sent out by two's to preach the Kingdom and heal the sick. He was definitely not instructing them to charge a fee for healing or for preaching. He was simply saying that, since even a laborer should receive wages, so also they should partake of the food and drink in the houses that receive them. They were to receive their upkeep, but the instructions do not even suggest that they were entitled to charge a price. In fact, when Jesus sent the twelve out to minister, He said, "Heal the sick, cleanse the lepers, raise the dead, cast out devils: freely ye have received, freely give" (Matt. 10:8). **We found no commentary that even suggests that the "labourer" can charge a fee.**

1 Corinthians 9:11-14, 18

Paul taught that there were clear biblical reasons for him to be supported by the church, even though he himself chose to give freely without reward.

> If we have sown unto you spiritual things, is it a great thing if we shall reap your carnal things? If others be partakers of this power over you, are not we rather? Nevertheless we have not used this power; but suffer all things, lest we should hinder the gospel of Christ. Do ye not know that they which minister about holy things live of the things of the temple? and they which wait at the altar are partakers with the altar? Even so hath the Lord ordained that they which preach the gospel should live of the gospel.... What is my reward then? Verily that, when I preach the gospel, I may make the gospel of Christ without charge, that I abuse not my power in the gospel.

Matthew Poole says, "It is the will of God, that those who are taken off from worldly employments, and spend their time in the study and preaching of the gospel, should have a livelihood from their labour."[15] They have a right to receive maintenance, but they are not under obligation to do so, for Paul went so far as to preach and teach without receiving compensation of any sort. He chose to "make the gospel of Christ without charge," meaning without expecting or accepting financial support. The words translated "without charge" mean "costless, i.e., gratuitous, without expense."[16] Therefore, one cannot say that Paul had the option to charge for his services, since the Greek word has nothing to do with exacting a fee for service. Instead, he had the option of ministering with or without receiving compensation or maintenance. In this instance he said that his reward was in preaching the Gospel freely at Corinth, without relating it in any way to receiving any livelihood from it. While he had every right to receive, he did not want there to be any misunderstanding whereby others might connect his preaching with some sort of monetary gain. In contrast, many biblical counselors blatantly and confidently connect money with ministry as they charge a set fee for their services in the same manner as their secular counterparts, and many require that the fee be paid in advance of the counseling.

"Filthy Lucre"

As we repeatedly say, there is nothing in the Bible that supports the practice of charging money for biblical counseling. Moreover, the Bible instructs those who minister not to do it for "filthy lucre." The apostle Peter exhorts the elders: "Feed the flock of God which is among you, taking the oversight thereof, not by constraint, but willingly; not for filthy lucre, but of a ready mind; neither as being lords over God's heritage, but being examples to the flock" (1 Peter 5:2). Thus, if a pastor, elder, or other believer is providing counsel, instruction, encouragement, and biblical admonition to fellow believers, such feeding of God's flock is not to be done for financial gain.

John Gill explains 1 Peter 5:2:

> ... not for filthy lucre; not from a covetous disposition, which is a filthy one; and for the sake of gaining money, and amassing wealth and riches, as the false prophets in Isaiah's time, who were never satisfied; and the false teachers in the apostle's time, who, through covetousness, made merchandise of men, and supposed that gain was godliness; whereas there is no such thing as serving God and mammon; and as the work of the ministry should not be entered upon, and continued in, with any such sordid view.[17]

Matthew Henry says regarding the elders: "These duties must be performed ... from a willing mind that takes pleasure in the work: *not for filthy lucre,* regarding the flock more than the fleece"[18] (emphasis in original).

William MacDonald, in the *Believers' Bible Commentary*, says:

> Financial reward must not be the motive for being an elder. This does not mean that an elder may not be supported by the local church; the existence of such "full-time elders" is indicated in 1Tim. 5:17-18. But it means that a mercenary spirit is incompatible with true Christian ministry.[19]

We are not judging hearts here, but rather actions regarding how the Lord's sheep are being tended. We are looking at people who are taking a position of leadership or authority ("counselor") over individual sheep. Many individuals take courses and earn certificates and/or degrees so that they can both minister to others and earn a living at the same time through being biblical counselors. While there is nothing wrong with earning a living through full-time ministry, **personal ministry should not be directly connected with money through charging or encouraging donations that are related to the counseling.** The exchange of money so blatantly connected with ministry sounds like "filthy lucre." Selling an hour of biblical counseling seems very much like a Christian selling prayer or selling friendship to a fellow believer. Since biblical counseling has in many ways usurped the biblical ministry of mutual care in the body of Christ, one wonders if it ends up being more like selling a substitute for mutual care, just as when professional counselors become substitutes for real friends. **If friendship should not carry a price-tag, should soul care in the body of Christ carry a price-tag?** Even some unbelievers along the way, as a matter of conscience, are opposed to charging. It is said that Ernest R. Groves, an early secular marriage counselor and advocate of marriage education, when he was asked if he charged for counseling, had decided not to because **"it seemed like taking pay for throwing a drowning man a rope"**[20] (bold added).

Those who are involved in ministry not only teach with their words but with their life. If they are charging money for personal ministry one to another, they are setting an example of charging for spiritual care. How much should one charge for praying for a fellow believer? Should the price-tag be dependent upon the length of the prayer or the words that are used? How much should one charge for a hospital visit? And, how can anyone put a price-tag on any spiritual activity? If the pastor were to charge each congregant for a Sunday message, how much might he charge? Would it be dependent on the quality of the sermon or the amount of seed sown?

Clearly, Scripture does not connect an act of ministry with charging a fee for it, even while the Bible gives clear instructions for supporting those who serve. What if a believer leads a person to the throne of grace and the individual believes in Jesus and is born again? Can a price-tag be put on that? **In fact, the most grievous aspect of charging for biblical counseling is that it cheapens the priceless work of Christ and makes merchandise of the Gospel. Selling the precious promises and precepts of Scripture for money reduces spiritual work to the level of ministering for mammon.**

Have not those who charge for biblical counseling reduced soul care to a commercial enterprise? Isn't placing a price tag on biblical counseling, i.e., charging for biblical counseling, commercializing personal ministry? The money, whether cash, check, or credit card, sounds like filthy lucre as it commercializes a person-to-person ministry in a manner for which there is no precedence in Scripture. As we keep demonstrating, **there is no evidence in any of the Bible commentaries that would even hint at the possibility of charging for mutual care in the body of Christ.**

We contend that charging money for biblical counseling is a form of simony (Acts 8) and have given biblical reasons as to why in our article titled "$$Simony & Biblical Counseling," which is available on our web site.[21] We have challenged the biblical counselors to respond, but none have done so to date. For further biblical analysis, we would suggest Debbie Dewart's article titled "Charging Fees for Biblical Counseling? Relationship, Responsibility, and Remuneration."[22]

While there are those individual biblical counselors and counseling organizations that are up-front about charging. some individuals and organizations do not charge up-front, but instead strongly encourage donations. The Institute for Biblical Counseling & Discipleship (IBCD) is one example. The IBCD web site says, "It costs us $65 per hour for these counseling appointments, and we therefore ask that you make a donation to IBCD for that amount when you receive counseling. If you are not able to afford that rate, we ask that you donate whatever you are able."[23] The Biblical Counseling and Educational Center (BCEC) in Visalia, California is another example. BCEC says:

> The extent that BCEC can provide a Biblical alternative to secular counseling is dependent upon the gifts of those who have benefited from the ministry of BCEC and those who believe in Biblical counseling.
>
> Counseling is a ministry of the body of Christ. The Scriptures teach that the laborer is worthy of his hire and that the person who is taught the Word of God should share with the one who teaches the Word (1 Timothy 5:18; Galatians 6:6).
>
> Donations are needed to keep the ministry going and growing.[24]

There are some biblical counseling centers that do not charge or encourage donations. Faith Baptist Church (FBC) in Lafayette, Indiana, provides free counseling through Faith Biblical Counseling Ministries. However, as part of the weekly homework in the course of counseling, those receiving counseling are required to attend at least one service at FBC, even if they are members of another church. Tithing is taught and encouraged during counseling and serves as a factor in evaluating their progress in counseling. Since both regular attendance and **tithing** are stressed and used in evaluating progress, free counseling should certainly be provided.

While the latter example is much closer to the Scriptures, there is always the danger of counseling becoming too closely related to financial gain, i.e., the counseling relying on the cash, check or credit card. The danger increases dramatically for those who charge or disguise the charging with suggested donations, to the point of ministry being reduced to a commercial enterprise, absolutely unsupported by Scripture.

Where is the Outrage?

Professor Jeffrey Kottler, in his book *On Being a Therapist*, says, **"Various studies of therapy dropouts estimate that roughly one-third of clients don't return after their initial interview, and close to half don't come back after the first two sessions"**[25] (bold added). Kottler also says, **"A therapist with a large turnover might require more than four hundred new referrals every year just to survive"**[26] (bold added). If truth be known, the same could be said about paid-for biblical counseling. For those who make a living at either psychological or biblical counseling, a prime motivating factor for the counselor is to keep each counselee in counseling as long as possible. While there is no scientific support for this idea, the justification involves the rationalization that the longer the counselee is in counseling, the greater good the counselor can do.

Underneath the rationalization is the reality of the revolving door of counselees, quickly and continually going out in large numbers and a need to have an equal number of counselees coming in. After all, the rent and utilities have to be paid and a sufficient income maintained. By our estimates, to make a decent living, a counselor would need to have at least 21 paying counselees per week. However, after the first counseling session, an average of 7 do not return, and after the second counseling session, the average increases to 10 non-returning counselees. Paid counselors not only have to "hold their breath" about the possibility of each new counselee not returning, but must be constantly on the prowl for new customers, as well as work on keeping old ones.

As pristine pure as the pay-as-you-go biblical counselors may think they are, the reality of the situation has to be that they, too, are caught in the revolving door phenomenon and need to pay the bills and the salaries. This hovering specter will no doubt affect the counseling process. Our readers are aware that, in addition to this chapter, we have demonstrated elsewhere clearly and concisely from Scripture that charging for biblical counseling has no examples, nor any support from the Bible, except for a few verses twisted out of context to cash in on a new meaning never before seen in the commentaries.[27] If one goes back a mere 50 years in the church, the biblical counseling movement did not exist and therefore no such Scripture twisting for pay was necessary.

There is a huge difference between a church or fellowship **paying** someone, such as a pastor or custodian, and a biblical counselor **charging** someone for services rendered. Can you imagine a pastor, elder, deacon, or church worker of any kind charging for ministries in the church? There is a vast number of church volunteers from leaders to functionaries of various kinds. If such individuals cashed in on the service-for-pay counselor mentality there would be "burglar" alarms going off throughout the church! Why, oh why, are there no alarms going off throughout the church over this crass cash-and-carry counseling mentality? We challenge our readers to find one well-known evangelical Christian leader who has publicly condemned the practice and publicly named individuals and organizations that are fleecing the flock.

Where is the outrage against such an unbiblical practice as charging for personal ministry? We would hope that those in influential positions regarding the training of biblical counselors would see the unbiblical nature of this practice of charging money for personal ministry and would speak out against it. Where are the Bible colleges and seminaries across America that discourage charging for personal ministry? Where is a Bible college or seminary in America that will publicly name names of those individuals and organizations that practice or support such charging and then clearly and publicly speak out against such a gross, unbiblical practice?

And, what about the individuals and churches that support these problem-centered, charging-for-ministry counselors and their organizations? Will they continue to be involved by supporting this filthy lucre process by failing to cry out against such an unbiblical activity? Are not those who cooperate with the counselors who charge enabling this filthy lucre practice to continue?

Shutting off the filthy lucre incentive would considerably disable the biblical counseling movement and those desiring to be trained to commercialize their training efforts. Shutting off the filthy lucre incentive could also reduce student enrollments at those Bible colleges and seminaries and thereby reduce their income. Is there a connection? We hope not. Moreover, **shutting off the filthy lucre incentive would close the door to referrals to biblical counseling outside the church and open the door to believers ministering mutual care to one another in local churches, which is where it should be.**

Separated-from-the-Church Biblical Counseling Centers (SBCC)

Prior to the rise of the biblical counseling movement, which followed on the heels of the psychological counseling movement, there were no separated-from-the-church biblical counseling centers. No one was sent away from a church for counseling because there was nowhere to send them. We trace the history of the cure of souls in *Against "Biblical Counseling": For the Bible* and find at no time was there a referral away from the church to a separated-from-the-church center for Christian care. Such ministry was and is a clear responsibility of the local church.

Referring individuals away from the church to a separated-from-the-church center to accomplish what the Lord has empowered His people to do in the local fellowship is a travesty on the teachings of the Bible and a failure on the part of the local fellowship. Yet, there are hundreds, if not thousands, of these separated-from-the-church counseling centers across America. There is no possibility in such a community center (which charges a fee) for ministering to people in the same way as in a local body of believers. There is no ministry beyond the 50-minute hour, no 24/7 availability, no availability of the usual services a church can provide, and no possibility to involve others as in a church fellowship.

There are relationships and ministries that exist in a local church that are absent in a separated-from-the-church biblical counseling center (SBCC). When, for sixteen years, we headed a mutual care ministry to those suffering from personal and interpersonal problems, those of us who ministered did things that do not happen in SBCCs. **We list only some of the many relational things that occurred that do not happen in SBCCs.**

Being available 24/7 was possible because the ministry was shared rather than one person having a "case load." Moreover, several different people may be involved in ministering to an individual in need.

Visiting a person at home, hospital, or work place would occur naturally as necessary because these are simply fellow believers experiencing problems of living. Neither a specified place nor restricted office hours interfered with ministry as in SBCCs.

Shared meals and coffee/tea/refreshment time were considered opportunities for fellowship and sharing both as fellow believers and as friends, whereas in SBCC settings, such activities would be discouraged and considered "unprofessional" or unnecessary.

Providing food, money, and such practical assistance as child or elder care, help with household chores, etc. are included in the benevolence activities of local churches. The person who ministers personally may be the one to perform these additional acts of love or they can be shared with other members of the Body of Christ. This does not happen in SBCCs.

Daily prayer for one another and opportunities to pray together personally or on the phone.

Expressions of love and care in the local fellowship, including hospitality, ongoing encouragement, sending cards for various occasions (from congratulations to condolences).

Relationships that continue on and develop further after the initial problems. The paid friendship in SBCC settings does not go beyond the counseling time, because continued friendship in SBCCs would be difficult because of time and distance and generally to the SBCCs "time is money" because bills and salaries must be paid.

The above are merely examples that biblically and practically distinguish the SBCC from the local church and **put to shame those who offer their 50-minute relationship hours (usually with a fee)** that pale in comparison to what happens in a truly biblical local church **free of charge**. These are all in addition to the vital worshipping and fellowshipping together, which would be absent from the SBCC.

The local church is the place for pastoral care and the mutual edification of all believers, under the authority of the foundation laid by Scripture and as given by Jesus Christ within the mutual ministry of the saints one to another, for the purpose of building up the Body of Christ through mutual encouragement, admonition, confession, repentance, forgiveness, restoration, consolation, and comfort.

Conclusion

"In cahoots" means "in partnership; in league."[28] The definition of "in partnership" is "being a partner with or in association with," and "in league"[29] is "working together, often secretly."[30] **Call it what you will regarding the problem-centered counseling, cross-gender counseling, charging for counseling, and separated-from-the-church counseling centers, the silence is deafening.** We are not saying that it is always an overt conspiracy, but rather an often covert (silent) concurrence. Nowhere can we find evidence of those in the biblical counseling movement raising a raucous over these grossly unbiblical practices by naming names. Even those who agree with us do not raise their voices in opposition to these unbiblical practices or publicly name those individuals and organizations that are guilty. So we conclude that they are **In Cahoots!**

8

Overcoming
Problem-Centeredness

For I determined not to know any thing among you, save Jesus Christ, and him crucified.   1 Corinthians 2:2

One of greatest difficulties in personal ministry and mutual care in the Body of Christ during this present era is overcoming the quagmire of problem-centeredness. Today most people expect to talk at length about their problems in a manner that ends up being unbiblical. They expect to give their unexpurgated versions of "life and love" as they see it and counselors encourage them to do so as they listen and explore. Because of this expectation, changing the conversation away from talking about the person's problems and towards talking about Christ and His life in the believer may seem very strange to both the one who seeks help and the one who ministers. Nevertheless, this is clearly how the apostles handled problems of living. Indeed, it was the "foolishness of preaching" (1 Cor. 1:21), rather than problem-centered counseling, that brought new life and nurtured believers. Believers who truly want to know the Lord in the midst of their problems and trials will see the value of focus-

203

ing on Christ instead of sinfully talking about their problems and the people involved. They will recognize that they will grow spiritually by turning to Him at every point.

Because of the influence of counseling theories and the public exposure of problems as discussed earlier, most people are accustomed to the idea that they must talk about their past and present emotional, personal, and interpersonal problems to obtain relief. Thus they will move in that direction at every opportunity. Their default setting is to focus on the problems and talk much about them in hopes of help. The counselors' default setting is similar, only for them it is the idea that with enough information they may be able to give wise counsel. In addition, playing the role of confident is a heady place to be and there is a natural inclination of the flesh to be enticed into listening to gossip. Problems are like magnets constantly drawing and demanding attention.

In our past writings we have criticized problem-centered counseling as being sinful because, beginning with the psychological counseling movement and mimicked by the biblical counseling movement, the expectation is for counselees to talk freely about their problems and for the counselors to freely pursue more and more details about the problems and the people involved.[1] Therefore, because we have spent so much time exposing the sinfulness of the problem-centered approach, some have assumed that we do not recommend hearing about problems or talking about them. **However, we have never said, "Do not talk about problems."** In our book *Competent to Minister* we say:

> While there are times when problems of living may be solved directly through exhortation and through applying specific verses that relate directly to those problems, we contend that personal ministry should move away from problems. **By saying this we do**

not mean that we overlook problems or merely sweep them aside.[2]

In our book *Christ-Centered Ministry versus Problem-Centered Counseling* we say:

> **Talking about problems should not be the central content of personal ministry in the Body of Christ. Problems should be seen as opportunities for drawing close to the Lord and growing spiritually. We are not saying, "Do not talk about problems!"** This is not an either-or situation; it is a matter of where the emphasis lies and how problems are addressed and used to motivate a believer to turn to the Lord, follow Him, and be further transformed into the likeness of Christ. **We are advising believers to minimize and generalize talking about problems and maximize and specialize in using problems as reminders to draw one closer to God.** Preoccupation with problems and seeking solutions through counseling often inhibit spiritual growth. Put simply, Christ must be the center of Christ-centered ministry whereas problems tend to be the center of problem-centered counseling.[3] (Bold in original.)

We repeat an important part of what we said back then: **"We are not saying, 'Do not talk about problems!'" We do say, "Do not talk about problems in the way that biblical counselors do," which leads to the Jeremiah 17:9 syndrome.**

Those who minister may certainly make suggestions and give advice when advice giving does not require information that would lead to sinful speaking or speculating. It should be made clear in ministry that the advice given is an option to consider rather than a mandate to follow unless there is serious sin involved. Much of what would be suggested or advised would be in the context of Scripture and from find-ing the Lord faithful in life experiences. And, there will be times when the one who ministers has no answers or advice to give and must honestly say, "I don't know. Let's bring this to the Lord and ask Him to show you."

One might ask, "Aren't you being problem-centered?" We say, "No," because **problem-centeredness as prac-ticed in biblical counseling opens the door for all kinds of unrestrained sinful talk on the part of the counselee and unrestricted questions and responses on the part of the counselor** to affirm what the individual says in order to pursue details in their attempt to understand and help. While it is usually not possible to prevent such talk from the ones in need who expect to be able to talk freely, **it is the counselors' problem-centered responses that promote and accelerate ongoing expressions of the Jeremiah 17:9 syndrome.** We call what we do "Christ-centered" or "Word-centered" min-istry because Christ is at the center of it and the Word is to control what is said by us and those who minister likewise. **While we cannot control what persons in need say about those not present or about themselves, we can control how we respond, what we say, and what we ask as we guide the conversation away from sinful talk.**

In the final section of this book, titled "Stop Counsel-ing! Start Ministering!" we give lists of Do Not's and Do's as guidelines for the conversations during personal minis-try. These should result in a clearly contrary direction from problem-centered biblical counseling. These Do not's and Do's will create an entirely different influence from what occurs in problem-centered counseling and will lead the conversation in a biblically sound direction to **encourage a daily walk with the Lord through the Word and the indwelling Holy Spirit.**

To clarify how we minister, we take two examples that are entirely different ways in which we may initially respond to those seeking help. **Prior to giving these two different examples, we recommend that, whatever the approach, the one who ministers should find out, as soon as possible, the spiritual condition of the one in need by asking about the person's salvation and daily walk with the Lord**. The first example is one in which an individual or couple generally describe why they are seeking help. Rather than asking questions about the details of the problem(s) they describe, we ask if it is alright if we take another approach before discussing the problem(s). We then describe the approach as Bible study and building a daily walk with the Lord. If the person(s) agree, we proceed to have a Bible study with them and to build a daily walk over the next few meetings. Sometimes it becomes necessary to return to discussing the problem(s) and sometimes not. As believers diligently turn to the Lord and attend to their daily walk with Him they find the answers to the initial problem(s) themselves without having to go into all the details with us.

The second example begins the same way, but because of the intensity of what is said by the individual or couple, we listen, exercising the Do Not's and Do's listed later. This unrestrained talk ("letting it all out") by the individual or couple may go on for several meetings. During each meeting we ask for the Lord to give us wisdom as to how much or how little we can begin to lead them in the direction of a Christ-centered daily walk, which we discuss in Chapter Ten. While this second example may involve the same kind of problem-centered talk on the part of the one in need, it **differs from problem-centered counseling in that those who minister do not encourage or amplify the problem-centeredness through questions and responses.**

There is a multitude of variations of the two entirely different examples and the question arises as to what to do. There are no rigid, for-certain answers to the question, except to say that if the one who ministers has a daily walk with the Lord and is growing in the things of the Spirit, the Lord will lead through His Word and Spirit and give discernment as to which of a number of possible ways may be followed in each and every unique situation. All the counseling manuals, certificates, degrees, and training will not be able to tell one what to do and how to proceed in each and every individual situation. **The ultimate goal is to get the individual into a daily walk with the Lord** as we discuss in Chapter Ten.

The default setting for the one who is ministering should be to turn the attention back to the Lord and His Word and the daily walk as soon as possible and as often as necessary. Of course there are exceptions, as when immediate action needs to be taken. For instance, if gross sin has been committed, such as a crime, physical or sexual abuse, or unfaithfulness in a marriage, there must be evidence and there must be action beyond the conversation of personal ministry. In other words, if there is an accusation of abuse, questions may have to be asked regarding the extent and type of abuse to determine who else (church leadership and/or civil authorities) may need to become involved. Marital infidelity would need to be referred to the pastor and/or elders. In fact, wherever church discipline is needed there must be evidence and referral to the pastor and/or elders. Talking extensively about such matters would not be helpful. However, talking about the Lord's work in the individual in need will always be beneficial and fruitful for spiritual growth and godly living.

Wheat and tares exist in every church fellowship. They may look much the same and do many of the same things. However, as it matures, wheat bends because of its fruitfulness. Likewise, believers who are like wheat will bend in humility. They will respond to the idea of turning to the Lord and talking more about Him and His will than the sins of others. As their daily walk is established and grows, they will not feel comfortable saying mean things about others because of a conscience influenced by the Holy Spirit. They will not be eager to cast blame on others and will be cognizant of the dangers of the tongue (James 3) and of how people will be accountable for their idle words (Matt. 12:36-37), especially if they are biased, backbiting, and blame-shifting.

Naturally there may be some true wheat that has not yet matured and has not had the conscience trained by the Spirit and the Word. Other believers may have become so comfortable with the world that they are not like "those who by reason of use have their senses exercised to discern both good and evil" (Hebrews 5:14). Such people may resist the truth about the Jeremiah 17:9 syndrome and continue sinfully speaking about others. However, as the one who ministers exercises patience and humility, the one in need is given the opportunity to see the value of personal ministry that leads to growing spiritually and becoming equipped in the Lord daily, without dwelling on problems and sinning with the mouth.

Those who resemble tares are the most difficult regarding spiritual matters because they may not be true believers. They are the most comfortable in the flesh, even as they are receiving ministry and proceeding to make external changes. That is why the truths of the Gospel need to be reiterated along the way in hopes that the Holy Spirit will show them where they are spiritually. However, if people continue to talk sinfully about their problems; if they are not willing to lay "aside all malice, and all guile, and hypocrisies, and envies, and all evil speaking"; if they show no "desire [for] the sincere milk of the word, that [they] may grow thereby" (1 Peter 2:1-2); if they do not want a daily walk with the

Lord; and if there is no response to the Gospel; then after a period of time it would be best to discontinue meeting for personal ministry. Why? Because they would continue to have an audience and even receive the listening as support for their sinful speaking, which would be detrimental to their own spiritual good.

Problem-centered counseling with its inevitable Jeremiah 17:9 syndrome is contaminated by the world and strengthens the flesh. In contrast, Christ-centered or Word-centered ministry does not rely on the ways of the world, but is dependent on the Lord Himself. Those who minister must do so by grace through faith and must depend on the Lord Himself working in and through them to minister what only the Lord knows is needful. This may sound a bit scary, as if there is no foundation, but this kind of ministry rests on the surest foundation ever: the Lord Himself! Just as believers are to walk by grace through faith, they are to minister to those in need by grace through faith. Colossians is clear about how the believer is to proceed in both the daily walk and in ministering to one another:

> As ye have therefore received Christ Jesus the Lord, so walk ye in him: Rooted and built up in him, and stablished in the faith, as ye have been taught, abounding therein with thanksgiving. Beware lest any man spoil you through philosophy and vain deceit, after the tradition of men, after the rudiments of the world, and not after Christ. For in him dwelleth all the fulness of the Godhead bodily. And ye are complete in him, which is the head of all principality and power (Col. 2:6-10).

In this brief section of Scripture, believers are given clear instruction about their position and walk: In Christ! They are to be "rooted and built up in him," "stablished in the faith," and "abounding therein with thanksgiving." This short list speaks about how to live, how to minister, and what to minister. The next verse tells what to avoid: "philosophy," which includes psychology, having come from philosophy; "vain deceit," which would include the emptiness and deception that goes on in problem-centered counseling; and "the rudiments of the world," under which we would categorize the various techniques of problem-centered counseling along with its inevitable Jeremiah 17:9 syndrome. The final two sentences reveal the power for life and ministry being in Christ and the fact that believers are "complete in Him"! Indeed the church traded its birthright for a pot of beans (Genesis 25:29-34) when it embraced problem-centered counseling and its rudiments of the world, whether such counseling is obviously psychological or simply a problem-centered biblical-counseling adaptation.

The Great Divide

When believers bring their problems to us, we listen and may give a word of advice. However, there is a great difference between being problem-centered and Christ-centered. We want to emphasize the Lord's work in the individual, not be an ongoing audience to people confessing the sins of others and playing the victim role, even if they are true victims of injustice and cruelty, which can best be dealt with at the cross of Christ. Problems are opportunities for spiritual growth and as believers mature in the Lord they will be handling life's issues through the indwelling Holy Spirit rather than the ways of the old nature. Those believers who understand the new life provided through Christ's death and resurrection and who are accustomed to walking according to the Spirit will not be dealing with problems in and of themselves, but rather according to their new life in Christ.

As they pass through the valleys and engage in spiritual conflict, they more and more know the truth of Paul's words: "I am crucified with Christ: nevertheless I live; yet not I, but Christ liveth in me: and the life which I now live in the flesh I live by the faith of the Son of God, who loved me, and gave himself for me" (Gal. 2:20).

Therefore we will focus on building up the individual's daily spiritual walk rather than on asking probing questions to hear details about the person's problems or to obtain an exhaustive and exhausting list of problems. **Talking about problems often leads to sinful speaking, self-effort, and carnal solutions.** In contrast, **we desire to help fellow believers to daily remember their resources in Christ, walk daily according to their new life in Him, and daily trust the Holy Spirit to bring forth fruit as they abide in Christ.**

As early as possible in the conversation we would turn to aspects of Christ's provisions, His constant presence, and His goal to bring every son and daughter to glory, conformed to His image. In Chapter Three we discuss three systems of biblical counseling with examples of the kinds of dialog that occur. Here we will delineate some of the differences between the biblical ministry of mutual care in the Body of Christ and the various biblical counseling methodologies.

Biblical counselors, along with their secular counterparts, want to know as much as possible about the problems so that they can direct the change. **In contrast, those who minister biblically generally want to know as little as necessary about the details of the problems as they encourage fellow believers to seek the Lord and trust the Holy Spirit to guide them daily.** Because they want to know as much as possible, many biblical counselors begin with Proverbs 18:13, "He that answereth a matter before he heareth it, it is folly and shame unto him." One glaring folly of using this verse to justify digging for more dirt is that counseling conversations are too filled with biased impressions, slanted stories, hearsay, and gossip about people who are not present for accurate information to be gleaned. Any understanding that comes forth will be filled with error, which can lead the counseling in the wrong direction and help solidify errone-ous perceptions. We would not use Proverbs 18:13 as a jus-tification for asking prying and probing questions, not only because of the above shortcomings, but also because we do not even need to know such details. There is no need to encourage expressions of the Jeremiah 17:9 syndrome, which are the inevitable outpourings when details are sought.

Counselors ask their counselees for more and more details regarding their problems and complaints about other people. In contrast we listen to what fellow believers may say about circumstances, self, and others, since we do not want to cut them off, but as soon as possible we redirect the conversa-tion back to Jesus Christ and what He might be doing by asking questions about their own daily walk with Him and how He would have them respond to the situation. Instead of dwelling on the sins of those not present, we would encour-age fellow believers to seek the Lord regarding their own walk and help them see the difference between when they are walking according to the flesh and when they are walk-ing according to the Spirit.

We would bring them back to the cross to consider all that Jesus accomplished for them to give them a right stand-ing with God (justification and imputed righteousness). We would talk about the indwelling Holy Spirit, who enables them to understand and apply Scripture, and about their brand new life in Christ whereby they are enabled to walk accord-ing to the Spirit. This is where the light needs to be shown rather than for counselors to imagine that they can know and understand all the details and inner workings of other people in order to solve their problems. Gleaning information from counselees saying bad things about others ends up being a detour that may never return to the path of spiritual growth. Some problems are unchanging. As someone once said, there is nothing so permanent as death and taxes. However, there are other life events that are often permanent and will not be alleviated through constant verbal airing. It is personally and spiritually detrimental to keep on talking about "woulda, coulda, shoulda," what one wished had happened rather than what actually did. Such talk compounds the detriment when a counselor listens over and over again to such mostly useless talk and pursues further amplification. Many people are just plain stuck in problems that may never have a solution and that cannot be undone. One must pray for a resolution or change if one is possible, but the one who ministers should draw the one in need to the Lord and His abundant storehouse to address all problems of living instead of pursuing the "woulda-coulda-shoulda's" of life.

As we repeatedly say, it is not necessary to know the details of those in need in order to help them deal with their problems. While there are instances in which details need to be heard and acted upon (sometimes immediately), the issues we are addressing are the usual counseling situations in which a person, usually a woman and usually alone, comes in and discusses personal and interpersonal issues week after week. We repeat what we said in *Person to Person Ministry: Soul Care in the Body of Christ*: Our goal in Christ-centered ministry is to nurture the spiritual life of believers, to equip them to fight the good fight of faith and thereby confront problems of living through exercising faith in Christ and obedience to His Word. To do this, the ministry must be Christ-centered rather than problem-centered.[4]

Different Questions, Comments, Responses

The intent of biblical counseling is to assist individuals to solve or deal with their problems of living through knowing much about their counselees and extensive details about their problems and relationships. The intent of biblical ministry is to assist individuals to grow spiritually and build their faith through their problems, while knowing as little as necessary about those problems. Biblical counselors typically **pursue** details of problems. According to anecdotes and dialogs that we have read, heard, and written about, biblical counselors often follow the lead of their counselees and often lead the way into the Jeremiah 17:9 syndrome, oftentimes with all sorts of sinful speaking as the lives of others are discussed. In contrast, those who minister should not be party to sinful speaking about others by asking leading questions to elaborate what is said and/or by ongoing listening without attempting to redirect the conversation. **Refraining from asking unnecessary questions about what is said, especially about others, will eliminate much sinful communication.**

Through eliciting details about people who are not present when problems are being discussed, problem-centered counselors lead their counselees into temptation, which usually results in sinful speaking. As early as possible those who minister should help those in need to avoid sinful speaking by guiding them away from the temptation to elaborate on problems that expose others unnecessarily.

Because of the Jeremiah 17:9 syndrome, no counselor can know much about, let alone understand completely, what is truly going on in anybody's life. Only the Lord knows! **Instead of questions that could elicit sinful speaking about others, we would ask questions regarding the person's understanding of the cross, the new life in Christ,**

the indwelling Holy Spirit, and a daily walk according to the Spirit. In other words, rather than prying into their private lives and circumstances, **we would probe into their biblical understanding and their moment-by-moment walk with the Lord, because, as they turn to Him and learn more of Him, they will be equipped to handle their problems according to His life in them, and they will be growing spiritually. Our ultimate goal would not be to solve their problems but for the Lord to work in the life so that they can solve their own problems His way!**

The questions, comments, and responses of those who desire to help others with personal and interpersonal problems reveal the differences between problem-centered counseling and biblical ministry. For example, a husband or wife comes into a session alone and in describing the reason for coming says, "My wife/husband and I are having marital problems." The general direction of the biblical counselor is to probe for details as Patten did by asking questions about the problems and directing the couple to "describe" (Chapter Three). In contrast, one who ministers biblically should avoid going down that path. Instead, if and when appropriate, one should ask questions that would draw the man or woman closer to God and bring forth truths from the Bible about the role of problems, trials, tribulation, and sufferings in a believer's life. Questions would thus be in the direction of the individual's spiritual life, such as:

"What might God be teaching you through this trial?"

"How do you think God sees this situation?"

"What are some good things you can say about your spouse?"

"Remembering that you have new life in Christ and the Holy Spirit indwells you, how might you respond or act differently?"

"Remembering that though you have new life, the flesh is there to war against the Spirit, what might you need to put off and put on?"

"Do you think much about the Lord and His ongoing presence during the day?"

"What kinds of thoughts run through your mind about God during the day?"

"What do you do daily in your walk with the Lord?"

"How do you pray for your spouse?"

"Do you desire your partner's good as much as your own?"

"What steps are you taking to follow your part of Ephesians 5:22-33?"

"How might you apply 1 Peter 2:19-24 to your situation?"

"What might the Lord be revealing to you about your own spiritual condition?"

"What provision has God given you to handle this situation?"

The above questions are merely possibilities. Questions should arise out of the conversation according to the Scripture truths brought to mind by the Holy Spirit. In addition to questions that could be asked during ministry, questions could be given to the one in need to take home to consider.[5] In Chapter Ten we discuss the need for a daily walk and give those in need ideas to build their own daily walk rather than homework that could amplify their problems, as biblical counselors sometimes do.

When counselors pursue the problems, often to the nth degree, they sympathize (or at least appear to sympathize) with the counselee, which is often an encouragement to say more and may be interpreted by the counselee as being in agreement. While sympathy (or apparent sympathy) does draw forth more details from the counselee, it is also received as support from the counselor. Even listening in an affirming manner often communicates support. The one who ministers needs to be careful about saying anything affirming when people say questionable things about other people. The default setting for most caring individuals is to believe what is said and to be sympathetic and supportive. Therefore those who minister need to remember Proverbs 18:17: "He that is first in his own cause seemeth just; but his neighbour cometh and searcheth him." **The one who ministers biblically may certainly express sympathy when a fellow believer is suffering, but care must be taken to ensure that the sympathy does not lend support to sinful speaking.** The support should be in the direction of encouraging the person to turn to the Lord daily in renewed faith and trust.

Becoming Christ-Centered

Moving from problem-centeredness to Christ-centeredness is a difficult process in ministering and at times takes a maximum amount of biblical discernment. However, this is necessary because it moves the conversation from the realm of darkness with its Jeremiah 17:9 expressions into the realm of light where the new man in Christ is enabled to deal with the problems from God's perspective and through God's power. Therefore this conflict is truly a spiritual battlefield where "the weapons of our warfare are not carnal, but mighty through God to the pulling down of strong holds" (2 Cor. 10:4). The truth to be brought forth must be the truth of the Gospel and of Christ in the believer by way of the indwelling Holy Spirit. The one who ministers enters the conflict with a clear understanding that the major work must be accomplished by God through a mere vessel, with the Holy Spirit bringing discernment and sensitivity to know when and what to say to guide and maintain a Christ-centered conversation. Problems often encompass the entire lives of those seeking ministry so that they are naturally occupied and preoccupied with their problems. **When appropriate, the one who ministers needs to be turning the conversation to Christ until those in need get the idea that He is their source of life and spiritual strength, and He is the one who must be first and foremost in thought, word, and deed in every situation.**

As we said earlier, we are advising believers to minimize and generalize conversing about problems and to maximize and emphasize using problems as reminders to turn to God and find His will and His way in and through the problems. The emphasis is to be on Christ and His work in the believer rather than on exploring circumstances and personalities and thereby trying to find solutions. We firmly believe that as people draw close to the Lord in faith and obedience they will know what to do. While personal knowledge and understanding regarding the person and the problem are limited, the one who ministers can be confident in the fact that God knows. His Word promises that as we trust and acknowledge Him, He will direct the conversation: "Trust in the LORD with all thine heart; and lean not unto thine own understanding. In all thy ways acknowledge him, and he shall direct thy paths" (Prov. 3:5-6). Acknowledging the Lord "in all thy ways," certainly includes all ministry as well as all of life! And while, biblical counselors do acknowledge the Lord in their counseling, they also depend upon certain problem-centered methods and pursuits and thereby encourage Jeremiah 17:9 syndrome responses. We are encouraging a stronger leaning on the Lord. After all, this is what we are attempting to communicate to the one in need—to lean on Christ, to be yoked with Him, to learn of Him (Matt. 11:28-30), and to walk according to His life in them daily.

In many cases there is an initial need to hear about the person's problems. To what degree and how long depends on what is being said and what information may be essential. Here there must be great discernment on the part of the listener, which comes through spiritual growth and experience in obeying the Lord's Word. For instance, there is a big difference between hearing about a problem and repeatedly discussing it through asking probing questions that would lead to sinful talk. Most problems discussed in counseling have to do with interpersonal relationships. Therefore some of what is said will no doubt be factual, but much is often subjective, skewed, unnecessary, unproductive, and downright sinful.

Those who minister need to be careful about what they ask and affirm. Nevertheless, if what they ask brings forth the Jeremiah 17:9 syndrome, they can change the direction of the conversation either through restructuring the question or asking another question all together. Or, perhaps a bit of teaching or reminding would be appropriate at the time. Of course, there must be teaching about the purpose of ministry being Christ-centered with His perspective, His involvement, His Word, and His life in the believer. Remembering the presence of the Lord Jesus Christ, through praying at the beginning of the meeting, will help guide what is discussed and how it is discussed. Those who are growing in Christ will be disturbed in their spirit by expressions of the Jeremiah 17:9 syndrome and will thereby be alerted to redirect the conversation themselves.

Getting Started

There is no one way of getting started, but we would begin at the foot of the cross and approach the throne of grace to "find grace to help in time of need" (Heb. 4:16). We need God's wisdom and His perspective. Thus we would begin and end with prayer and also pray along the way as needed. If the one in need seems ready, we might ask something general, such as "How do you want the Lord to work in your current situation?" Questions could be asked to find out generally but not specifically if the problem is a regular problem of living, such as a relational problem (which is often the case, especially in marriage), or, if appropriate, whether it is of a more serious nature, which would require intervention on the part of church leadership or civil authorities. One way to begin could be that, after the very general nature of the problem has been described, the person who is ministering might describe Christ-centered ministry and how it differs from usual forms of counseling. This could involve explaining about how talking about problems can lead to the Jeremiah 17:9 syndrome, how problems can be used for good in a believer's life, and how a daily walk with the Lord will not only please Him, but will enable them to deal with their problems. Then the conversation could proceed with a discussion of the Lord's involvement in the problematic situation, His perspective, how He might be using this situation in the person's life, and how the person can grow spiritually through a daily walk.

In the case of "Trey and Deb," who came in for marriage counseling (Chapter Three), what might have happened if the counselor had asked some direct questions at the beginning to see if this was a relationship problem that could be solved if each were to seek and follow the Lord? In the case of Trey and Deb, it was a relationship problem. In that situation the one who ministers could explain the difference

between usual counseling and personal ministry and then
proceed to talking about the life of Christ in them with the
goal of spiritual growth leading to a godly marriage.

This could be more of an interactive Bible study, perhaps beginning with passages having to do with the Gospel
and the new life. Various passages could be used, but it is
most helpful to establish the person IN Christ before instructions of how His life is to be worked out in the believer.
For instance: Romans 6-8 clearly teaches about the new
life which is then enabled by the Lord to follow Romans
12; Ephesians 1-3 teaches about the new life which is then
enabled by the Lord to follow Ephesians 4-6. In other words,
the person needs to learn to recognize the difference between
the old life that is to be put off and the new life that is to be
put on and exercised. The believer must not only have a clear
understanding, but experiential knowledge that comes from
putting truth into practice through obedience to the Word on
a daily basis. As believers learn to walk according to their
new life in Christ daily, they will relate with others in a more
Christ-like manner and deal with problems of living from the
place of spiritual wisdom, understanding, and power. Along
the way the one who ministers will see what Scriptures need
to be taught, explained, or reviewed.

As mentioned earlier, at some point along the way when
it seems appropriate, verses having to do with verbal communication could be read and discussed. One could begin with
one or more of the following: Psalm 19:14: "Let the words
of my mouth, and the meditation of my heart, be acceptable
in thy sight, O LORD, my strength, and my redeemer"; Matthew 12:36-37, "But I say unto you, That every idle word
that men shall speak, they shall give account thereof in the
day of judgment. For by thy words thou shalt be justified,
and by thy words thou shalt be condemned"; and James 3:2,
"For in many things we offend all. If any man offend not

in word, the same is a perfect man, and able also to bridle the whole body"? Then what if words were added about the control of one's tongue being a barometer of the spiritual maturity of a person?

Diverting Away from Problems and Onto Christ

Each person will have a different manner of redirecting the conversation. However, **foremost must be a strong intent to avoid the Jeremiah 17:9 syndrome and foster spiritual growth rather than to fix the problem.** Yes, it may be difficult to turn a person around. It may take time. Ongoing reminders of the purpose of this kind of ministry may be needed so that both the one who ministers and the recipient will be moving in the same direction. We have found that once those who seek ministry begin to understand the process, they will catch themselves and redirect the conversation themselves. While one may be giving and the other receiving, personal ministry should be a cooperative effort, remembering always that the Lord is the primary one who is truly ministering to both.

There must be great humility and care in diverting the conversation. After all, this kind of ministry is not what most people expect when they seek help because of all the problem-centered counseling that is promoted and done. Thus, rather than pursuing the sinful talk, the one who ministers could say something like: "Perhaps we should shift gears here and talk about the presence and provisions of the Lord and about your new life in Christ." At that moment the one who is ministering could suggest that they pray together for the Lord's leading in the conversation. This would make room for the Holy Spirit to do the convicting.

Paul's advice to Timothy is very appropriate to consider when ministering to anyone who is involved in any kind of sin, because all ongoing sin is a form of captivity from which one may "recover" oneself through turning to the Lord and repenting.

> And the servant of the Lord must not strive; but be gentle unto all men, apt to teach, patient, in meekness instructing those that oppose themselves; if God peradventure will give them repentance to the acknowledging of the truth; and that they may recover themselves out of the snare of the devil, who are taken captive by him at his will (2 Tim. 2:24-26).

Much of this captivity involves erroneous thinking, and that is why the process of turning from the ways of the old man to walking according to the new life in Christ takes being "renewed in the spirit of your mind" (Eph. 4:22-24).

All ministry must be clothed with gentleness and humility, especially the personal ministry of mutual care. If the ministry is to be Christ-centered, humility and love must be uppermost, because they are intrinsic to the life and presence of Christ. Therefore, another passage of Scripture to be kept in mind is this:

> Brethren, if a man be overtaken in a fault, ye which are spiritual, restore such an one in the spirit of meekness; considering thyself, lest thou also be tempted. Bear ye one another's burdens, and so fulfil the law of Christ. For if a man think himself to be something, when he is nothing, he deceiveth himself (Gal. 6:1-3).

Notice that the one who ministers is "**nothing**" in himself. Those who minister must come to a realization of their own nothingness so that Christ may be all. There is absolutely no room for any one-upmanship or sense of superiority in any Christian ministry as often happens in biblical counseling.

The counselors referred to in Chapters Three and Four generally took the position of a one-up expert who is able to diagnose and fix people's problems. Pride is a great temptation for biblical counselors, and that temptation is there even when one believer attempts to minister to a fellow believer without all the accoutrements of being a trained biblical counselor. Christ, who is perfect in love and humility, must always be central. Therefore, the one who ministers is to reflect Him, be empty of self, and serve as a mere vessel "meet for the master's use and prepared unto every good work" (2 Tim. 2:21).

We give suggestions for diverting from problem-centeredness to Christ-centeredness in *Person to Person Ministry*.[6] **However, we are convinced that as believers become more and more Christ-centered in their own lives and in their attitude and intent during personal ministry, the Holy Spirit will enable them to redirect the conversation biblically.** Christ-centered ministry will come forth, but since people generally need to be educated in this area, the challenge will always be there. At first, such redirection may not be easy, but the more it is done, the more progress towards Christ-centered ministry will be made. The following are a few things to keep in mind to encourage a Christ-centered direction:

Keep Christ ever in mind as the primary person present.

Remember that you are "**nothing**" in yourself.

Trust God to do the essential inner work.

Be compassionate without compromise or condescension.

Avoid probing questions that may lead to the Jeremiah 17:9 syndrome.

Learn to watch for aspects of the Jeremiah 17:9 syndrome, so as not to fall into the trap of pursuing it or being supportive of what is being said.

Ask the Lord to give you questions to ask that would lead to spiritual growth.

Talk about Christ and His presence and provisions.

Teach and remind the individual aspects of doctrine that need emphasizing.

Bring forth Scripture that the Holy Spirit may use to convict the individual regarding sin.

Always be encouraging the fellow believer in spiritual growth.

Remember eternity and speak of it often.

Because of the usual focus on problems and a driving desire to fix or get rid of them, great effort may be needed to turn the attention to Christ. The tendency to drift back into talking sinfully about problems is always a temptation. **Evidence of progress in ministry will be when there is an absence of problem-centered discussions during ministry and a greater desire to talk about the Lord and His will in the believer.** Problems may continue to be brought up by the one in need, but as believers learn to avoid expressions of the Jeremiah 17:9 syndrome, they will find satisfaction in walking more according to the Spirit than the flesh, and they will be sharing what the Lord is teaching them.

"Forgetting Those Things Which Are Behind"

Examining the contents of the heart and exploring the past in counseling are two of the murkiest and most misleading unbiblical excursions. We have already discussed the biblical errors of attempting to know another person's heart regarding its deceitfulness in Chapter Two and regarding the idols-of-the-heart counseling in Chapter Three. In this section we examine the fleshly futility of delving into the past.

The history of every individual is important to that person. The Lord knows that some people have extremely painful histories and **we do not want to minimize what people may have suffered throughout their lives. Nevertheless, we do not believe that it is helpful to dwell on the past or to search for details of the past to explain or improve the present. One cannot undo the past or even fix it by revisiting it. What every person needs is a brand new life and that is what Jesus came to give.**

Mutual care in the body of Christ should serve as an ongoing encouragement to one another, especially those who have suffered greatly. People who have suffered abuse need the compassion of Christ as well as the truth. They need truth wrapped in mercy, kindness, and gentleness. Jesus was careful not to break a bruised reed or quench a smoking flax (Matt. 12:20). Some people are like bruised reeds and flickering lights. Christ is in the business of making all things new, not only at salvation but each day as believers are learning to walk according to the Spirit. When the "ghosts" of the past intrude into their thoughts, feelings, and actions, they need to be reminded of Christ and His great love for them, of His life in them, and of the hope of eternity He has secured for them. One does not have to find out how a reed was bruised or how a light was almost extinguished in order to speak the truth of "Christ in you, the hope of glory" (Col. 1:27).

Believers do not need to revisit or understand their past in order to walk according to their new life in Christ, to be filled with the Spirit, and to bear the fruit of love, joy, and peace. Those who have had difficult childhoods often feel quite miserable about themselves and may carry a nagging bitterness about others, but going backwards will not give them what they truly need. The Gospel was exactly what freed early believers from bondage to a past that, for many, was filled with horror and abuse. Nevertheless, people who have been influenced by worldly psychological theories of personality erroneously believe that exploring and understanding one's past are necessary. In our concern about counselors' penchant for exploring the past to gain insight into the present, we have often quoted Paul's words:

> Brethren, I count not myself to have apprehended: but this one thing I do, forgetting those things which are behind, and reaching forth unto those things which are before, I press toward the mark for the prize of the high calling of God in Christ Jesus" (Phil. 3:13-14).

Those biblical counselors whose methods depend on gaining insight into the person's past in their search for clues to the inner drives and the motivations of the heart disagree that Paul was referring to a person's past circumstances. They tend to limit the verse to Paul's early commitment to the Old Testament law. In Philippians 3:3 Paul is speaking about confidence in the flesh, by which he formerly sought righteousness. Therefore that which is to be left behind is the flesh, including past circumstances that may have influenced the flesh, as well as having had confidence in the flesh. The new life in Christ Jesus is the theme of Philippians 3, and the goal of the pursuit is Jesus Christ Himself. Therefore, all that is of the flesh and its past are to be left behind. Indeed, when people in need seek to understand the present by searching their past they are back into the flesh, looking for answers back in the flesh, and being limited to the flesh fixing the flesh.

Various commentaries on Philippians 3:12-13 do not limit "forgetting those things which are behind" to Paul's former commitment to the law or even to the covenant given to Israel. **Paul is forgetting everything in his past that would hinder him**. The analogy Paul is giving in this verse is of a man running a race for the prize. In such a race all looking behind would be a distraction. The *Tyndale Concise Commentary* says:

> Paul forgot the past, Christian and non-Christian, because his goal was continual present-tense obedience that yields the knowledge of Christ. Each new moment is fresh and powerful for gaining the fruit of righteousness. Paul used the image of a runner with hopes of winning the prize stretching for the finish line to describe his Christian walk.[7]

The *Jamieson, Fausset, Brown Commentary* gives the following regarding "forgetting those things which are behind":

> *Looking back* is sure to end in *going back* (Luke 9:62): So Lot's wife (Luke 17:32). If in stemming a current we cease pulling the oar against it, we are carried back. God's word to us is as it was to Israel, "Speak unto the children of Israel that they go forward" (Ex. 14:15). The Bible is our landmark to show us whether we are progressing or retrograding (emphasis in original).[8]

Just as a runner in a race must be looking forward rather than backward, so must believers keep their eyes on Jesus.

> Wherefore seeing we also are compassed about with so great a cloud of witnesses, let us lay aside every weight, and the sin which doth so easily beset us, and let us run with patience the race that is set before us, looking unto Jesus the author and finisher of our faith; who for the joy that was set before him endured

230 Stop Counseling! Start Ministering!

the cross, despising the shame, and is set down at the right hand of the throne of God (Heb. 12:1-2).

Here "laying aside" every hindrance would include "forgetting those things which are behind," particularly the ways of the flesh. **While this must not eliminate remembering the cross and all Christ accomplished there for sinners or remembering other blessings of the Lord, it should eliminate all thinking about oneself that would keep one's eyes from Jesus and the calling that He has on every believer's life.**

A common misbelief of our era is that one must explore the past and thereby gain insight into the self to find reasons for present behavior in order to change oneself or to help another person change. This belief drives much of the counseling industry both in the world and in the church. Many biblical counselors have gleaned various ideas and methods from the world of psychological counseling. One of these is exploring a person's early circumstances and feelings in hopes of gaining insight into the why's and wherefore's of present feelings and behavior. Since most biblical counselors are eclectic even in methods of biblical counseling, we find that the past is often explored in biblical counseling. Those biblical counselors who are behavioristic may want to know the person's background to determine possible patterns of cause and effect. Those who follow a "psychoanalytic" model (idols of the heart) will attempt to see how the inner person developed as they seek insight into the inner drives and motivations of the heart. The Bible does not support this backward search and accompanying speculation as a method to move forward spiritually. Christ's solution for a bad past is the same remedy every person needs, and that is the new life in Him and a present daily walk in His presence.

A person need not be trapped in negative patterns of thinking, feeling, and behaving established during the early years of life, for the Bible offers a new way of life. Put off the old man; put on the new. Jesus said to Nicodemus, "Ye must be born again" (John 3:7), and He said elsewhere that new wine could not be put into old wineskins (Matt. 9:17). Jesus offers new life and new beginnings. One who is born again has the spiritual capacity to replace old ways and develop new ones through the action of the Holy Spirit, the fruit of the Spirit, and the sanctification of the believer. One wonders why so many have given up the hope of Christianity for the hopelessness of early life determinism and the futility of trying to fix the flesh by going back to early life experiences.

While we agree that the past may influence the present and that some people have suffered extremely difficult and cruel early circumstances, we do **not** agree that what happened in a person's past **causes** the person to sin in the present. Circumstances may give rise to temptations and they may even provide sinful examples. Nevertheless, no matter what abuse has been committed against one, that abuse does not **cause** the victim to sin; neither should it be used as an excuse for sinful ways of dealing with life's current challenges. Neither is it helpful to talk repeatedly about it in counseling or personal ministry. If that were so, there would be much about that in Scripture.

From whence comes sin and its consequences? Does a person's sinful behavior come from outside the person through circumstances and hurtful treatment by others? While bad company corrupts morals and while other people's behavior may influence a person, sin is a natural proclivity of the natural man (called the "old man" and the "flesh" in Scripture). Therefore, whenever people give much attention to the past to figure out why they are feeling miserable and behaving in unsuccessful ways, they are limiting themselves to their flesh. First of all the flesh, with its proclivity to defend itself against all blame, will seek to find the reasons outside self. Next comes an untrustworthy memory that will cooperate in one's own defense (Chapter Two). Then comes speculation regarding how what happened to them in the past may explain their present situation. Then this tainted insight into the self (aka "flesh") gets in the way of the truth that sets people free: the cross and all that Christ accomplished for believers.

While there are admonitions against all forms of evil committed against others, none of those admonitions include the suggestion that any sin committed by anyone who has been abused is not one's own sin that has come from within. Matthew 15:19 is clear about the source of sin: "For out of the heart proceed evil thoughts, murders, adulteries, fornications, thefts, false witness, blasphemies" (Matt. 15:19). Ironically those biblical counselors who specialize in searching the inner man use this very verse with the misunderstanding that they can know another person's heart if they just find out enough about how the person developed from early childhood on into the present. In their attempt to discover the reasons why a person sins in a particular way, they proceed to speculate which of a host of possible idols of the heart may be driving the person's behavior. However, they are going against Scripture, which is to "look unto Jesus," forget the past, put off the "old man," be renewed in the mind, and walk according to the new life in Christ Jesus. Looking back to one's past circumstances and how one has been treated to figure out how to change the present will only lead to further discouragement and deception in the flesh, that is, the "old man, which is corrupt according to deceitful lusts" (Eph. 4:22).

Indeed there is much evil around us that can have various affects on us. Evil will particularly affect the natural man or the flesh. However, whatever evil comes into the life of one who has been given new life in Christ Jesus can be used for good as the Lord is in the process of conforming His children into the image of Christ (Rom. 8:28-29). Searching the past for reasons for a miserable life and rummaging around the memory to fix the present will lead backwards spiritually. At most the flesh will be strengthened and fortified, but the new life will not be nurtured and God will not be glorified. Therefore believers need to be following Paul's example of "forgetting those things which are behind."

The Lord has far better things for people to remember. Instead of dwelling on one's own painful past, the Bible gives believers much encouragement to remember what He has done from before the foundation of the world. Instead of remembering the sins committed against oneself, people are to remember their own sinfulness for the purpose of realizing their need for a Savior and for their need for repentance. Then, instead of continuing to remember sins that have been forgiven and continuing to feel guilty, which is a sign of unbelief, believers need to remember the cross of Christ and the new life He procured for sinners. Instead of trying to live the Christian life through self-effort, believers are to remember the indwelling Holy Spirit, the promises of Scripture, and the whole counsel of God. They need to remember to walk by faith in the Son of God and not according to the traditions of men (Col. 2:6-10). Believers need to remind themselves and one another daily about the essence of the new life in Christ and of their hope of eternity. Intentional remembering these truths can be a strong antidote to being preoccupied with remembering and talking about personal painful circumstances in the past, as promoted in problem-centered counseling.

Thinking in the present should replace dwelling on the past as one considers Paul's words: "whatsoever things are true, whatsoever things are honest, whatsoever things are just, whatsoever things are pure, whatsoever things are lovely, whatsoever things are of good report; if there be any virtue, and if there be any praise, think on these things" (Phil. 4:8). **Paul does not have any such list as the following**: "Think about sins committed against you, list each one by name, write down the name of the perpetrator next to the sin, remember how you felt, write down how you felt and the ways each one has affected your life...." Some biblical counselors present such exercises in their attempt to help their counselees forgive those who have sinned against them. However, such remembering and listing may only serve to magnify the idea of having been sinned against, which would greatly detract from realizing one's own sinfulness, for which Christ paid the penalty and for which every believer must repent and from which every believer must turn, so that righteousness may be served rather than sin.

The direction throughout the New Testament is on one's own turning from sin and walking according to the new life instead of remembering and talking about the sins committed against oneself, as in problem-centered counseling. The emphasis is on Christ who fits Paul's description in Philippians 4:8, for He is true, honest, just, pure, lovely, of good report, perfect in virtue and worthy of ongoing praise. Yes, the race is always forward into glory to that day when we will see Jesus face to face.

> Beloved, now are we the sons of God, and it doth not yet appear what we shall be: but we know that, when he shall appear, we shall be like him; for we shall see him as he is" (1 John 3:2).

Let us then with Paul press forward, walking according to the Spirit rather than looking back at the old flesh.

Conclusion

As we said at the beginning of this chapter, one of greatest difficulties in personal ministry and mutual care in the Body of Christ during this present counseling era is overcoming the quagmire of problem-centeredness. We have shown in this chapter ways of moving away from problem-centeredness to a Christ-centered, Word-centered, daily walk with the Lord. We have also revealed how challenging it is to resist the fleshly inertia to talk sinfully about problems with the Jeremiah 17:9 syndrome. Vigilance is needed not only for getting off the problem-centeredness but for staying off and replacing it with an ongoing daily walk.

As we have shown in *Person to Person Ministry* and in this book, biblical counselors by their problem-centered questions permit and even encourage their counselees to expose sins and shortcomings of people who are not present, which are often biased and colored with many false hues. **It is essential for the one who ministers biblically to lead fellow believers away from talking about the sins and shortcomings of others and to assist them to see their own need for spiritual growth as the Holy Spirit working together with the Word convicts them of their own sinfulness and enables them to think and act daily according to their new life in Christ.**

9

Ministering Biblically

But we all, with open face beholding as in a glass the glory of the Lord, are changed into the same image from glory to glory, even as by the Spirit of the Lord.

2 Corinthians 3:18

Many believers are already equipped to minister mutual care in the body of Christ through all that God provides through salvation and ongoing sanctification. As believers mature in walking according to the new life He has given in Christ Jesus by grace through faith, they are enabled by the Holy Spirit to minister Christ to one another. The Lord equips believers with both the way to live and the way to minister accordingly. Their text is the Bible; their teacher is the Holy Spirit; their course is living their new life by grace through faith; and their primary subject is Jesus Christ. That is why we are not interesting in training Christians to be biblical counselors, but rather desire to encourage those in the church who are already called and equipped by God to minister to fellow believers as needs arise.

Ministering biblically is ministering the Lord Jesus Christ through the Word empowered by the Holy Spirit. Because the Lord does the primary work in bringing about godly change and spiritual growth, both the one who ministers and the one receiving ministry will be changed as they behold "as in a glass the glory of the Lord." They will become like a mirror reflecting Jesus as they behold His glory, which includes His attributes of love, mercy, grace, kindness, forgiveness, generosity, power, justice, and tender care. As believers attend to Him, think about His character, and His relationship to them, they are changed "from glory to glory," which implies that the change is not instant but rather a growing change that comes from purposefully gazing on His gracious personhood. This is a glorious promise! The response to such a glorious promise must be a purposeful intent to think about Jesus and His attributes more than dwelling on problems and problem people.

People naturally pick up characteristics of those they pay attention to. They sometimes even pick up the very characteristics that irritate them if they spend time thinking about those people with whom they have problematic relationships. How much more edifying to be thinking about Jesus than about problem people! How much better to be talking about Him than "them"! As we minister to one another in the Body of Christ we want to help one another look for Jesus in every circumstance, because those who find Him will be changed "from glory to glory" (2 Cor. 3:18).

Much of what we say in this chapter will be familiar to you who have been walking with the Lord and ministering mutual care. However, we believe that all of us need to be reminded of these great truths so that we will not slip back into walking after the flesh and following the ways of the world or a legalistic works mentality. **We again want to make it clear that what we are presenting in this book and in our**

other writings is not the final word. It represents how we function and what we have found to be God-honoring to bring the one in need into an authentic, daily spiritual walk with the Lord. If you have found another means of ministering that is biblically based without being sinfully problem-centered, we encourage you to use it.

Many of our readers have told us that they are not only in agreement with what we have been writing, but it matches the knowledge they have had and the means of ministry they have been using for years. One pastor told us recently that when individuals or couples ask for personal ministry they must already be active in the services of the church or become active prior to receiving personal ministry. He knew that the most important thing for them was their own walk with the Lord. If believers are walking daily with the Lord and growing in the things of the Spirit according to God's Word, the Holy Spirit will draw out of them what needs to be done in the many ministry variations of all the situations that occur.

As we have said elsewhere:

> **We do not want to intimidate those who are ministering biblically by introducing a new or competing system that must be learned and mastered by those who read it.** There is already too much intimidation in the church by those who have developed elaborate approaches to biblical counseling that require courses, certificates, and the reading of many books and counseling cases. **We are simply presenting some ideas to complement what others who minister biblically are already doing. We give suggestions on how the one who draws alongside may assist in change and growth with the understanding that God does the primary work and that the**

person in need has the opportunity and responsibility to follow Him. Some or all of what we present are already being done by those who are not caught in the unbiblical web of psychological integration or the contemporary problem-centered biblical counseling movement.[1]

In ministering biblically, a member of the Body of Christ can minister Jesus Christ to one who is presently living in the kingdom of darkness under the influence of Satan or to a fellow believer in whom Christ lives. **If the ministry recipient has not yet been born again by the Holy Spirit and thereby placed into the Body of Christ and into the kingdom of light, then evangelism is the primary goal in every encounter,** through opportunities to present the Gospel, to pray, and to express the life of Christ by walking according to His indwelling Holy Spirit. When unbelievers seek help, believers have a ready opportunity to speak forth the Gospel.

When believers seek help, fellow believers have the opportunity to edify them by reminding them of their great and wonderful possessions in Christ for meeting the challenges of life. Here we will primarily discuss ministering to fellow believers in the Body of Christ. Whether the reason a person has come for help is simply for a word of advice or whether the reason is for complex personal and/or interpersonal problems, the intent of ministry is to gain God's perspective, beginning with the person's relationship with the Lord and His ongoing work of growing His children into godly maturity. **Therefore we begin with these objectives in mind: to edify one another in the Lord, to amplify one's understanding of all that Christ accomplished on the cross, and to encourage fellow believers to walk daily according to their new life in Christ. This is simply minis-**

tering God's truth in love on a more personal basis than that of public proclamation through preaching, teaching, and evangelizing.

Biblical Antidote to Problem-Centered Counseling

The solution to the problem of sinning and being sinned against is not found by one person trying to figure out the make-up of another person's fleshly nature. The solution to sinning and being sinned against is to receive Christ by grace through faith and then to walk according to the new life in Christ. Jesus declared to Nicodemus, "Verily, verily, I say unto thee, Except a man be born again, he cannot see the kingdom of God" (John 3:3). Jesus never attempted to fix anyone's flesh. Instead he knew it had to be replaced with new life. Even God's Holy Law could not fix the flesh in that the flesh was incapable of keeping the law (Romans 8:7). Therefore, Christ bore the punishment of sin, died in the place of sinners and gave them new life in Him so that in identifying themselves with Him they could count themselves dead to sin and alive to God (Romans 6:11).

Studying Romans 6-8 together during personal ministry would be beneficial. Here Paul explains the process of the believer's identification with Christ in His death, burial, and resurrection, whereby believers have a new way of life because they have a new source of life.

> Knowing this, that our old man is crucified with him, that the body of sin might be destroyed, that henceforth we should not serve sin. For he that is dead is freed from sin. Now if we be dead with Christ, we believe that we shall also live with him.... Likewise reckon ye also yourselves to be dead indeed unto sin, but alive unto God through Jesus Christ our Lord.

> Let not sin therefore reign in your mortal body, that ye should obey it in the lusts thereof. Neither yield ye your members as instruments of unrighteousness unto sin: but yield yourselves unto God, as those that are alive from the dead, and your members as instruments of righteousness unto God (Rom. 6:6-8, 11-13).

Notice how volitional and active this is! Paul is not describing a passive life, but one that has been made alive as never before.

Another section of Scripture to talk about in personal ministry clearly states that God has indeed equipped His children with all they need to live the Christian life and also to minister to those suffering from problems of living.

> Grace and peace be multiplied unto you through the knowledge of God, and of Jesus our Lord, according as his divine power hath given unto us all things that pertain unto life and godliness, through the knowledge of him that hath called us to glory and virtue: Whereby are given unto us exceeding great and precious promises: that by these ye might be partakers of the divine nature, having escaped the corruption that is in the world through lust (2 Peter 1:2-4).

We desire through ministry to help believers remember their spiritual resources and to encourage them to use these resources actively and volitionally as they walk with Him. Having been given all they need for life and godliness, believers are then to participate: "giving all diligence, add to your faith virtue; and to virtue knowledge; and to knowledge temperance; and to temperance patience; and to patience godliness; and to godliness brotherly kindness; and to brotherly kindness charity" (2 Peter 1:5-7). Then Peter says that their experiential knowledge of Christ will grow: "For if these things be in you, and abound, they make you that ye shall neither be barren nor unfruitful in the knowledge of our Lord Jesus Christ" (1 Peter 1:5-8). God gives the promises; the believer is to act upon them by faith. When believers truly believe God, they become both willing and able to obey Him, not in order to become acceptable to Him, but because they have already been "accepted in the beloved" (Eph. 1:6).

Paul explains that believers are not under the law, but under grace and are thereby enabled to obey the Lord by means of the indwelling Holy Spirit. They can choose to put off the old ways of the flesh and put on the ways of the new life in Christ, as described in Ephesians 4:25-32 and Colossians 3:1-16. Indeed believers have a new life and they have the Word of God, which nurtures, guides, and empowers them. Paul summed it all up when he wrote: "Therefore if any man be in Christ, he is a new creature: old things are passed away; behold, all things are become new" (2 Cor. 5:17). Ministry must emphasize and remind over and over again these truths of the new life.

The Importance of Reminding

After Peter described the completeness of the believer's divine resources (2 Peter 1:3-4, quoted above) and what their response should be in the ensuing verses, he said that he would "not be negligent to put you always in remembrance of these things, though ye know them, and be established in the present truth" (2 Peter 1:12). Peter knew how essential it is for believers to continue to remember what they have been taught regarding their identity in Christ and their spiritual provisions and power to walk according to His ways. When Christians wonder how they might help fellow believers in need without focusing on problems and probing into the details, we wonder why they do not talk about those things that Peter believed were so important. Peter determined to remind them while he was still living so that they might remember them after he would no longer be with them (2 Peter 1:13-14).

The Bible is full of truths to be remembered and applied. Even new believers often know plenty to remember and apply. Those who have been walking with the Lord over the years should be well-equipped, not only with the essentials of the faith, but with experience in applying God's Word in their lives through the indwelling Holy Spirit. They also know what it is to have slipped back into their old ways of the flesh and to choose once again to make the vital transition from the flesh to the Spirit through confession (admitting), repentance (turning), and faith (believing God) (1 John 1:9). Every time they make this transition, they start out spiritually clean and further seasoned in the ways of the Lord.

As believers minister to those in need they should be endeavoring to encourage them to remember all that God has done and given through His Word, through Jesus Christ, and through the Holy Spirit. Remembering and reminding, teaching and exhorting the truths from God's Word will strengthen believers to walk according to their new life by grace through faith. In contrast, **problem-centered counseling tends to weaken the believer's spiritual walk. Conversation centered in Christ and in all that God has done and given will edify, equip, and encourage.** As the content of remembering is the Lord Jesus Christ, believers will become more like Him (2 Cor. 3:18). Yes, there is much to remember that will serve Christians in their walk with the Lord in the direction of eternity with Him. The following are some of the truths to minister to those in need.

Remembering the Great Commandment

"God is love." The new life in Christ will reflect His love. In fact 1 John 4:8 goes so far as to say, "He that loveth not knoweth not God; for God is love." For the believer love is not an option: "Thou shalt love the Lord thy God with all thy heart, and with all thy soul, and with all thy strength, and with all thy mind; and thy neighbour as thyself" (Luke 10:27). However the Great Commandment is impossible for the natural man to obey. Love for God and others comes from God Himself: "Herein is love, not that we loved God, but that he loved us, and sent his Son to be the propitiation for our sins. Beloved, if God so loved us, we ought also to love one another" (1 John 4:10-11). Love is the identifying mark of Christians. As Jesus said, "By this shall all men know that ye are my disciples, if ye have love one to another" (John 13:35). The source of this love is Christ's life in the believer, but the believer must nevertheless choose to love. Love also reveals whether one is walking according to the new life or abiding in the death of the flesh: "We know that we have passed from death unto life, because we love the brethren. He that loveth not his brother abideth in death" (1 John 3:14).

Interpersonal problems generally arise because of misdirected love. In other words, the flesh tends to love itself more than God and others. The new life will love God and others by the indwelling power of the Holy Spirit. The kind of love we are talking about here is a giving love, agape, translated "charity." 1 Corinthians gives a clear description of this love.

> Charity suffereth long, and is kind; charity envieth not; charity vaunteth not itself, is not puffed up, doth not behave itself unseemly, seeketh not her own, is not easily provoked, thinketh no evil; rejoiceth not in

iniquity, but rejoiceth in the truth; beareth all things, believeth all things, hopeth all things, endureth all things (1 Cor. 13:4-7).

Believers can discern whether they are walking according to the Spirit or according to the flesh by comparing their own attitude, thoughts, words, and actions with the above description. To help with this, the one who ministers could go over various aspects of this description, such as "suffereth long" and ask, what does it mean to suffer long? What long-suffering may be called for in the present circumstances? Then, if there is a lack of longsuffering, the person can put off the ways of the flesh and put on longsuffering, by grace through faith. While this is a spiritual activity, this putting off and on can be instantaneous, like turning around, because the new life is there ready to be lived as soon as a believer chooses to mortify the flesh (Rom. 8:13).

Kindness goes a long way in human relationships and quite often the problems people experience are relationship problems. People often call these "communication problems," but in most cases they could be solved with kindness and the attributes of love found in 1 Corinthians 13. As one believer ministers to another, there must be much agape love and kindness. The one who ministers must be careful not to preach down to a believer in need. After all, every believer is still in the process of growth. No one has yet arrived at the point of perfect love aside from Jesus Christ Himself, who is and was love from the beginning. **Therefore, in discussing biblical principles, there must be a sense of "we," as in "we can all benefit from this passage."** We all need the Lord to work in our lives so that we will reflect Him more than we do. We all need to be walking according to the Spirit and putting off the old ways of the flesh.

Discussing these verses having to do with love will equip believers for dealing with problems according to their new life in Christ. Commentaries may also be useful to bring forth the full meaning of each aspect of love, especially for what might be included in "beareth all things, believeth all things, hopeth all things, endureth all things." What is meant by "all things"? One will find that the phrase "all things" must be limited by the context of the entire Bible. A brief sampling here of "beareth all things" comes from *Adam Clarke's Commentary on the Bible*:

> Love conceals every thing that should be concealed; betrays no secret; retains the grace given; and goes on to continual increase. A person under the influence of this love never makes the sins, follies, faults, or imperfections of any man, the subject either of censure or conversation. He covers them as far as he can; and if alone privy to them, he retains the knowledge of them in his own bosom as far as he ought.[2]

Albert Barnes Notes on the Bible adds that the "all things" here "refers to private matters," not public matters.[3]

A brief sampling of "believeth all things" comes from *John Gill's Exposition of the Entire Bible*:

> **Believeth all things**; that are to be believed, all that God says in his word, all his truths, and all his promises; and even sometimes in hope against hope, as Abraham did, relying upon the power, faithfulness, and other perfections of God; though such a man will not believe every spirit, every preacher and teacher, nor any but such as agree with the Scriptures of truth, the standard of faith and practice; nor will he believe every word of man, which is the character of a weak and foolish man; indeed, a man of charity or love is willing to believe all the good things reported of men;

he is very credulous of such things, and is unwilling to believe ill reports of persons, or any ill of men; unless it is open and glaring, and is well supported, and there is full evidence of it; he is very incredulous in this respect.[4]

Clarke gives the following commentary on "hopeth all things":

When there is no place left for believing good of a person, then love comes in with its hope, where it could not work by its faith; and begins immediately to make allowances and excuses, as far as a good conscience can permit; and farther, anticipates the repentance of the transgressor, and his restoration to the good opinion of society and his place in the Church of God, from which he had fallen.[5]

This kind of hope should be very evident in those who minister to others. In fact this hope is a grace that all believers should develop in their walk with the Lord.

Gill lists some of the **"all things" that love endures**:

All things; that are disagreeable to the flesh; all afflictions, tribulations, temptations, persecutions, and death itself, for the elect's sake, for the sake of the Gospel, and especially for the sake of Christ Jesus.[6]

Some trials believers go through are not always solved but rather must be endured in ways that express love for God and others. We recommend that all Christians give great attention to this passage on love, for as they keep these things in mind they will more easily walk according to the Spirit and more easily discern when they have shifted back into the flesh. By God's grace and by the empowerment of the Holy Spirit believers are enabled to follow the Great Commandment to love God and neighbor.

Being Mindful of Spiritual Warfare

Those who minister need to remember that they and the ones to whom they minister are in a spiritual battle. If believers do not realize that they are in a spiritual battle, they are already failing to "fight the good fight of faith" (1 Tim. 6:12) and are thereby already losing much ground. Those who minister need to remind themselves and those to whom they minister that every believer is in the midst of spiritual warfare every day, whether there is obvious conflict or not.

Galatians 5 describes the inner conflict between the Spirit and the flesh.

> Walk in the Spirit, and ye shall not fulfil the lust of the flesh. For the flesh lusteth against the Spirit, and the Spirit against the flesh: and these are contrary the one to the other: so that ye cannot do the things that ye would (Gal. 5:16-17).

While there is a conflict between the flesh and the Spirit, the indwelling Holy Spirit gives the power to do what is right. However, the believer must choose to follow the Spirit rather than the flesh. The clause "ye cannot do the things that you would" shows that the believer is not truly an independent agent, but always under the influence of either the flesh or the Spirit. That is why the very next verse says, "But if ye be led of the Spirit, ye are not under the law" (Gal. 5:18). While this conflict may be fierce, the Holy Spirit gives the power to act according to the new life. In other words, being under the law does not empower one to do what is right, but the Holy Spirit does. There is such a vast contrast between the works of the flesh listed in Galatians 5:19-21 and the fruit of the Spirit: "love, joy, peace, longsuffering, gentleness, goodness, faith, meekness, temperance: against such there is no law" (Gal. 5:22-23). The fruit bearing comes from the Holy Spirit indwelling believers, but believers have a responsibility to "walk in the Spirit." The inner battle is won by remembering and acting according to the following: "And they that are Christ's have crucified the flesh with the affections and lusts. If we live in the Spirit, let us also walk in the Spirit" (Gal. 5:24-25).

To fight the good fight of faith, believers need to "be strong in the Lord, and in the power of his might" and: "Put on the whole armour of God, that ye may be able to stand against the wiles of the devil" (Eph. 6:11). Believers have power in the Lord and spiritual armor for the conflict, and they have been given the identity of the enemy, "For we wrestle not against flesh and blood, but against principalities, against powers, against the rulers of the darkness of this world, against spiritual wickedness in high places" (Eph. 6:12). Behind every external conflict lurks the wiles of the devil, tempting people to sin, bringing misunderstanding, confusion, and anything to destroy God's plan and therefore His people. That does not mean that the person with whom one is having a disagreement is "of the devil," but rather that the devil is behind discord, misunderstanding, and even sinful behavior through his crafty temptations and subtle deceptions. So often when believers are involved in conflicts they forget who their real enemy is. That is one reason why people argue and fight with one another and why they may be filled with bitterness, anger, wrath, and an unforgiving attitude. While believers may know these verses very well, they often forget them when they are in conflict with people.

Just as God has given His children all they need for life and godliness, He has given them all they need for spiritual warfare.

> Wherefore take unto you the whole armour of God, that ye may be able to withstand in the evil day, and having done all, to stand. Stand therefore, having

your loins girt about with truth, and having on the breastplate of righteousness; And your feet shod with the preparation of the gospel of peace; Above all, taking the shield of faith, wherewith ye shall be able to quench all the fiery darts of the wicked. And take the helmet of salvation, and the sword of the Spirit, which is the word of God: Praying always with all prayer and supplication in the Spirit, and watching thereunto with all perseverance and supplication for all saints (Eph. 6:13-18).

One may find it very helpful to talk about each item of armor that God has given the believer. The armor described in Ephesians 6:13-17 describes the new life of the believer being in Christ. The loins "girt about with truth" describe the integrity of the new man in Christ as he walks in all truthfulness and sincerity according to the truth of Scripture. The "breastplate of righteousness" is not only the righteousness imputed to the believer at salvation, but is also the righteousness that comes from walking according to the new life Christ has given. Having one's "feet shod with the preparation of the gospel of peace" is especially needful when people are in conflict with one another. They need to have a sure footing in the "gospel of peace," which includes peace with God (Romans 5:1), and not only a readiness to proclaim the Gospel (Rom. 10:15), but a readiness to walk in peace with others, with the peace of God ruling the heart (Col. 3:15), and to "follow after the things which make for peace, and things wherewith one may edify another" (Romans 14:19). The "shield of faith" is faith in God Himself and in all that God has said and promised, for only the truth of God can "quench all the fiery darts of the wicked." The "helmet of salvation" keeps the mind fixed on the victory that Christ has already wrought, on the hope of the saving work of Christ continuing to sanctify the believer, and on the hope of the final stage of salvation: glorification with Christ in eternity. Keeping those thoughts in mind in the midst of trials will not only protect the mind, but will keep the battle in perspective. The only weapon listed here is the only one believers need: "the sword of the Spirit, which is the word of God." Believers do not need to add such weapons of the world as found in psychological counseling theories and therapies.

While prayer is not part of the armor or weaponry, prayer is being in touch with the "Commander in Chief." Notice how believers are to be "watching ... with all perseverance." In any conflict the enemy will try surprise attacks. How many times people are blindsided and react before considering what God has directed in His Word. While salvation is a free gift, spiritual warfare takes ongoing "perseverance and supplication for all saints," including those with whom one may be in present conflict. When people talk about their problems, it is good to remind them that they are indeed in a spiritual battle. And when we minister to one another, we must realize that we are entering into the spiritual battle so that we will want to remind ourselves and one another to use the resources God has given.

Growing Spiritually through Problems

Most biblical counselors become problem solvers either through giving advice and directing the change or through searching out the unrecognized motivation of the person's heart. We encourage believers to see problems as opportunities for spiritual growth and for discovering more of what they possess in Christ for life and godliness and for handling problems themselves through faith in Him. While there may be instances when a word of advice will be helpful, we urge believers to evaluate all advice they receive from us or others with Scripture, to search the Scriptures daily, to become established in the faith, walking more and more according to the Word of God and the indwelling Holy Spirit. **The following consists of some of the many teachings regarding the opportunity for spiritual growth during trials that can be spiritually beneficial to discuss during ministry. Not all of them will necessarily be used.**

Reasons Why Christians Suffer

Christians should not be surprised when they are assailed with trials and suffering. Believers can expect problems of living simply because they are living in a fallen world where "the whole creation groaneth and travaileth in pain together until now" (Rom. 8:22). Christians are bound to suffer because they are Christians involved in a cosmic battle (Eph. 6:12) and many will suffer because of their testimony for Christ. Furthermore God uses trials to purify His saints and teach them to trust Him in the most difficult circumstances. Christians also suffer under the direction and discipline of their loving heavenly Father. God uses all trials for His glorious purposes and for the good of His people (Rom. 8:28-29). Suffering gives believers a unique opportunity to walk by faith rather than by sight.

Jesus warned His disciples that they would face much conflict in the world because they "are not of the world" (John 15:19). He taught them about His life in them as the life of the vine and about their dependence on Him to the degree that without Him they could do nothing (John 15:5). He taught them about His love for them and then said, "These things have I spoken unto you, that my joy might remain in you, and that your joy might be full" (John 15:11). He went before them in suffering and said that they would also suffer as they followed Him. As believers follow Jesus today they too will suffer, but not needlessly, for God will use that suffering for His glory and their ultimate good.

God's Purposes and Benefits
    When believers are in the midst of problems of living, God is neither absent nor uninformed. He is present in believers and actively involved to bring about His glorious purposes. Therefore whenever Christians encounter trials they need to remember God's purposes and benefits. Many sections of Scripture having to do with trials and suffering are useful to remember, remind, and talk about with one another. We will review a few of them here.
    James clearly tells how trials and suffering can be used for spiritual growth:

> My brethren, count it all joy when ye fall into divers temptations; Knowing this, that the trying of your faith worketh patience. But let patience have her perfect work, that ye may be perfect and entire, wanting nothing (James 1:2-4).

"Diverse temptations" would include both temptations to sin and various problems of living with their own temptations to act in ways apart from Christ. These verses are truly amazing! They assure the believer that the very trials of life are used to bring them to maturity ("perfect and entire") where they lack nothing. This truth goes counter to the world's way of thinking. But, notice what happens when the faith is tried (tested and strengthened) and results in patience. That very patience comes as believers learn to wait on God.
    Then, as people learn to wait expectantly on God by faith they grow in their spiritual walk. We need to remind one another about the marvelous fruitfulness that can come through trials, especially when problems themselves tend to make us all impatient and/or miserable, especially if we are

focused on the problems and trying to solve them through self-effort and the kind of counseling that relies on sinful speaking.

Paul gives the following spiritual benefits of tribulations:

> Therefore being justified by faith, we have peace with God through our Lord Jesus Christ: By whom also we have access by faith into this grace wherein we stand, and rejoice in hope of the glory of God. And not only so, but we glory in tribulations also: knowing that tribulation worketh patience; And patience, experience; and experience, hope: And hope maketh not ashamed; because the love of God is shed abroad in our hearts by the Holy Ghost which is given unto us (Rom. 5:1-5).

Why would Paul "glory in tribulations"? He certainly had experienced more tribulation than most with all the beatings, even to the brink of death, rejection, persecution, physical hardship, false accusations, shipwreck, pain, and imprisonment (2 Corinthians 11:23-28). Paul lists the effects of tribulation leading to patience, leading to experience, leading to hope, and leading to "the love of God … shed abroad in our hearts by the Holy Ghost which is given unto us."

Believers need to remember that through all the suffering God is with them and nothing can separate them from God's love. There is hope in every trial as presented in such Scriptures as the following:

> Who shall separate us from the love of Christ? shall tribulation, or distress, or persecution, or famine, or nakedness, or peril, or sword? As it is written, For thy sake we are killed all the day long; we are accounted as sheep for the slaughter. Nay, in all these things we are more than conquerors through him that loved

us. For I am persuaded, that neither death, nor life, nor angels, nor principalities, nor powers, nor things present, nor things to come, nor height, nor depth, nor any other creature, shall be able to separate us from the love of God, which is in Christ Jesus our Lord (Rom. 8:35-39).

Experiencing God through Trials

Painful circumstances in a Christian's life can serve as great opportunities to know Christ better. Paul did not waste time licking his wounds in self pity. One can find numerous passages that extol the usefulness of suffering, not only for spiritual growth, but for usefulness in ministry and for future glory. He revealed an eternal perspective:

... though our outward man perish, yet the inward man is renewed day by day. For our light affliction, which is but for a moment, worketh for us a far more exceeding and eternal weight of glory; while we look not at the things which are seen, but at the things which are not seen: for the things which are seen are temporal; but the things which are not seen are eternal (2 Cor. 4:16-18).

Believers want to experience God, but too often they seek emotional experiences rather than the kind of experience one gains by walking with God through the depths of suffering. Paul knew what it was to suffer loss for the excellency of knowing Christ to the point where he said: "That I may know him, and the power of his resurrection, and the fellowship of his sufferings, being made conformable unto his death" (Phil. 3:10). There is a blessed and very personal knowing that comes from suffering with Christ. Those who have suffered in Christ have known the close fellowship with Him that comes and the great comfort and inner strength He gives. Knowing Christ in this way is experiencing our unity with Him in both His death and resurrection, as we reckon ourselves "to be dead indeed unto sin, but alive unto God through Jesus Christ our Lord" (Rom. 6:11).

Developing a Grateful Heart

As believers experience God in the midst of trials they also develop a grateful heart. Their gratitude comes from knowing and trusting Him. Their thanksgiving is wrapped up in their relationship with Him so that when the Bible says, "In every thing give thanks: for this is the will of God in Christ Jesus concerning you" (1 Thes. 5:18), they respond with thanksgiving: "Giving thanks always for all things unto God and the Father in the name of our Lord Jesus Christ" (Eph. 5:20); "abounding therein with thanksgiving" (Col. 2:7); and praying "with thanksgiving" (Phil. 4:6). These verses on thanksgiving have much to do with the believer's relationship with Christ and all His promises and provisions. Therefore the one who ministers will help those in need to see the connection and to give their own reasons for thanking God in difficult places.

When everything seems wrong and out of kilter one of the most strengthening things to do is look for things for which to be grateful. These may be little things or things we generally take for granted, such as whatever is functioning in the body (eyes, ears, lungs, limbs, etc.) even when they could be functioning better than they are. Creation is filled with beauty that is often clouded by pain and sorrow, but if one begins to thank and praise God for aspects of His creation, one is at least for the moment living above the circumstances. We remember one individual who tolerated a difficult transition in her life by marveling over the beauty of the trees, so that when asked how she was doing she would talk about the magnificence of the trees and the sky and the clouds. Contemplating the person of Christ with all His marvelous attributes and thinking about Him can bring forth praise and thanksgiving even in the most dire circumstances. Of course there is always a great deal for which to be grateful in the spiritual realm, such as all the spiritual blessings reserved in heaven for believers (Eph. 1:3), His constant love and presence (Heb. 13:5), and the hope of eternity with Him. Christians have so much for which to be grateful that can shine light even on the darkest days.

Long-Term Suffering

Many believers experience long-term trials, not just an hour or a day or a week, but years upon years. They may be living in very challenging conditions where there is much temptation to argue and be in conflict either in the home or at work. Many live in dire circumstances where they endure much physical, emotional, and relational suffering. It is in these long-term trials that believers need the analogy and exhortation found in Hebrews:

> Wherefore seeing we also are compassed about with so great a cloud of witnesses, let us lay aside every weight, and the sin which doth so easily beset us, and let us run with patience the race that is set before us, looking unto Jesus the author and finisher of our faith; who for the joy that was set before him endured the cross, despising the shame, and is set down at the right hand of the throne of God. For consider him that endured such contradiction of sinners against himself, lest ye be wearied and faint in your minds. Ye have not yet resisted unto blood, striving against sin (Heb. 12:1-4).

The intensity can be seen in that the description is not about walking, but about running in a race. This race is not just a short sprint, but likely a marathon, where the runners must keep their eyes on the goal for a long time. Any backward or sideways look at circumstances could pull them down and tempt them to turn back to the old ways of the flesh. When believers remember all that Christ did for them they can be strengthened in the inner man to run by faith in the power of the Lord. Discussing these verses and their application to an individual's life would be far more edifying than talking about problems.

The verses having to do with suffering can comfort, lift, and empower those who are enduring pain and agony of soul. However, they cannot just be quoted in a cavalier manner. Believers need to identify with one another in Christ and in His death and resurrection. We are called to "weep with those who weep" (Rom. 12:15) because we are members of Christ. As Christ is touched with "the feeling of our infirmities" (Heb. 4:15), we are also to be merciful and compassionate with those who are enduring trials. Every attempt to help a fellow believer must be in the spirit of meekness, remembering one's own natural proclivity to sin (Galatians 6:1). Such an attitude is especially necessary when believers may be suffering under our Father's discipline.

The Father's Loving Discipline

Not all problems are due to one's own sin. Job's three friends were wrong when they chastised him. However, there are times when believers may be receiving the "chastening of the Lord" for purposes of restoration and further spiritual growth. Moreover they may need to be reminded that such discipline is an expression of God's love and an indication that one is a true child of God.

> My son, despise not thou the chastening of the Lord, nor faint when thou art rebuked of him: For whom

the Lord loveth he chasteneth, and scourgeth every son whom he receiveth. If ye endure chastening, God dealeth with you as with sons; for what son is he whom the father chasteneth not? But if ye be without chastisement, whereof all are partakers, then are ye bastards, and not sons. Furthermore we have had fathers of our flesh which corrected us, and we gave them reverence: shall we not much rather be in subjection unto the Father of spirits, and live? For they verily for a few days chastened us after their own pleasure; but he for our profit, that we might be partakers of his holiness. Now no chastening for the present seemeth to be joyous, but grievous: nevertheless afterward it yieldeth the peaceable fruit of righteousness unto them which are exercised thereby (Hebrews 12:5b-11).

You may want to spend time talking about this Scripture. Emphasize all the benefits of being disciplined by the Lord through problems of living: being "partakers of His holiness" and receiving "the peaceable fruit of righteousness." Such Scripture passages from God's word are effective for restoration and increased maturity.

Becoming Equipped to Handle Problems of Living

As believers draw close to Christ and learn from Him in their trials, they will become mature so that they will be able to "solve" their own problems and/or learn to endure trials that may continue over time. Even here we must remember and remind one another that just as Jesus endured the cross for the joy that was set before Him, we need to keep the joy that is set before us, that is, the hope that He has given in His Word.

> Wherein ye greatly rejoice, though now for a season, if need be, ye are in heaviness through manifold temptations: That the trial of your faith, being much more precious than of gold that perisheth, though it be tried with fire, might be found unto praise and honour and glory at the appearing of Jesus Christ: Whom having not seen, ye love; in whom, though now ye see him not, yet believing, ye rejoice with joy unspeakable and full of glory (1 Peter 1:6-8).

Here is a hope greater than any human promise that if we do such and such we will solve the problem. Here is a hope that surpasses all hopes. This hope is secure and will not fade away, but will be fully realized in Eternity:

> Behold, what manner of love the Father hath bestowed upon us, that we should be called the sons of God: therefore the world knoweth us not, because it knew him not. Beloved, now are we the sons of God, and it doth not yet appear what we shall be: but we know that, when he shall appear, we shall be like him; for we shall see him as he is. And every man that hath this hope in him purifieth himself, even as he is pure (1 John 3:1-3).

Therefore let us lift up one another with God's sure Word, His many promises regarding the usefulness of trials, the hope He gives, and the goal that will be reached by all who are in Christ Jesus, no matter how rough the terrain or how many obstacles in the course. He will bring us through! Therefore we can trust Him to do a glorious work in us through all problems of living, whether small and brief or agonizing and long-term. And, when we suffer, let us remember the future—Eternity!

> The Spirit itself beareth witness with our spirit, that we are the children of God: And if children, then heirs; heirs of God, and joint-heirs with Christ; if so be that we suffer with him, that we may be also glorified together. For I reckon that the sufferings of this present time are not worthy to be compared with the glory which shall be revealed in us (Rom. 8:16-18).

Seeking God's purposes more than personal preferences prepares believers for those times when following Christ seems to make circumstances worse. Moses was puzzled and grieved when God allowed the Pharaoh to further burden the Israelites after Moses had asked Pharaoh to let the Israelites leave Egypt. Moses' obedience appeared to make matters worse and the Israelites blamed him for it, but God showed forth His power and glory far more through the series of plagues and the seeming entrapment by the shore of the Red Sea than if everything had gone smoothly after the first request or even after the first plague. God had a greater plan. Quite often obedience to the Lord does make matters worse because God is performing a far greater work in the lives of His children.

Believers need to be prepared for setbacks in circumstances when they truly turn to God in the midst of trials. The spiritual battle may get hotter. But when that happens, believers need to trust God even more. Here is where faith is truly tested. For instance, when one person in a relationship becomes a Christian or grows in faith, others may not understand or appreciate what is happening. They may not like the person who becomes Christ-like because it may be like a kind of mirror revealing their own sin. Friends and relatives may prefer the believer's old ways of the flesh. When circumstances seem to backfire while a believer is learning to follow Christ through the trial, one discovers whether one is using the Lord or is willing to be used by the Lord for His purposes.

The Ministry of Prayer

Those who minister Christ without needing to pursue all the details about the problems, as generally happens in problem-centered counseling, will find that their ministry is totally dependent on the Lord, their own walk with Him, and prayer, "Praying always with all prayer and supplication in the Spirit, and watching thereunto with all perseverance and supplication for all saints" (Eph. 6:18). Not only will those who minister pray for the Lord Himself to work mightily in those to whom they minister; there must be prayer regarding their own walk with the Lord. Since those who minister are merely vessels for the Lord to work, they must attend to whether they are walking according to the Spirit (Ps. 19:14; Ps. 139:23-24). If there is any known sin, they must confess to the Lord and be cleansed (1 John 1:9). They must divest themselves of those personal interests and desires that may interfere with Christ's work in and through them. Even innocent seeming entertainments may be one of the distractions that may have to be set aside. Moreover, they will need to yield themselves to be Spirit controlled. Using such Scriptures as the following, they can check their own attitudes and actions:

> I therefore, the prisoner of the Lord, beseech you that ye walk worthy of the vocation wherewith ye are called, with all lowliness and meekness, with longsuffering, forbearing one another in love; endeavouring to keep the unity of the Spirit in the bond of peace (Eph. 4:1-3)

Whatever is to be ministered to a fellow believer, must first touch and further transform the one who ministers, so that ministry can flow unimpeded through the channel and not get clogged up by any sinful ways of the flesh. If those who minister in any way encourage expressions of the Jeremiah 17:9 syndrome, as in problem-centered counseling, they will be aiding and abetting sin and they will be grieving the Holy Spirit.

Besides praying prior to ministering, both spoken and silent prayer should be going on throughout any ministry of personal care. As believers pray expectantly and wait on the Lord, He will work His purposes. As believers pray and trust Christ, they can be confident that He will hear, answer, and work, whether or not they see results, as so much of the Lord's work is an inner work that takes time. The Lord knows what He is doing. That is why Paul could be confident about the results of His own ministry:

> Now thanks be unto God, which always causeth us to triumph in Christ, and maketh manifest the savour of his knowledge by us in every place. For we are unto God a sweet savour of Christ, in them that are saved, and in them that perish: To the one we are the savour of death unto death; and to the other the savour of life unto life. And who is sufficient for these things? For we are not as many, which corrupt the word of God: but as of sincerity, but as of God, in the sight of God speak we in Christ (2 Cor. 2:14-17).

As believers, we are always encouraged and comforted to know that someone else is praying for us. Therefore those who minister should be praying daily for those to whom they are ministering. In fact, all believers need to be praying daily for one another, especially for those who are experiencing problems of living. One does not have to know the details of the problems in order to pray, because God knows.

Conclusion

Because believers have been given new life in Christ and are indwelt by the Holy Spirit they are enabled to grow spiritually. **They absolutely do have all they need for life and godliness and for mutual care in the Body of Christ.** As they look more and more to Christ through His Word they will not only grow in walking according to the Spirit, they will find God faithful in trials and tribulations. They will believe what God has said in His Word about the usefulness of trials and trust Him in the midst of dire circumstances. Instead of looking for answers in the world, they will be finding truth and direction in God's Word and gain experience in walking by faith rather than by sight. As they avail themselves of all the Lord provides, including the spiritual armor and the Sword of the Spirit, they will learn how to walk with Him through trials, disappointments, and problems of living in such a way as to meet them God's way and to become as pure gold in the process. As they minister His life to one another, they will be encouraging one another to fight the good fight of faith and to live according to the new life He has given. As believers experience the truth of Colossians 2:10, "And ye are complete in him, which is the head of all principality and power," in difficult circumstances they will become further equipped to minister to fellow saints along the way of biblical sanctification, and all the praise and glory will go to God.

10

The Believer's Daily Walk

If ye then be risen with Christ, seek those things which are above, where Christ sitteth on the right hand of God. Set your affection on things above, not on things on the earth. For ye are dead, and your life is hid with Christ in God. When Christ, who is our life, shall appear, then shall ye also appear with him in glory.

Colossians 3:1-4

Believers need to give their attention to Christ and what He has done for them every day. They need to remember and act according to their position in Him daily. They need to remember their eternal hope daily: "When Christ, who is our life, shall appear, then shall ye also appear with him in glory." As believers set their "affection on things above, not on things on the earth," they will be equipped to handle difficulties and trials from God's perspective and through Christ's life in them. **Therefore, one of the most important things that believers can do for fellow believers who are in the midst of problems and trials is to encourage a daily**

walk that would include communicating with Him and being strengthened by Him through His Word and Holy Spirit on a daily basis. A daily walk in fellowship with the Lord should be the norm for Christians. Lack of a daily walk with the Lord is probably one of the biggest shortcomings in many believers' lives and this lack is frequently more pronounced when people are experiencing personal and/or interpersonal problems. **We encourage those in the dire circumstances of life to diligently seek God daily so that they might grow in the things of the Spirit, rather than being swallowed up by the trials, tribulations, and sufferings of life.**

The way through suffering is truly the daily walk with the Lord, not the weekly rehashing with a counselor. In contrast to sinfully discussing the problems, as biblical counselors do, we believe that talking about and encouraging the daily walk will serve to mature believers and put them into a position where the necessary wisdom and knowledge for what to do will come from the Lord. Those who minister to fellow believers should themselves have a very definite walk with the Lord each day. Then, as the daily walk is discussed, those who minister will know what to encourage and to suggest, especially in weak areas where changes may need to be suggested.

The daily walk is so essential to Christian living that we have on occasion started ministering to a person or couple by saying that we would like to begin with talking about their daily walk so that we can put everything into that perspective first. If those seeking help have a consistent daily walk, we could discuss the problems within that perspective, which would curtail expressions of the Jeremiah 17:9 syndrome. However, we have often found that when people are experiencing problems of living their daily walk has deteriorated or been suspended during the trial. They have, in essence, lost touch with their True Counselor. In that case we would want to see if they understand the truth of Colossians 3:1-4, quoted above, and make suggestions regarding how they might establish or reestablish their daily walk with the Lord even before talking about their problems.

The believer's daily walk is concisely expressed in Colossians 3:17: "And whatsoever ye do in word or deed, do all in the name of the Lord Jesus, giving thanks to God and the Father by him." Believers have been given new life enabling them to be servants of righteousness (Romans 6:4, 18). Believers are called to walk with God daily both as "joint heirs with Christ" (Romans 8:17) and as "servants of Christ, doing the will of God from the heart" (Eph. 6:6). After all, believers are born again through faith, which should, by God's grace and provision, result in good works that follow (Eph. 2:8-10).

Complaining and speaking evil of others, as often occur in counseling sessions, are contrary to the spiritual life and only empower that which is to be put off and reckoned dead (Col. 3:8-9; Romans 6:11). Ministry should be encouraging believers to grow in the faith and act as God's dear children, following Him and loving one another (Eph. 5:1-2). **Therefore great emphasis should be placed on the daily walk of the one who is suffering from problems of living more than on the problems themselves.**

Rather than dwelling on problems, those who are ministering biblically to another person will talk much about the provisions, privileges, and practices of the believer's daily walk with the Lord. Oneness with Christ is so profound and continuous that He promised, "I will never leave thee, nor forsake thee" (Heb. 13:5). Just the idea of the Creator of the universe even bothering to notice one person in His entire cosmos is astounding! Add to that the tremendous privilege of prayer. Believers can be in communication with God throughout the day. In addition, there is the confidence and security of knowing that God watches over each believer and knows everything that is going on, both in the circumstances and in the accompanying thoughts, emotions, and attitudes. There is the wonderful benefit of being indwelt by the Holy Spirit to guide and to prick the conscience when there is sin. The believer's provisions in Christ for walking in a manner pleasing to God are available moment by moment so that the daily walk does not have to be one of self-effort and constant failure. Of course these are privileges available to those who are seeking to please God and to walk according to the Spirit. They all come by grace through faith exercised through obedience and through turning to Him in every situation.

The Christian life consists of doing what Christians are enabled to do day by day by grace through faith according to the Word. Therefore those who minister need to teach, remind, and encourage fellow believers to be walking by faith daily. Encouraging faith in Christ is the most essential aspect of any personal ministry. After all, whatever individuals truly believe will show up in their words and actions. Those who truly believe that Christ is in them will act accordingly. Thus obedience to Christ's commands follows faith in Him. A Christian's behavior is therefore the practical outworking of what is truly believed because true believers have been given all that is necessary to act according to their faith in Christ. This is the essence of the daily walk.

Ministering the Daily Walk

In discussing the daily walk with those in need, questions can be asked about what the individuals are already doing and what has been particularly helpful in the past. Some people use a daily devotional guide and/or a Scripture reading calendar. Others plan their own Bible reading and prayer time. Many worship and praise God by singing and/ or listening to recorded hymns and spiritual songs. Another suggestion would be to set aside time during the day to listen to a sermon through available media in addition to attending services at church. There is so much available right on the internet. People can sign up to receive daily devotionals by email from various ministries. They can download sermons. They can obtain Bible software for Bible study. The resources are vast! Nevertheless, **the believer's greatest resource for the daily walk is the Lord Himself and His Word.**

Instead of having specific homework related to problems, those who minister biblically will encourage a daily walk emphasizing the elements without prescribing details. The daily walk can be summed up in a few words: **trust and obey throughout the day.** While this may be a consistent manner of life for those who have been walking with the Lord over a period of time, all believers need to give intentional attention to the Lord and His Word early in the day and throughout the day. They need to remember Christ Himself, consider His glorious attributes, and His life in them:

> That Christ may dwell in your hearts by faith; that ye, being rooted and grounded in love, may be able to comprehend with all saints what is the breadth, and length, and depth, and height; and to know the love of Christ, which passeth knowledge, that ye might be filled with all the fulness of God (Eph. 3:17-19).

We received the following reminder at the bottom of an email from a woman requesting to be added to the *PsychoHeresy Awareness Letter* mailing list:

> Happy moments, PRAISE GOD!
> Difficult moments, SEEK GOD!

> Quiet moments, WORSHIP GOD!
> Painful moments, TRUST GOD!
> EVERY MOMENT, THANK GOD!

What a great reminder! Later we learned that these words are not unique to this person. In fact, there are so many people using this at the end of their emails that it was listed in a book about human-computer interaction as one of the examples of "E-mail signatures."[1] What a blessing that believers are reminding one another to praise, seek, worship, trust and thank God throughout the day!

Actually, praising, seeking, worshipping, and trusting God are right for any moment, whether it be happy, difficult, quiet, or painful. Believers need to encourage one another to fill their minds and hearts with the Lord and His Word rather than ongoing stewing and talking sinfully about problems of living. **Encouraging those in need in their daily walk may include the following, but not necessarily every single one or in this order, because they are interconnected.**

DAILY SEEKING GOD.

DAILY READING AND FOLLOWING GOD'S WORD.

DAILY LOVING GOD AND OTHERS.

DAILY PRAYING TO GOD.

DAILY DENYING SELF AND WALKING ACCORDING TO THE SPIRIT.

DAILY BEING CLEANSED BY GOD.

DAILY BEING PREPARED FOR SPIRITUAL WARFARE.

DAILY PRAISING GOD.

DAILY WORSHIPPING GOD.

DAILY TRUSTING GOD.

DAILY THANKING GOD.

DAILY SERVING GOD AND ONE ANOTHER.

Because these elements of the daily walk are interconnected, believers will find that as they are doing one, they are also doing others. In fact as they are doing any of the above in truth and sincerity, they will be walking according to the Spirit. Each person will have a different emphasis, a different combination, and a different plan, based upon available time, which may involve giving up some entertainment or other less important activities, **especially during times of trial**. As believers commit themselves to a daily walk, they will find that they will be trusting and obeying God more and more each day.

Daily Seeking God

Instead of arranging one problem-centered counseling appointment after another, believers need to remind one another of Jesus words:

> Come unto me, all ye that labour and are heavy laden, and I will give you rest. Take my yoke upon you, and learn of me; for I am meek and lowly in heart: and ye shall find rest unto your souls. For my yoke is easy, and my burden is light (Matt. 11:28-30).

Unlike paid counselors, Jesus is available 24/7. What better way to plow through a problem than by being yoked together with Jesus?

Those who seek the Lord will find Him (Prov. 8:17), and those who diligently seek Him in faith are rewarded (Heb. 11:6). Numerous Bible verses urge believers to seek the Lord. Seek to know Him more and more. Seek Him who is the source of all wisdom. Those who are experiencing problems need wisdom from above, not just human opinion. While wisdom may be gleaned from other believers, such wisdom needs to be tested with Scripture. In the final analysis, God gives wisdom to those who trust and obey:

> If any of you lack wisdom, let him ask of God, that
> giveth to all men liberally, and upbraideth not; and it
> shall be given him. But let him ask in faith, nothing
> wavering. For he that wavereth is like a wave of the
> sea driven with the wind and tossed. For let not that
> man think that he shall receive any thing of the Lord
> (James 1:5-7).

Many believers begin by seeking God, but they become impatient and want some human answers that will solve the problems as quickly as possible. They turn to problem-centered counselors, who specialize in problems and begin to trust the counselor to bring about the solutions more than they trust God to work through His provisions. There are other times when people seek wisdom from God, but they want it to agree with their own wishes and desires. In fact, there are times when people know clearly what the Word says and look for another way.

Seeking God first thing in the morning even as one is rising brings one immediately into the right perspective. He is here and He is here to help, guide, and comfort. Seeking God to know Him better and better each day, to know His will, and follow His ways is a glorious adventure. Sometimes, however, the adventure can be painful as one's honest seeking may reveal much that the Father has yet to work in His children. Possible questions to ask in "difficult moments" might be, "What do you want to teach me, Lord? What are you working in me through this difficulty? What would you have me to do? Am I operating according to the flesh or the Spirit?"

Daily Reading and Following God's Word
Believers need to develop the habit of thinking about God throughout the day. For thoughts about God to be cor-

rect, one needs to be reading the Word. Therefore helping establish a time and pattern for reading the Bible can be one of the elements of conversation during ministry. Memorizing portions of Scripture provides much for thinking about God during the day. **A planned time for reading the Bible, thinking about God, and praying is not meant to "take care of it" for the day, but rather to "fill the vessel" so that Christ may be followed and His will fulfilled throughout the day.**

> For God, who commanded the light to shine out of darkness, hath shined in our hearts, to give the light of the knowledge of the glory of God in the face of Jesus Christ. But we have this treasure in earthen vessels, that the excellency of the power may be of God, and not of us (2 Cor. 4:6-7).

Daily reading the Word is very necessary for it gives both instruction and power:

> For the word of God is quick, and powerful, and sharper than any two-edged sword, piercing even to the dividing asunder of soul and spirit, and of the joints and marrow, and is a discerner of the thoughts and intents of the heart (Heb. 4:12).

The Word is the sustenance for the new life in Christ. Nevertheless, to be effective, it must be digested, remembered, and followed. It is commendable when Christians do their morning reading, but for some that's all there is to it. There is little or no thinking about it afterwards, little or no remembering, and little or no following.

James was concerned about those believers who were not also "doers of the word."

> But be ye doers of the word, and not hearers only, deceiving your own selves. For if any be a hearer

of the word, and not a doer, he is like unto a man beholding his natural face in a glass: For he beholdeth himself, and goeth his way, and straightway forgetteth what manner of man he was. But whoso looketh into the perfect law of liberty, and continueth therein, he being not a forgetful hearer, but a doer of the work, this man shall be blessed in his deed (James 1:22-25).

Here James puts together the idea of doing the Word with the new man in Christ. A "doer of the word" is also a "doer of the work" because good works are to follow faith (Eph. 2:10). Those Christians who are neither "doers of the word" nor "work" by faith have evidently forgotten who they are in Christ or they have not understood the essential teachings of what it means to be a Christian. If they are hearers only, or readers only, they are truly deceiving themselves and depriving Christ of His rightful place and themselves of the blessings that follow obedience that comes through relationship.

Daily Loving God and Others.

Daily remembering God's love for us and His life in us enables us to love Him and to love one another. Loving another person is easier when we are being loved and being treated lovingly by them. However, during relationship problems, loving others can be difficult. Expressing sacrificial love and forbearance are the fruit of the spirit. Therefore, one must be volitionally walking according to the Spirit to love God's way. To turn the other cheek (Luke 6:29), to suffer wrong (1 Peter 2:20), to excuse another's weakness (1 Peter 4:8), and to forgive sin (Eph. 4:32) will go a long way in dealing with interpersonal problems. To do so may in some cases be an expression of loving one's enemies as believers are commanded to do (Matt. 5:44).

Believers would do well to remember and even memorize 1 Corinthians 13:4-7, as discussed in Chapter Nine and again quoted here:

> Charity suffereth long, and is kind; charity envieth not; charity vaunteth not itself, is not puffed up, doth not behave itself unseemly, seeketh not her own, is not easily provoked, thinketh no evil; rejoiceth not in iniquity, but rejoiceth in the truth; beareth all things, believeth all things, hopeth all things, endureth all things (1 Cor. 13:4-7).

Making this an intent early in the day helps one remember to respond according to the Spirit rather than react in the flesh. Whenever believers react in an unloving manner, they have recourse with God, because they can turn to Him at any moment, confess, be forgiven, and be filled again with the Spirit. They also have recourse with one another as they can ask for forgiveness for their reaction. However, this must even be done in love with the right attitude so that one does not justify oneself and cast blame on the other while asking for forgiveness.

Forgiveness is an essential aspect of loving one another. "And be ye kind one to another, tenderhearted, forgiving one another, even as God for Christ's sake hath forgiven you" (Eph. 4:32). The attitude of forgiveness with a readiness to extend forgiveness to those who ask forgiveness for their sin is based on what Christ has done for every believer and is an expression of His love. Forgiveness is not an option, but a command. Until forgiveness is requested, an attitude and readiness to forgive must be maintained in the heart daily so that thoughts towards the one who has sinned will yet be hopeful and kind rather than hostile, bitter, or revengeful. "Keep thy heart with all diligence; for out of it are the issues of life" (Prov. 4:23). When love for God and others reigns in the heart, loving words and actions will follow.

Daily Praying to God

Prayer is an essential part of a believer's daily walk with the Lord. There are many admonitions to pray and many promises throughout Scripture. Jesus directs His followers to ask God the Father for what they need.

> Ask, and it shall be given you; seek, and ye shall find; knock, and it shall be opened unto you: For every one that asketh receiveth; and he that seeketh findeth; and to him that knocketh it shall be opened (Matt. 7:7-8).

Believers are told to "Pray without ceasing" (1 Th 5:17), which means to never give up, but to continue to pray. Instead of rehearsing wrongs, complaining about others, and dwelling on problems, believers are to:

> Be careful for nothing; but in every thing by prayer and supplication with thanksgiving let your requests be made known unto God. And the peace of God, which passeth all understanding, shall keep your hearts and minds through Christ Jesus (Phil. 4:6-7).

Notice all the promises that accompany the admonitions to pray.

In addition to promises regarding prayer, there are also certain restrictions, as James points out: "Ye ask, and receive not, because ye ask amiss, that ye may consume it upon your lusts" (James 4:3). Asking amiss would be for selfish, fleshly purposes. And, when people are dwelling sinfully on their problems and thinking bad thoughts about others, they are likely to ask amiss. When they are focused on Christ, they are far more able to ask according to His will and purposes.

The Bible contains many prayers that would be helpful for believers to pray. David cried out to the Lord during times of great duress. Many of his Psalms can be helpful to those in dire spiritual battles and suffering from various problems of living. In Psalm 143 David cries out to the Lord in his distress as he was being persecuted by his enemy and feeling overwhelmed and desolate (vv. 3-4). But then in the next verse David shifts his attention and says: "I remember the days of old; I meditate on all thy works; I muse on the work of thy hands" (v. 5). He cries out to the Lord to help him and then says:

> Cause me to hear thy lovingkindness in the morning; for in thee do I trust: cause me to know the way wherein I should walk; for I lift up my soul unto thee…. Teach me to do thy will; for thou art my God: thy spirit is good; lead me into the land of uprightness. Quicken me, O LORD, for thy name's sake: for thy righteousness' sake bring my soul out of trouble (Ps. 143:8, 10-11).

David speaks of literal enemies and asks for them to be destroyed at the end of the Psalm. However, Paul reminds us that in this age of grace "we wrestle not against flesh and blood, but against principalities, against powers, against the rulers of the darkness of this world, against spiritual wickedness in high places" (Eph. 6: 12). Keeping that in mind, one who is going through serious struggles would find both comfort and strength in praying this Psalm. Other prayers we would suggest are found in Ephesians 1:15-23; 3:14-21 and Colossians 1:9-13. And, of course we would encourage fellow believers to pray as Jesus taught His disciples (Matt. 6:9-13, followed by vv 14-15, and Luke 11:2-4). We suggest spending time meditating on each phrase of The Lord's Prayer and considering how it applies to one's life.

Daily Denying Self and Walking According to the Spirit
The fleshly self is always ready to take over. Thus there is a need for denying self daily. Jesus said:

> If any man will come after me, let him deny himself, and take up his cross daily, and follow me. For whosoever will save his life shall lose it: but whosoever will lose his life for my sake, the same shall save it (Luke 9:23-24).

Jesus said these words before He went to the cross. How much could the disciples have understood this statement regarding the cross? They understood something of the idea of putting Christ before their own wants, desires, and even needs. They surely understood something of the nature of the self life that had to be put aside. However, after Jesus went to the cross and died in their place they grew in their comprehension, not only of the literal death but of identifying so much with Christ's death, they were to count their old life as dead and worthless.

Denying self for the believer is the equivalent of putting off the old man, the old nature, or the flesh. Taking up one's cross is remembering one's identification with Christ's death to the degree that one has "been crucified with him" (Rom. 6:6) and is counted dead as in Colossians 3:3 quoted above. While having been crucified with Christ by faith and receiving new life occurred once and for all at conversion, denying the old self and taking up one's cross is to be daily. **The word daily here does not just mean once during the day, but throughout the day.**

Believers are thus equipped to live the new life daily by grace through faith rather than according to a form of legalism. Christ already died in the believer's place and has taken the condemnation upon Himself at Calvary. Thus Paul explains:

> There is therefore now no condemnation to them which are in Christ Jesus, who walk not after the flesh, but after the Spirit. For the law of the Spirit of life in Christ Jesus hath made me free from the law of sin and death. For what the law could not do, in that it was weak through the flesh, God sending his own Son in the likeness of sinful flesh, and for sin, condemned sin in the flesh: That the righteousness of the law might be fulfilled in us, who walk not after the flesh, but after the Spirit (Romans 8:1-4).

Whereas the law could not enable them to do what is right, the life of Christ in believers enables them to do so. As believers deny self and lose their life for His sake, they are following what Paul wrote in Romans 12:

> I beseech you therefore, brethren, by the mercies of God, that ye present your bodies a living sacrifice, holy, acceptable unto God, which is your reasonable service. And be not conformed to this world: but be ye transformed by the renewing of your mind, that ye may prove what is that good, and acceptable, and perfect, will of God (Romans 12:1-2).

The phrase "be not conformed to this world" is an important aspect of denying self. Every day believers may be barraged with all kinds of worldly ideas, entertainments, distractions, and temptations. Therefore, as they daily present their "bodies a living sacrifice unto the Lord" they need to be watchful regarding what they are putting into their minds and hearts and lives. They need to follow Paul's admonition to "walk circumspectly, not as fools, but as wise, redeeming the time, because the days are evil" (Eph. 5:15-16). For instance, at the end of the day many people turn on television and mindlessly watch whatever is available. They probably have little idea how much they are absorbing without critical evaluation. Christians can easily be tempted to relax in front of TV, to allow their minds to be contaminated with worldly ideas and images, and to waste precious time during which they might otherwise be involved in filling their minds with the things of the Lord or being involved in Christian service or other edifying activities.

The A. C. Nielson Company reports that "the average American watches more than 4 hours of TV each day…. In a 65-year life, that person will have spent 9 years glued to the tube."[2] How many of those TV years might be feeding the flesh, fouling the mind, and frittering away the years God has graciously given? While there may be educational programs on television and some possibly wholesome or at least noncontaminating programs, believers need to be wise in selecting and watching. Believers also need to consider how much of their time should be devoted to various forms of recreation, entertainment, and other leisure time activities. In fact wisdom would call believers to evaluate everything they do with Colossians 3:17: "And whatsoever ye do in word or deed, do all in the name of the Lord Jesus, giving thanks to God and the Father by him."

When warning of the wrong way ("be not conformed to this world") the Bible also gives the right way: "but be ye transformed by the renewing of your mind, that ye may prove what is that good, and acceptable, and perfect will of God." There is the put off and the put on, the do not's and the do's. Quite often one must put off before putting on. However, as believers are consistently mindful of the Lord and turning to Him during the day, they will be walking in a manner pleasing to Him and growing spiritually. However, if believers mindlessly absorb the world around them they are in danger, for they are then walking according to the flesh and are vulnerable to temptation. **In fact, as one increases the daily feeding of the flesh, one will impede the daily** growing in the Spirit. Thus, believers need to be encouraging one another to be walking in the Spirit daily, being mindful of the Lord Jesus Christ (2 Cor. 3:18), and having their affections fixed on "things above" (Col. 3:2). This is especially needful in times of trouble when people tend to assuage their discomfort with self-indulgence.

Denying self includes the most subtle ways that self seeks its own and that is the independent self and the self that seems to be doing so well, at least to itself. This is the self that not only thinks well of itself for its seemingly good and virtuous deeds, but expects to be well thought of by others as well. The obvious picture of this self that must be denied is in the parable of the Pharisee and the publican. In contrast those who desire to please God must be willing to be unrecognized, ignored, and dishonored, for the reason that they are nothing apart from Christ (Gal. 6:3). John the Baptist's words, "He must increase, but I must decrease" (John 3:30), should ring in the heart—no trumpet sound for us at all until the final call to glory.

Daily Being Cleansed by God

Because sin can cloud the sweetness of relationship with the Lord, cause the believer to be more vulnerable to temptation, and grieve the Spirit, Christ has provided for daily, even moment-by-moment, cleansing and purifying. God uses His Word to cleanse His children (Eph. 5:26-27) as the Holy Spirit brings conviction and repentance. As the Holy Spirit brings conviction to the conscience, the believer has the privilege to confess and receive forgiveness and cleansing. Believers need to encourage one another to come to the throne of grace without delay to receive the promise of 1 John 1:9: "If we confess our sins, he is faithful and just to forgive us our sins, and to cleanse us from all unrighteousness." We need to encourage one another to do this right away, as soon as sin is committed or as soon as unconfessed sin is remembered. Instead of waiting until the end of the day or a special quiet time with the Lord, believers can follow 1 John 1:9 immediately on the spot, any time, any place.

Daily Being Prepared for Spiritual Warfare

Believers can be blindsided if they are not cognizant of ongoing spiritual warfare. They need to be watchful even when all seems to be peaceful and pleasant, so that when something unexpected and unpleasant suddenly crosses their path, they don't fall back into the flesh and react with a vengeance. When believers are not prepared they are vulnerable to attack and they may not only forget the fact of ongoing spiritual warfare; they may forget who they are in Christ, the identity of the enemy, and their armor. While we discussed spiritual warfare in Chapter Nine, we mention it here because there must be a daily readiness. **Believers need to "be strong in the Lord, and in the power of his might" daily. They need to "put on the whole armour of God" daily so that they "may be able to stand against the wiles of the devil" (Eph. 6:10-11).**

Paul declared that the "the weapons of our warfare are not carnal, but mighty through God to the pulling down of strong holds" (2 Cor. 10:4). The weapons are not physical, natural weapons. Neither are they made up of human wisdom. They are the spiritual weapons of truth and primarily the spiritual weapon of the Gospel to tear down the strongholds of sin, idolatry, and the teachings of the Judaizers who were enticing believers back into the bondage of the Law (such as circumcision). Armed with His spiritual weapons, Paul was also "casting down imaginations, and every high thing that exalteth itself against the knowledge of God, and bringing into captivity every thought to the obedience of Christ" (2 Cor. 10:5). By extension, the spiritual weapons of believers today are the very Words of God, His truth as revealed in Scripture, and specifically the Gospel of salvation and sanctification. The very Word of God is not only for instruction and power to obey; it is the spiritual weapon believers are to use to wage war against falsehood and idolatry as they encounter falsehood and idolatry in their external environment and in their own thinking. **To keep the spiritual weaponry sharp, believers must daily equip themselves by reading, studying, and obeying the Word of God.**

Daily Praising God

Praising God not only glorifies God. Praising God places the mind on His glorious attributes and power and thereby strengthens faith so that, when the arch enemy shoots his darts, tempting believers to dwell on past hurts, injustices, and conflicts leading to bitterness, anger, wrath, clamor, evil speaking, and malice (Eph. 4:31), they can hold up their shield of faith, trust Christ to give them His wisdom, and grow in their love for one another. For some people, singing hymns inspires worship and praise, particularly those hymns that speak of God's attributes and all He has done and is doing for His children. As believers fill their hearts and minds with God's Word, praise will come forth, for Jesus says that "out of the abundance of the heart the mouth speaketh" (Matt. 12:34) and continues with these words:

> A good man out of the good treasure of the heart bringeth forth good things: and an evil man out of the evil treasure bringeth forth evil things. But I say unto you, That every idle word that men shall speak, they shall give account thereof in the day of judgment (Matt. 12:35-36).

Ministry should always encourage fellow believers to be putting good things into their minds and hearts rather than thinking evil of others. In fact, if one is filled with bitterness, anger, wrath, and malice rather than love, praise may end up being empty words. In contrast, when one's focus is on Christ and the truths of Scripture, praise will flow forth in worship.

Daily Worshipping God

Worshipping God is honoring Him for who He is. Whenever believers attribute worth to God in thought, attitude, word, and action, they are worshipping Him. Therefore it is possible to worship God throughout the day, not only in "quiet moments," but even in busy, noisy times. Attributing worth to God early in the day sets the attitude for actively recognizing His presence, power, holiness, love, mercy, truth, wisdom, and glory. Worshipping God reveals the right perspective in every situation: His eternal greatness and sovereignty over His creation. Therefore His own dear children will bow before Him in lowliness and humility when they consider who He is, and they will renew their confidence in Him who is their high priest:

> For we have not an high priest which cannot be touched with the feeling of our infirmities; but was in all points tempted like as we are, yet without sin. Let us therefore come boldly unto the throne of grace, that we may obtain mercy, and find grace to help in time of need (Heb. 4:15-16).

Worship attributes worth to God. The more believers think about Jesus and remember all He has done for them, the more worship will flow out to the Lord and the more they will be filled with wonder and awe. They will be worshipping Him even as they are going about their daily affairs because they will be attributing worth to Him by their attitudes, thoughts, and actions. Believers also attribute worth to God by how they use their time. If they spend countless hours on pleasing themselves, they are attributing more worth to themselves than to God. If they are more enthusiastic and devoted to various forms of entertainment, sports, and other leisure-time activities than the Lord, one can see that their worship is sinfully misdirected. Believers need to consider what and whom they are really worshipping. Then, if they are off the mark they can turn to the Lord, confess their sin, and worship Him "in spirit and in truth" (John 4:23).

Worship is shown throughout Scripture in all sorts of situations. David worshipped the Lord throughout many of his Psalms and also as he danced before Him with much rejoicing as he accompanied the ark as it was being carried to Jerusalem. Job worshipped God in response to his tragic loss of all things including his children:

> Then Job arose, and rent his mantle, and shaved his head, and fell down upon the ground, and worshipped, and said, Naked came I out of my mother's womb, and naked shall I return thither: the LORD gave, and the LORD hath taken away; blessed be the name of the LORD (Job 1:20-21).

But, when Job complained to his "counselors" and talked about his problems, his misery increased. The answers to his problems were in God's timing, at the end of the testing, and they were "exceeding abundantly above all that [he could] ask or think" (Eph. 3:20). Finally near the end, God revealed Himself to Job, and Job worshipped God and said:

> I have heard of thee by the hearing of the ear: but now mine eye seeth thee. Wherefore I abhor myself, and repent in dust and ashes (Job 42:5-6).

In the vision given to him as recorded in Revelation, the apostle John saw the glorious scene of worship in heaven:

Holy, holy, holy, Lord God Almighty, which was, and is, and is to come. And when those beasts give glory and honour and thanks to him that sat on the throne, who liveth for ever and ever, the four and twenty elders fall down before him that sat on the throne, and worship him that liveth for ever and ever, and cast their crowns before the throne, saying, Thou art worthy, O Lord, to receive glory and honour and power: for thou hast created all things, and for thy pleasure they are and were created (Rev. 4:8b-11).

One day all believers will join that magnificent chorus. The splendor and beauty of the Lamb upon the throne will be so tremendous that there will be a continual flow and outburst of worship. Even now, believers have the privilege of worshipping the God of Creation and as they do they will be one with the heavenly host. Their perspective on the daily grind will change, and they will begin to see things from a heavenly viewpoint.

When the believer's goal is the Lord Himself and eternity with Him, one's outlook changes dramatically even regarding pressing problems. Even the problems themselves will appear quite different from a heavenly perspective and the solutions and/or strength to endure will come from the Lord. Believers may listen and advise. They may sympathize (weeping with those who weep), but it is the Lord Himself who will work in every circumstance as the believer seeks Him, worships Him, trusts Him, and thereby obeys Him.

Daily Trusting God

Notice how seeking, praising, and worshipping God encourage faith so that the believer will more and more trust the Lord. As fellow believers talk about their daily walk, the one who ministers will be listening for where they are beginning to trust Christ more in their circumstances. And, when people bring up problems, there may be a need for asking questions about their level of trust in the Lord and how much they are depending on other people and responding independently. Without saying, "You need to trust God more," the one who ministers might ask, "For what aspects of this situation do you think you could trust Christ?" or "Where is Christ in this picture?"

Much of the discussion during personal ministry can be about the trustworthiness of Christ. Examples from Scripture may be reviewed and Psalms having to do with reasons why we can trust God in every circumstance. David's Psalm 139 comes to mind here.

> O LORD, thou hast searched me, and known me. Thou knowest my downsitting and mine uprising, thou understandest my thought afar off. Thou compassest my path and my lying down, and art acquainted with all my ways. For there is not a word in my tongue, but, lo, O LORD, thou knowest it altogether. Thou hast beset me behind and before, and laid thine hand upon me. Such knowledge is too wonderful for me; it is high, I cannot attain unto it (Psalm 139:1-6).

What comforting, strengthening words for every believer! Besides engendering trust, such words may also convict the conscience as the believer remembers that the Lord knows every word that is uttered, every thought conceived, and every action taken. This every-present intimacy with the Lord, whether comforting or convicting, needs to be emphasized since God is there and He is able to work in every situation.

David further says that no matter where he is God is right there leading him: "Even there shall thy hand lead me, and thy right hand shall hold me. If I say, Surely the darkness shall cover me; even the night shall be light about me" (vv. 10-11). Yes, there were times when God's guidance was not clear, but as David trusted Him, he found that God could always be trusted. One could go further into this Psalm and turn to many other places in Scripture to stimulate trust.

Daily Thanking God

How much better to be thanking God than talking sinfully about and stewing over problems! In fact, not being thankful to God can lead to "vain imaginations" and a darkened, foolish heart (Romans 1:21). An unthankful heart towards God opens the mind to much deception and to the whole gamut of the Jeremiah 17:9 syndrome. As people dwell on and continue talking sinfully about their problems and dissatisfactions they sink further and further into the mire. Therefore, when ministering to one another, conversation should include that for which one is thankful. Simply listing the basics of the Gospel gives much for which to be grateful. God deserves all thanksgiving and praise, and that is reason enough to thank Him. But God also knows the benefits of praising and thanking Him, because it enables believers to see the whole picture, not just the knotty, frustrating, painful moment, but God Himself and eternity. It's like looking at the panorama of mountains, sky, and sea and God's overpowering control and love in contrast to a dark black crack in the earth. This does not mean that problems are ignored, but that they are put in the correct perspective.

Thanking God helps believers to see things more clearly and follow Him more closely. The mind, heart, and life will be lifted to a higher plane of living as one considers all that God is and has done. Thanking God should become the usual response to any circumstance, as believers are to be "abounding therein with thanksgiving" (Col. 2:7). God's will is that we are to be grateful to Him at all times and in every situation: "In every thing give thanks: for this is the will of God in Christ Jesus concerning you" (1 Thes. 5:18). Thus we are to be "Giving thanks always for all things unto God and the Father in the name of our Lord Jesus Christ" (Eph 5:20). Since God uses all things to conform believers to the image of Christ (Rom. 8:28-29), believers can by faith thank Him in every situation. If a fellow believer is in the dumps and overwhelmed with problems the one who ministers could ask something like this: "In the midst of all the pain you are experiencing, can you think of anything to thank God for?" Then the person who is ministering could suggest that they pray and thank God for these blessings in the midst of the problems.

Daily Serving God and One Another

Paul and the other apostles referred to themselves as servants of the Lord. Serving Him was their greatest calling and greatest joy. In explaining the believers' former life as being servants of sin, Paul clearly reveals that they are now servants of God: "But now being made free from sin, and become servants to God, ye have your fruit unto holiness, and the end everlasting life" (Romans 6:22).

Believers are not saved simply to sit around and bask in their new life. No! They are created to serve: "For we are his workmanship, created in Christ Jesus unto good works, which God hath before ordained that we should walk in them" (Eph. 2:10). Every believer has been given gifts for service (Romans 12). Not every act of serving God is within the confines of the local church. In fact, a great deal of service happens within families, neighborhoods, and places of work as people find ways to serve God right where they are. Just as servants during the first century were to serve their masters as unto the Lord, so also those believers who are employed may serve God even as they are serving their employers, "With good will doing service, as to the Lord, and not to men: Knowing that whatsoever good thing any man doeth, the same shall he receive of the Lord, whether he be bond or free" (Eph. 6:7-8). Even kindnesses extended to one another are forms of service. All believers need to be both hearers and doers. They need to sit at the feet of Jesus, learn from Him, and worship Him. They also need to be serving, but service should never take the place of fellowship with the Lord, for the service should flow out from the life of Christ in the believer.

Example of Faith

Another encouragement for those who are experiencing difficult circumstances comes from examples of believers who have responded to suffering by trusting God and seeking to know Him more. We mention only one here, as reported in three issues of *Moody Bible Institute Monthly*. The September 1930 issue described the progress of Arthur and Ethel Tylee's pioneering a work with the Nhambiquara Indians in Brazil. They had made some good progress in "overcoming prejudice, cultivating confidence, acquiring a smattering of their language, and giving the first demonstrations of Christian love."

However, the December 1930 issue reported the tragic deaths of Arthur Tylee, Mildred Kratz (a nurse who had joined the work), and the Tylees' baby at the hands of the very Indians they loved and served. While the Tylees had made some progress gaining their confidence, conflict developed between the Indians and government workers who were attempting to erect a telegraph line through the area. Evidently the tribe's animosity towards outsiders confused them and led them to attack the missionaries, who were easy targets as they opened their home to the Indians. Mrs. Tylee was

seriously wounded, but survived. The following is quoted
from the June 1931 issue of *Moody*. It is Mrs. Tylee's letter
of January 4, 1931, **written from the very place where she
lost her husband, baby, and friend**:

Dear Friends:

To you who have been so faithful in your inter-
cession for us and the work in Juruena, I am sending
this message that you may know that your prayers
have not been in vain. I want to tell you how I have
been sustained and kept by the mighty outpouring
of His love and grace in answer to your prayers. I
also want you to know how Arthur counted on you
and your prayer fellowship in the task God gave him
to perform. I do not think a single Wednesday night
passed that he did not think of you as you were meeting for prayer and praise.

But I long especially that not one of you should
allow yourself to feel that there has been any failure
on the part of those in Juruena or the prayer helpers
in the homeland. We must believe that all happened
according to the plan of an all-wise and loving Heavenly Father, even to the smallest detail. I do not say
we must understand, but only believe.

I know many of you have wondered if we had
any warning or any preparation for what happened.
To that question I have to answer both yes and no. As
to warning, we were just a little puzzled by some of
the things that occurred in the two preceding days,
and yet we had no grave apprehensions. Arthur is
now in the presence of his Lord and to him all has
been made plain, while I am still groping in the darkness, yet even in the darkness I can trace the working

of my Father's loving hand, and not one thing would I have different.

How distinctly I recall each movement of my loved one on that last morning as he attended faithfully to the little everyday details of our life. There was his quiet time with the Word, sitting at his desk; the transplanting of some young trees; the work in the garden. All went on as it had for so many days previous, but as it never was to again. Then came breakfast. We ate it as we had eaten many another meal, surrounded by Indians.

As Arthur ate his breakfast, the chief sat by him discussing the work on the auto road which had been planned for the day. He arose from the table to attend to the final preparations. My meal had been interrupted several times so the others excused themselves and left me to finish. I had not left the table when the signal was given and in a few minutes all was over. To you it may seem ghastly, but to me it was not so. No long, lingering illness accompanied by suffering and the wasting away of his strength. One swift, clean blow and he was ushered into the presence of his Lord. How I love to remember him as I saw him last, in the strength of his manhood!

As for our preparation, I wonder if there could have been a better one? I think not. What so prepares us for the big things of life, whether they be joys or tragedies, as a quiet daily walk with our Father, meeting each temptation or each danger in the strength of the Lord and faithfully performing each day's task. The years we had spent in Juruena, often facing danger, gave us a quiet, calm assurance in His keeping power that was with us to the last. (Bold added.)

For Arthur, I am sure no further preparation was needed to meet his Lord, nor did it seem the least bit strange to him to find the veil removed and to see Him face to face. As I came back from the darkness of unconsciousness to find myself not only without my own family but to find my entire household gone, it was to know a Father's care so tender, so gentle, that even the intense loneliness of the first day's separation were made sacred and hallowed. The "Kindly Light" that never fails made even those days luminous with His presence. So I ask you to believe with me that no accident has happened but only the working out of our Father's will. To you who knew and loved Arthur I beg you not to mourn him as dead, but to rejoice with me that he has been called to higher service.

But what of the work he laid down? Are the years of patient labor and unceasing prayer to be lost? That is for us to answer. Shall we not dedicate ourselves anew to the task of bringing the Gospel to the Nhambiquara Indians, for if anything can add to Arthur's joy in the Gloryland it will be to share the joys of heaven with the dark friends he so dearly loved and to whom he gave "the last full measure of devotion."

Sincerely,

Ethel Canary Tylee

Notice how prior trials and her daily walk with the Lord had prepared Ethel Canary Tylee for this most devastating attack and grievous loss. What might have happened if this had occurred after instead of before the modern-day church had embraced the counseling mentality? She probably would have been returned to the states and required by her mission agency to go for extensive psychological counseling, reliving the experience, and talking about the dreadful circumstances and people involved. The pain would have increased and she probably would never have returned to the field. What a blessing that she had not been indoctrinated into the counseling mindset and forced into treatment! In Christ she knew where to look and where to turn and how to glorify Christ in the situation. Instead of wallowing in self pity and reliving the horror, she stayed on to continue the work she and her husband had begun. Her love for her savior and for the Indians increased day by day because she was able to hang on to her hope for eternity—not only for herself and her family, but for those she had come to serve.

Conclusion

Do we serve a different Savior and Lord in the 21st Century? Or can we yet choose the way of the Lord and His Word rather than using problem-centered counseling that can hinder spiritual growth and lead to expressions of the Jeremiah 17:9 syndrome? Our desire is to help others know the Savior in such a way as to trust Him and walk by faith as so many Christians have done through the ages. If those who are suffering from problems of living are walking **daily** with the Lord and growing **daily** in the faith, they will not even want to have unbiblical conversations on a weekly basis with a problem-centered counselor. A **daily walk devoted to the Lord** is essential for believers to grow, serve, and please God. **May all of us remember the many elements of the daily walk, beginning early in the day, extending throughout the day, and ending in worship, praise and thanksgiving.**

Stop Counseling!
Start Ministering!

Let the word of Christ dwell in you richly in all wisdom; teaching and admonishing one another in psalms and hymns and spiritual songs, singing with grace in your hearts to the Lord. And whatsoever ye do in word or deed, do all in the name of the Lord Jesus, giving thanks to God and the Father by him. **Colossians 3:16-17**

We offer the following goal and suggestions for ministering to those suffering from the various issues of life: **One primary goal for ministering to fellow believers is to lead those in need away from sinful problem-centeredness into a daily walk of faith through the Word of God and the work of the Holy Spirit in the fellowship of the saints, so that God may be glorified in their lives and in the lives of others through them.**

To accomplish this goal, we give a one-sentence reminder of each chapter along with one-sentence suggestions for ministry. **Then, after that we give additional suggestions to aide those who wish to minister to those with personal problems of living.**

297

Chapter 1: "The Public Undressing of Private Lives"

Because we live in a transparent society where the most private matters are readily and often eagerly shared publically, it will be difficult to stop individuals from blabbing about their private lives and even their private thoughts about others and themselves. **Therefore**, be aware that the typical person comes in for help with an "anything-goes," "no-holds-barred" attitude about what can be said.

Chapter 2: "The Heart Is Deceitful"

As long as the counseling centers on sinful problem-centeredness, the Jeremiah 17:9 syndrome, along with its concomitant unbiblical faults in the flesh, will influence both the counselor and counselee. **Therefore**, remember that both the helper and the one helped are still living in the flesh and will be tempted to say and respond in a sinful manner when problems are discussed.

Chapter 3: "Problem-Centered Biblical Counseling"

Problem-centered counseling will inevitably lead to sinful talk, which becomes readily apparent when the literal descriptions and dialogs of problem-centered counseling are examined. **Therefore**, listen carefully to what is said by the one in need and compare what is said with what the Bible says about it and exercise care in your response and leading.

Chapter 4: "The Myth of Problem-Centered Counseling"

The one fatal error of biblical counseling is that from its very beginning it mimicked the problem-centeredness of psychological counseling and adopted the lynchpin of hearing all about and knowing all about problems, which inevitably involves sinful communication. **Therefore**, divert away from sinful problem-centered talk as much as possible and continually consider the biblical implications of what is said.

Chapter 5: "Cross-Gender Counseling"

Cross-gender, problem-centered biblical counseling was "inherited" from the psychological counseling movement and has no precedence in or support from Scripture and should be avoided for both biblical and practical reasons. **Therefore**, do not cross-gender minister to those who come to you to discuss their problems.

Chapter 6: "Research Against Counseling"

Research reveals numerous fallacies and fictions regarding psychological counseling, some of which also apply to biblical counseling. **Therefore**, remember and recognize these fallacies and fictions about both psychological and biblical counseling since both are problem-centered and involve sinful communication.

Chapter 7: "In Cahoots"

Two particularly egregious unbiblical practices of biblical counselors are charging for biblical counseling and separated-from-the-church biblical counseling centers, and, while many are aware of these two outrageously unbiblical practices, almost no one is crying out in opposition or naming the perpetrators of these two practices and all seem to be in cahoots to protect each other and these practices. **Therefore**, do not charge or seek donations from those who seek personal ministry and do not minister in a separated-from-the-church counseling center.

Chapter 8: "Overcoming Problem-Centeredness"

One of the greatest difficulties in personal ministry and mutual care in the Body of Christ is overcoming the quagmire of sinful problem-centeredness. **Therefore**, make it a high priority to notice when the problem-centeredness involves sinful talk and divert away from it towards building up the person's faith.

Chapter 9: "Ministering Biblically"

Ministering biblically must include the reasons Christians suffer, the role of suffering in a believer's life, and a review of sound doctrine regarding salvation and sanctification. **Therefore** talk about the role of suffering and how believers can grow spiritually through the trials of life and remind those in need about the truths from Scripture and encourage them to apply those truths even when others may be sinning against them.

Chapter 10: "The Believer's Daily Walk"

When trials, troubles, and sufferings occur, the **best ministry to those in need is to help them build a daily walk with the Lord though the Word so that they can grow in the Spirit, mature in the faith, honor God, and be a blessing to others. Therefore**, help the one in need to build faith by developing a daily walk with the Lord using the various spiritual resources presented in Scripture.

Stop Counseling!

Because the biblical counseling movement has copied the psychological movement in being problem-centered, it is necessary to deal with **what not to do** to clear the ground so that biblical teachings can be built upon a clean slate rather than contaminated with worldly ways. We are restricting ourselves to examples from Chapter Three from the National Association of Nouthetic Counselors, the Christian Counseling and Educational Foundation, and the Biblical Counseling Foundation because they are representative of what goes on in the biblical counseling movement. **Our overall most important warning is not to mimic the psychological or biblical counseling movement and their sinful problem-centered preoccupation and fetish.** The "Do Not's" that follow will equip you to do that.

While the following cautions have already been discussed, we are gathering them together as a quick and brief review. These are not in order of importance except for the first one. **These cautions to consider are not meant to be hard and fast rules, because there may be exceptions. This list is suggestive but not exhaustive. However, in most cases of personal ministry, we would say, "Do not" for the following:**

- **Do not minister like a problem-centered biblical counselor.**

- Do not ask questions that will elicit a Jeremiah 17:9 syndrome response, including the kangaroo court, hearsay, self-bias, evil speaking, the mote and beam, and the victim mentality (see Chapter Two).

- Do not be deceived into thinking you can fully know and understand anyone or any situation through asking enough "right questions."

- Do not charge money or suggest that a donation is needed as a result of personal ministry (see Chapter Seven).

- Do not make assumptions or speculations about those to whom you minister, such as when Tripp concludes that "Joe was the kind of guy who lived for the respect of other people" and he "sought to get it at home…by establishing a violent autocracy."

- Do not assume that you can get an accurate picture of a third party who is not present, as in Tripp's example of Greta describing her husband as being "critical and demanding," etc., and as in the BCF example where the counselor gives Mary a platform for talking sinfully about her husband.

- Do not give a comment or compliment that would support or lead to sinful talk.

- Do not sympathize at inappropriate times, such as when questionable information about the past or others is being shared or when the one in need is bad-mouthing people not present, because it may be interpreted as affirmation and support for what is said.

- Do not feel obligated to take a plethora of notes during a ministry conversation as Tripp had with Mike and Martha, after which he said, "I don't think I took as many notes in my theology classes at seminary as I did that afternoon!"

- Do not go into the past for reasons given in Chapter Eight.

- Do not use an intake form that will lead individuals down the path of sinful thinking and expression as with the Personal Data Inventory used by NANC and other biblical counselors.

- Do not pursue details about family members who are not present, such as when "Trey and Deb" are being critical of their parents.

- Do not assume that what is being said about someone who is not there is accurate, such as when a person complains about or blames in-laws as "Trey" did.

- Do not look for bad stuff to talk about and fix, because enough bad stuff will come up spontaneously and quite often the "bad stuff" will fade away as people talk about what is right and good in a problem relationship and as they learn to walk according to the Spirit.

• Do not ask for opinions regarding what is wrong with another person or what is wrong in a relationship, as Tripp does when asking, "What things in your marriage make you sad?" and "What do you see as the weaknesses of your marriage?" because such questions lead to tale-bearing and saying mean things and tend to lead the person deeper into the problem.

• Do not ask about what other issues may be problems besides the ones already discussed, as when Patton asks, "What's another issue?" as he is attempting to get a full picture of their problematic relationship, and when the BCF counselor gives Mary additional opportunities to speak evil about her husband behind his back by asking her about other "specific problems."

• Do not attempt to get a full picture of a couple's problematic relationship, because that is too elusive to achieve and you do not need all those details if the couple is willing to turn to the Lord and begin to walk according to the Spirit rather than the flesh.

• Do not attempt to fix issues such as finances when the couple is walking and talking according to the flesh, such as in the examples from NANC and BCF.

• Do not ask for details about conflicts as Patton did in asking "Trey and Deb" to tell him how they fight, how often, and over what and, "Do you throw things?" since no one needs to know the details for the couple to learn to walk according to the Spirit.

304   Stop Counseling! Start Ministering!

- Do not seek self-disclosure, as Tripp does by asking "questions that cannot be answered without self-disclosure.

- Do not seek private information about a person who is not there.

- Do not attempt to pierce the privacy barrier, which would include prying questions about sexual intimacy in a marriage, as Patton did with "Trey and Deb," because discussing something as personal and intimate as sex may cause more harm than good and be extremely hurtful, especially when the Jeremiah 17:9 syndrome is expressed.

- Do not engage in cross-gender person-to-person ministry for reasons given in Chapter Five.

- Do not dictate behavior as one who has authority over the person seeking ministry, as Patton did when he told "Trey," "No Bible, no TV."

- Do not think that those who seek ministry will not be able to make changes or progress without you.

- Do not be intimidated into studying ponderous and intimidating manuals and books, such as the BCF Manual and the required reading for NANC and CCEF certification.

- Do not assume that an individual who claims to be a Christian and gives a reply such as in the BCF example of Mary is necessarily truly born again.

- Do not be deceived into thinking you can know another person's heart through asking "Some Good Questions," as Tripp does.

- Do not attempt to explore the idols of the heart to find out why people do what they do, because humans cannot and do not need to know the heart of another person and because the root cause of sinful behavior is clearly given in Scripture as being the flesh or the "old man" and the way of change is learning to walk according to the new life in Christ.

Start Ministering!

The Lord is clear in His Word how the church is to function with evangelists, pastors and teachers equipping the saints "for the work of the ministry, for the edifying of the body of Christ: Till we all come in the unity of the faith, and of the knowledge of the Son of God, unto a perfect man, unto the measure of the stature of the fulness of Christ" (Eph. 4:11-13). Those in leadership could not possibly accomplish all the work of the ministry to bring every believer "unto the measure of the stature of the fulness of Christ." Those who are maturing in the faith are called and equipped to come alongside and serve one another. In addition to Galatians 6:1-2, there are other verses that direct believers to comfort, edify, admonish, teach, and exhort one another, all as expressions of love and care for one another's spiritual well-being and growth (e.g., 1 Thes. 5:11; Heb. 3:13; 10:24).

1 Peter not only says to minister to one another, but tells how to speak "as the oracles of God," meaning according to the Word of God, not according to the prevailing wisdom of men:

> As every man hath received the gift, even so minister the same one to another, as good stewards of the manifold grace of God. If any man speak, let him speak as the oracles of God; if any man minister, let him do it as of the ability which God giveth: that God in all things may be glorified through Jesus Christ, to whom be praise and dominion for ever and ever. Amen (1 Peter 4:10-11).

The following **reminders of what to do** are not in the order of importance, except for the first one, and certainly do not have to be memorized. These reminders will come naturally as you minister spiritually, because they should closely relate to your own spiritual walk with the Lord. Also, there is some overlap with what has already been said. As with the list of "Do Nots" this list of "Dos" is made up of suggestions and it is not exhaustive.

- **Do make sure that you yourself are walking daily with the Lord.**

- **Do lead the one in need in establishing a daily walk with the Lord, if they do not already have one.**

- Do keep Christ ever in mind as the primary person present.

- Do remember that you are nothing in yourself, but rather a vessel for the Lord's use.

- Do trust the Holy Spirit to do the essential inner work.

- Do talk about the usefulness of trials.

- Do encourage the fellow believer in spiritual growth.

- Do teach about and remind believers of the presence of Christ, the work of the cross, the new life He has given, and the Holy Spirit living in them.

- Do teach and remind the individual aspects of doctrine that need emphasizing.

- Do help believers learn to recognize whether they are walking according to the Spirit or according to the flesh (such as when there is an expression of the Jeremiah 17:9 syndrome) by asking themselves if they are walking according to the flesh or the Spirit at that moment.

- Do make sure that the person in need understands the biblical teachings regarding human depravity and sinfulness.

- Do bring forth Scripture that the Holy Spirit may use to convict the individual regarding sin.

- Do help believers to recognize their own sins so that they can change by God's grace and choose to walk according to the Spirit rather than the flesh.

- Do teach believers about putting off the old and putting on the new through confession (1 John 1:9) and renewing the mind (Eph. 4:23).

- Do remember that what is said will be skewed according to the person's viewpoint and bias, and therefore important information may be left out and unimportant information may be exaggerated.

- Do watch for aspects of the Jeremiah 19:9 syndrome, so as not to fall into the trap of pursuing it or being supportive of what is being said.

- Do ask about their relationship with the Lord.

- Do ask about ways God has blessed them.

- Do listen briefly when people spontaneously begin to speak negatively about those not present, but then change the direction of the conversation.

- Do refrain from asking unnecessary leading questions to obtain information about the past or about others who are not present.

- Do ask the Lord to give you questions to ask that would lead to spiritual growth.

- Do be compassionate without compromise or condescension.

- Do sympathize when appropriate.

- Do divert the conversation as much as possible away from sinfully talking about problems and into a daily building up of faith through the Word of God and the work of the Holy Spirit in the fellowship of the saints.

- Do encourage one another to serve, remembering that part of walking daily in the faith involves service of some kind, even if it is just to bring a little help, encouragement, or joy to someone.

- Do pray before, at the beginning and end of the conversation, and midway when needed.

- Do trust and acknowledge the Lord.

- Do remember eternity and speak of it often.

- Do continue to pray for one another.

Conclusion

We urge all believers to grow in grace, in faith, and in the knowledge of our Lord Jesus Christ and to be ready to minister to one another as the Lord provides opportunities and wisdom. New believers can certainly testify of the Lord's work in them, which can be a great encouragement to others. As believers talk with one another they will find opportunities to give a word of comfort, encouragement, and exhortation. They may have opportunities to remind one another of essential truths of Scripture that need to be emphasized. And, they may find themselves sought out for personal ministry by those who are enduring trials and various problems of living. Those who are trusting the Lord and His Word, are giving themselves as ready vessels for the Holy Spirit to work through them, and have been walking daily with the Lord through both sunny and stormy days are equipped to minister in some of the most difficult situations that fellow believers may be experiencing.

We thank God for those individuals who, without counseling certificates, degrees, manuals, books or programs, are **not intimidated** by a lack of counseling education and training and who minister to others just as believers were doing prior to the rise of the psychological and biblical counseling movements. We say to all who have been prepared by the Lord and are dependent on Him rather than on the wisdom of men: **Go forth and minister by grace through faith.**

> Now the God of peace, that brought again from the dead our Lord Jesus, that great shepherd of the sheep, through the blood of the everlasting covenant, make you perfect in every good work to do his will, working in you that which is wellpleasing in his sight, through Jesus Christ; to whom be glory for ever and ever. Amen (Heb. 13:20-21).

START MINISTERING!

FREE NEWSLETTER

For a sample copy of *PsychoHeresy Awareness Letter*,
a FREE bimonthly newsletter about the intrusion of
psychological counseling theories and therapies
into the church, please write to:

PsychoHeresy Awareness Ministries

4137 Primavera Road

Santa Barbara, CA 93110

or call:

1-800-216-4696

www.psychoheresy-aware.org

Notes

What This Book Is All About

1 Martin and Deidre Bobgan. *Christ-Centered Ministry versus Problem-Centered Counseling.* Santa Barbara, CA: EastGate Publishers, 2004, p. 80.

Chapter 1: The Public Undressing of Private Lives

1 Phone call to the United States Conference of Catholic Bishops, 202-541-3200.
2 Robert C. Fuller. *Mesmerism and the American Cure of Souls.* Philadelphia: University of Pennsylvania Press, 1982, p. 1.
3 *Ibid.*, p. 3.
4 *Ibid.*, p. 146.
5 Eva S. Moskowitz. *In Therapy We Trust: America's Obsession with Self-Fulfillment.* Baltimore: The Johns Hopkins University Press, 2001, p. 22.
6 Thomas Szasz. *The Myth of Psychotherapy.* Garden City: Doubleday/Anchor Press, 1978, p. 43.
7 Donald K. Freedheim, ed. *History of Psychotherapy: A Century of Change.* Washington, DC: American Psychological Association, 1992, p. 32.
8 E. M. Thornton. *The Freudian Fallacy.* Garden City: The Dial Press, Doubleday and Company, 1984, p. ix.
9 www.wikipedia.org.
10 Karin G. Coifman et al, "Does Repressive Coping Promote Resilience? Affective-Autonomic Response Discrepancy During Bereavement," *Journal of Personality and Social Psychology*, 2007, Vol. 92, No. 4, p. 745.
11 Moskowitz, *op. cit.*, pp. 2-3.
12 *Ibid.*, p. 71.
13 *Ibid.*, p. 78.
14 *Ibid.*, p. 77
15 *Ibid.* pp. 81-82.
16 *Ibid.* p. 83.
17 *Ibid.*, p. 3.
18 *Ibid.*, p. 161.

19   *Ibid.*, p. 162.
20   *Ibid.*
21   *Ibid.*, p. 170.
22   *Ibid.*, p. 164.
23   *Ibid.*, p. 169.
24   *Ibid.*, p. 171.
25   *Ibid.*, p. 173.
26   *Ibid.*, p. 172.
27   Joyce Milton. *The Road to Malpsychia: Humanistic Psychology and Our Discontents.* San Francisco: Encounter Books, 2002, 2003, p. 135.
28   Carl Rogers, quoted in *ibid.*, p. 135.
29   "The Most Influential Therapists of the Past Quarter-Century," *Psychotherapy Networker*, March-April, 2007.
30   *Ibid.*
31   *Ibid.*
32   Fuller, *op. cit.*, p. 140.
33   Moskowitz, *op.cit.*, p. 8.
34   Sudhir Kakar, "Western Science, Eastern Minds," *The Wilson Quarterly*, Vol. XV, No. 1, p. 114.
35   Skye Stephenson. *Understanding Spanish-Speaking South Americans: Bridging Hemispheres.* Yarmouth, ME: Intercultural Press, Inc., p. 47.
36   *Ibid.*, pp. 60-61.
37   G. Hofstede and G.J. Hofstede. *Cultures and Organizations: Software of the Mind.* New York: McGraw Hill, 2005, p. 76.
38   *Ibid.*, p. 98.
39   Neil Postman. *Amusing Ourselves to Death: Public Discourse in the Age of Show Business.* New York: Viking Penguin, Inc., 1985, pp. 110, 111.
40   *Ibid.*, p. 138.
41   *Ibid.*, p. 74.
42   Janice Peck. *The Age of Oprah: Cultural Icon for the Neoliberal Era.* Boulder. CO: Paradigm Publishers, 2008, p. 15.
43   *Ibid.*
44   *Ibid.*
45   *Ibid.*
46   *Ibid.*

47   Vicki Abt, "How TV Talkshows Deconstruct Society," *Research/ Penn State*, Vol. 17, No. 1, March, 1996, http://www.rps.psu.edu/ mar96/tvtalk.html.
48   *Ibid.*
49   Janice Peck, *op. cit.*, p. 16.
50   Abt, *op. cit.*
51   Peck, *op. cit.*, p. 16.
52   Moskowitz, *op. cit.* p. 267.
53   *Peck, op. cit.*, p. 31.
54   *Ibid.*, p. 35.
55   *Ibid.*, p. 9.
56   Abt, *op. cit.*
57   Peck, *op.cit.*, p. 126.
58   *Ibid.*, p. 127.
59   Austin Considine, "The Emotions of a Facebook 'Defriending,'" *Santa Barbara News-Press*, Sept. 15, 2010, p. D8.
60   Kent L. Norman. *Cyberpsychology: An Introduction to Human-Computer Interaction.* New York: Cambridge University Press, 2008, p. 288.
61   *Ibid.*, p. 288.
62   Brian Snider, quoted in "Church News Notes," August 13, 2010, www.wayoflife.org.
63   Norman, *op. cit.*, pp. 288-289.
64   Peck, *op. cit.*, p. 18.
65   Steven Stosny, "Case Studies," *Psychotherapy Networker*, Vol. 33, No. 2, p. 65.

Chapter 2: The Heart Is Deceitful

1   Matthew Poole. *A Commentary on the Holy Bible*, Vol. II. Peabody, MA: Hendrickson Publishers, p. 549.
2   *Ibid.*
3   *Webster's Encyclopedic Unabridged Dictionary of the English Language.* New York: Gramercy Books, 1996, p. 1928.
4   http://en.wikipedia.org/wiki/Kangaroo_court.
5   *Webster's Encyclopedic Unabridged Dictionary, op.cit.*, p. 882.
6   *Ibid.*, p. 1680.
7   *Ibid.*, p. 882.
8   Matthew Henry. *Matthew Henry's Commentary on the Whole Bible.* E-Sword—the Sword of the Lord with an electronic edge, http://www.e-sword.net.

9   Francis Foulkes. *The Epistle of Paul to the Ephesians: An Intro-duction and Commentary*. Grand Rapids, MI: W. B. Eerdmans Publishing Company, 1963, p. 137.

10   Gordon H. Clark. *Ephesians*. Unicoi, TN: The Trinity Foundation, 1985, p. 162.

11   Albert Barnes. *Notes on the Bible*. E-Sword, *op. cit.*

12   Adam Clarke. *Commentary on the Bible*. E-Sword, *op. cit.*

13   William MacDonald. *Bible Believer's Commentary: New Testament*. Nashville: Thomas Nelson Publishers, 1990, p. 756.

14   *Webster's, op. cit.*, p. 1928.

15   Cordelia Fine. *A Mind of Its Own: How Your Brain Distorts and Deceives*. New York: Norton & Norton Company, 2006, inside jacket cover.

16   *Ibid.*, p. 2.

17   *Ibid.*, p. 4

18   *Ibid.*, p. 7.

19   *Ibid.*, p. 8.

20   *Ibid.*, p. 9.

21   *Ibid.*, p. 11.

22   *Ibid.*, p. 12.

23   Carol Tavris and Elliot Aronson. *Mistakes Were Made (but not by me)*. New York: Harcourt, Inc., 2007.

24   Charles G. Lord, Lee Ross, and Mark R. Lepper, "Biased Assimilation and Attitude Polarization, *Journal of Personality and Social Psychology*, Vol. 37, No. 11, p. 2098.

25   *Ibid.*

26   George Orwell, quoted in Tavris and Aronson, *op. cit.*, p. vii.

27   Tavris and Aronson, *op. cit.*, p. 2.

28   *Ibid.*, p. 4.

29   *Ibid.*, p. 13.

30   Carol Tavris and Elliot Aronson, "'Why Won't They Admit They're Wrong' and Other Skeptics' Mysteries," *Skeptical Inquirer*, Vol. 31, No. 6, p. 12.

31   Tavris and Aronson. *Mistakes Were Made, op. cit.*, p. 18.

32   Tavris and Aronson, "'Why Won't They Admit They're Wrong,'" *op. cit.*, p. 12.

33   Tavris and Aronson. *Mistakes Were Made, op. cit.*, p. 6.

34   *Ibid.*, pp. 104-105.

Chapter Three: Problem Centered Biblical Counseling

1   "Biblical Counseling Observations," Faith Biblical Counseling, Faith Baptist Church, Lafayette, Indiana, Session One.

2   http://www.paultrippministries.org.

3   Paul David Tripp. *Instruments in the Redeemer's Hands.* Phillipsburg, NJ: P & R Publishing, 2002.

4   *Ibid.*, pp. 174 ff.

5   *Ibid.*, p. 175.

6   *Ibid.*, pp. 175-176.

7   *Ibid.*, p. 183.

8   *Ibid.*, p. 206.

9   *Ibid.*, pp. 176-177.

10   *Ibid.*, pp. 188-189.

11   *Ibid.*, p. 188.

12   *Ibid.*, p. 189.

13   *Ibid.*, p. 222.

14   *Ibid.*, p. 273.

15   Carol Tharp, "*Broken-Down House* by Paul David Tripp Reviewed," Parts One and Two, *PsychoHeresy Awareness Letter*, March-April, 2010, Vol. 18, No. 2; May-June, 2010, Vol. 18, No. 2, http://www.pamweb.org/articles.html.

16   John C. Broger. *Self-Confrontation Syllabus: Biblical Counseling Training – Course One.* Rancho Mirage, CA: Biblical Counseling Foundation, 1991.

17   John C. Broger. *Self-Confrontation: a manual for in-depth discipleship.* Nashville: Thomas Nelson Publishers, 1994.

18   *Level 2 Instructor's Guide Weekly.* Rancho Mirage, CA: Bibilcal Counseling Foundation, 1999, 2010.

19   Broger, *op. cit.,* both editions, Lesson 9, p. 12.

20   *Ibid.*, Lesson 12, p. 14.

21   *Ibid.*

22   *Ibid.*, Lesson 12, p. 15.

23   *Ibid.*

24   *Ibid.*, Lesson 13, p. 24.

25   *Ibid.*, Lesson 14, p. 7.

26   *Ibid.*, Lesson 15, p. 10.

27   Martin and Deidre Bobgan, "Confronting the Biblical Counseling Foundation's *Self-Confrontation* Manual: A PsychoHeresy Awareness Position Paper," http://www.pamweb.org/images/bcfpaper.pdf.

Chapter 4: The Myth of Problem-Centeredness

1   *Webster's Encyclopedic Unabridged Dictionary of the English Language*. New York: Gramercy Books, 1996, p. 1272.

2   Martin and Deidre Bobgan. *PsychoHeresy*. Santa Barbara, CA: EastGate Publishers, 1987. Martin and Deidre Bobgan. *Person to Person Ministry*. Santa Barbara, CA: EastGate Publishers. 2009. Also see www.psychoheresy-aware.org.

3   Robert C. Fuller. *Mesmerism and the American Cure of Souls*. Philadelphia: University of Pennsylvania Press, 1982.

4   Henri F. Ellenberger. *Discovery of the Unconscious: The History and Evolution of Dynamic Psychiatry*. New York: Basic Books/ HarperCollins Publishers, 1970, p. 892.

5   Harold I. Kaplan and Benjamin J. Sadock. *Concise Textbook of Clinical Psychiatry*. Baltimore: Williams & Wilkins, 1996, p. 376.

6   Christina Hoff Sommers, "The Republic of Feelings," *American Enterprise Institute for Public Policy Research*, AEI Online, Jan. 1, 2001.

7   Emily Nussbaum, "Good Grief! The Case for Repression," *Lingua Franca*, October, 1997.

8   Sommers, *op. cit.*

9   Nussbaum, *op. cit.*

10   Jay Lebow. "War of the Worlds: Researchers and Practitioners Collide on EMDR and CISD." *Psychotherapy Networker*, Vol. 27, No. 5, p. 79.

11   Rogers H. Wright and Nicholas A. Cummings, eds. *The Practice of Psychology: The Battle for Professionalism*. Phoenix, AZ: Zeig, Tucker & Theisen, Inc., 2001, p. 3.

12   *Ibid.*, p. 76.

13   Charles J. Sykes. *A Nation of Victims: The Decay of the American Character*. New York: St. Martin's Press, 1992, p. 34.

14   Ellen Herman. *The Romance of American Psychology*. Berkeley: University of California Press, 1995, p. 3.

15   *Ibid.*, p. 5.

16   Cara Marcano, "Growing Christian Shrinks," *Opinion Journal* from *The Wall Street Journal* Editorial Page, http://opinionjournal.com.

17   Wright and Cummings, eds., *op. cit.*, p. 270.

18   Jay E. Adams. *Update on Christian Counseling*, Vol. 1 and 2. Grand Rapids: Zondervan, 1977, 1979, 1981, Introduction to Vol. 2.

19   "Biblical Counseling Observations," Faith Biblical Counseling, Faith Baptist Church, Lafayette, Indiana,

20   John C. Broger. *Self-Confrontation Syllabus: Biblical Counseling Training – Course One*. Rancho Mirage, CA: Biblical Counseling Foundation, 1991, Supplement 1, p. 3.

21   Matthew Henry. *Commentary on the Whole Bible*, Leslie F. Church, ed. Grand Rapids, MI: Zondervon Regency Reference Library, 1960, p. 766.

22   Martin and Deidre Bobgan. *Person to Person Ministry*. Santa Barbara, CA: EastGate Publishers, 2009, p. 19.

23   Jacqueline Olds and Richard S. Schwartz. *The Lonely American*. Boston: Beacon Press, 2009, pp. 164-165.

24   *Ibid.*, p. 165.

25   Thomas Szasz. *The Myth of Psychotherapy*. Garden City: Anchor Press/Doubleday, 1978, p. 11.

26   "Should Therapists Self-Disclose?" *Psychotherapy Networker*, Vol. 34, No. 2, p. 14.

27   Olds and Schwartz, *op. cit.,* p. 166.

28   American Psychological Association, www.apapracticenet.net.

29   Email response from *Family Therapy Magazine,* September 9, 2009, on file.

30   David Wexler, "Shame-O-Phobia," *Psychotherapy Networker*, Vol. 34, No. 3, p. 23.

31   Holly Sweet, "Women Treating Men," *Psychotherapy Networker*, Vol. 34, No. 3, p. 34.

32   David Wexler, *op. cit.*, p. 23.

33   Carl Sherman, "Man's Last Stand," *Psychology Today*, Vol. 37, No. 4, p. 71.

34   Terrence Real quoted by Sherman, *ibid.*

35   Gary R. Brooks. *A New Psychotherapy for Traditional Men*. San Francisco: Jossey-Bass Publishers,1998, pp. 41, 42.

36   Sherman, *op. cit.*, p. 71.

37   Steven Stosny, "Case Studies," *Psychotherapy Networker*, Vol. 33, No. 2, p. 65.

38   *Ibid.*

Chapter 5: Cross-Gender Counseling

1   Survey of the Association for Clinical Pastoral Education, Inc., the International Association of Biblical Counselors, and the National Association of Nouthetic Counselors.

2   Janet Raloff, "Chemicals from plastics show effects in boys," *Science News*, Vol. 176, No. 13, p. 10.

3   "The Neural Roots of Intelligence," *Scientific American Mind*, Vol. 20, No. 6, p. 30.
4   Larry Cahill, "His Brain, Her Brain," *Scientific American*, Vol. 292, No. 5, p. 40.
5   *Ibid.*, p. 41.
6   *Scientific American Mind*, Vol. 21, No. 2, cover.
7   Cristof Koch, "Regaining the Rainbow," *Scientific American Mind*, *ibid.*, p. 16.
8   Deborah Tannen, "He Said, She Said," *Scientific American Mind*, *ibid.*, p.56.
9   Louann Brizendine. *The Female Brain*. New York: Morgan Road Books, 2006, inside jacket cover.
10   *Santa Barbara News-Press*, Feb. 24, 2009, p. B5.
11   Jan Donges, "You Are What You Say," *Scientific American Mind*, Vol. 20, No. 4, p. 14.
12   *Ibid.*, p. 15.
13   "Gender Differences," http://en.wikipedia.org/wiki/Gender_differences.
14   Jeffrey A. Kottler. *On Being a Therapist*, Fourth Edition. San Francisco, CA: Jossey-Bass, 2010, p. 144.
15   Alexandra G. Kaplan and Lorraine Jasinski in *Women and Psychotherapy: An Assessment of Research and Practice*. Annette M. Brodsky and Rachel T. Hare-Mustin. New York: The Guilford Press, 1980, p. 210.
16   Henri F. Ellenberger. *Discovery of the Unconscious: The History and Evolution of Dynamic Psychiatry*. New York: Basic Books/HarperCollins Publishers, 1970, p. 152.
17   *Webster's Encyclopedic Unabridged Dictionary of the English Language*. New York: Gramercy Books, 1996.
18   Garry Cooper, "Your Inner Therapist," *Psychotherapy Networker*, Vol. 34, No. 3, p. 11.
19   *Ibid.*
20   *Ibid.*
21   Ellenberger, *op. cit.*, p. 490.
22   http://en.wikipedia.org/wiki/Transference.
23   Jeffrey A. Kottler, *op. cit.*, p. 151.
24   Matthew Poole. *A Commentary on the Holy Bible*, Vol. III. Peabody, MA: Hendrickson Publishers, Inc., 2008, p. 28.

25   William MacDonald. *Bible Believer's Bible Commentary: New Testament*, Revised Edition. Nashville: Thomas Nelson Publishers, 1990, pp. 40-41.

26   Susan K. Golant, "Therapists Admit Sex Lure," *Los Angeles Times*, June 24, 1986, Part V, p. 1.

27   "Should Psychotherapist-Patient Sex Be a Crime?" *The Harvard Mental Health Letter*, Vol. 8, No. 9, p. 8.

28   "License to Harm," *The Seattle Tim*es, April 23, 2008.

29   Paul David Tripp. *Broken-Down House*. Wapwallopen, PA: Shepherd Press, 2009, p. 100.

30   *Ibid.*, p. 222.

31   Leslie Vernick. *How to Live Right When Your Life Goes Wrong* and *How to Act Right When Your Spouse Acts Wrong*. Colorado Springs: WaterBrook Press, 2003.

32   Holly Sweet, "Women Treating Men," *Psychotherapy Networker*, Vol. 34, No. 3, p. 34.

33   Concluded as a result of phone calls to or web site searches of all those organizations.

Chapter 6: Research Against Counseling

1   Martin and Deidre Bobgan. *PsychoHeresy: The Psychological Seduction of Christianity*. Santa Barbara, CA: EastGate Publishers, 1987. *The End of "Christian Psychology*," Santa Barbara, CA: East-Gate Publishers, 1997.

2   Michael Lambert, ed. *Bergin and Garfield's Handbook of Psychotherapy and Behavior Change*, Fifth Edition. New York: John Wiley & Sons, Inc., 2004, p. 6.

3   Bobgan and Bobgan, *The End of "Christian Psychology," op. cit.,* Chapter 2.

4   *Ibid.*, pp. 21, 21.

5   Henry D. Schlinger, Jr., "Of Planets and Cognitions: The Use of Deductive Inference in the Natural Sciences and Psychology," *Skeptical Inquirer*, Vol. 22, No. 5, p. 51.

6   Karl Popper, "Scientific Theory and Falsifiability" in *Perspectives in Philosophy*. Robert N. Beck, ed. New York: Holt, Rinehart, Winston, 1975, p. 342.

7   *Ibid.*, p. 343.

8   *Ibid.*, p. 344.

9   *Ibid.*, p. 345.

10   *Ibid.*, p. 343.

11 *Ibid.*, p. 346.
12 Jerome Frank, "Therapeutic Factors in Psychotherapy," *American Journal of Psychotherapy*, Vol. 25, 1971, p. 356.
13 E. Fuller Torrey. *The Mind Game.* New York: Emerson Hall Publishers, Inc., 1972, p. 8.
14 Adolf Grünbaum. *The Foundations of Psychoanalysis: A Philosophical Critique.* Berkeley: University of California Press, 1984; Adolf Grünbaum, personal letter on file
15 David E. Orlinsky, Klaus Grawe, and Barbara K. Parks, "Process and Outcome in Psychotherapy—Noch Einmal" in *Handbook of Psychotherapy and Behavior Change*, Fourth Edition. New York: John Wiley & Sons, Inc., 1994, p. 365. H. J. Eysenck, "Meta-Analysis Squared—Does It Make Sense?" *American Psychologist,* February, 1995, p. 110. H. J. Eysenck, "The Outcome Problem in Psychotherapy: What Have We Learned?" *Behavioural Research and Therapy*, Vol. 32, No. 5, 1994, p. 477. American Psychiatric Association Commission on Psychotherapies. *Psychotherapy Research: Methodological and Efficacy Issues.* Washington: American Psychiatric Association, 1982, p. 228.
16 Bruce E. Wampold, Zac E. Imel, and Scott D. Miller, "Barriers to the Dissemination of Empirically Supported Treatments: Matching Messages to the Evidence," *The Behavior Therapist*, Vol. 32, No. 7, p. 144.
17 APA Commission on Psychotherapies. *Psychotherapy Research: Methodological and Efficacy Issues.* Washington, DC: American Psychiatric Association, 1982.
18 Mary Sykes Wylie interviewing Martin Seligman. "Why Is This Man Smiling?" *Psychotherapy Networker*, Vol. 27, No. 1, p. 51.
19 Personal letter on file.
20 Lewis Carroll, *The Complete Alice.* Topsfield: Salem House Publishers, 1987, p. 30.
21 Michael J. Lambert and Allen E. Bergin, "The Effectiveness of Psychotherapy," *Handbook of Psychotherapy and Behavior Change*, Fourth Edition, Allen E. Bergin and Sol L. Garfield, eds. New York: John Wiley & Sons, Inc., 1994, p. 156.
22 Allen E. Bergin and Sol L. Garfield, "Overview, Trends, and Future Issues," *Handbook of Psychotherapy and Behavior Change*, Fourth Edition, *op. cit.*, p. 822.
23 Bobgan and Bobgan, *PsychoHeresy* and *The End of "Christian Psychology," op. cit.*

24   Henri F. Ellenberger. *Discovery of the Unconscious: The History and Evolution of Dynamic Psychiatry*. New York: Basic Books/ HarperCollins Publishers, 1970, p. 152.

25   *Ibid.*, p. 65.

26   *Ibid.*, p. 69.

27   *Ibid.*, p. 111.

28   *Psychotherapy Networker*, Vol. 31, No. 6, p. 2.

29   Kathleen McGowan, "The Power Couple," *Psychology Today*, November/December, 2004, p. 20.

30   Jay Lebow, "Big Squeeze: No Research? No Treatment," *Psychotherapy Networker*, Vol. 34, No. 1, p. 33.

31   "Therapeutic Alliance and Treatment Preference," *Harvard Mental Health Letter*, Vol. 24, No. 1, p. 7.

32   *Psychotherapy Networker*, Vol. 31, No. 6, p. 2.

33   John C. Norcross and Marvin R. Goldfield, eds. *Handbook of Psychotherapy Integration*, Second Edition. Oxford: Oxford University Press, 2005, p. 87.

34   "Clinician's Digest," *Psychotherapy Networker*, Vol. 34, No. 5, pp 10-11.

35   *Ibid.*, p. 11.

36   Marilynn Marchione, "Experts: Placebo effect behind many natural cures," *Santa Barbara News-Press*, November 11, 2009, p. B1.

37   Robyn M. Dawes, *House of Cards: Psychology and Psychotherapy Built on Myth.* New York: The Free Press/Macmillan, Inc., 1994, p. 62.

38   *Ibid.*, p. 52.

39   Larry E. Beutler, Paulo P. P. Machado, and Susan Allstetter Neufeldt, "Therapist Variables" in *Handbook of Psychotherapy and Behavior Change*, Fourth Edition, *op. cit.*, p. 259

40   Dawes, *op. cit.*, pp.101-102.

41   Jerome Frank, "Mental Health in a Fragmented Society: The Shattered Crystal Ball," *American Journal of Orthopsychiatry,* July, 1979, p. 406

42   Walter Mischel, "Connecting Clinical Practice to Scientific Progress," *Perspectives on Psychological Science*, Vol. 4, No. 6.

43   Scott O. Lilienfeld, "Psychological Treatments that Cause Harm" *Perspectives on Psychological Science*, Vol. 2, No. 1, pp. 53-70. Review of G. J. Devilly and P. Cotton, "Caveat Emptor, Caveat Venditor, and Critical Incident Stress Debriefing/Management" from *Australian Psychologist* , Vol. 39, pp. 35-40, *The Scientific Review of Mental Health Practice*, Vol. 3, No. 1, p. 76. Jeffrey M. Lohr, Wayne

Hooke, Richard Gist, David F. Tolin, "Novel and Controversial Treatments for Trauma-Related Stress Disorders" in *Science and Pseudoscience in Clinical Psychology*, Scott O. Lilienfeld et al, eds. New York: The Guilford Press, 2003, p. 259.

44 Derek Hatfield, Lynn McCullough, Shelby H.B. Frantz and Kenin Krieger, "Do We Know When Our Clients Get Worse? An Investigation of Therapists' Ability to Detect Negative Client Change," *Clinical Psychology and Psychotherapy*, Vol. 17, p. 25, published online, November 13, 2009, in Wiley InterScience, www.interscience.wiley.com.

45 Sharon Begley, "Get Shrunk at Your Own Risk," *Newsweek*, June 18, 2007, http://www.newsweek.com/id/34105.

46 Christina Hoff Sommers and Sally Satel. *One Nation Under Therapy: How the Helping Culture is Eroding Self-Reliance*. New York: St. Martin's Press, 2005, p. 6.

47 *Ibid.*, p. 7.

48 "Born Again Adults Less Likely to Co-Habit, Just as Likely to Divorce," Barna Research Online, August 6, 2001, www.barna.org.

49 Richard Simon, "From the Editor," *Psychotherapy Networker*, Vol. 26, No. 6, p. 2.

50 Brent Atkinson," "Brain to Brain," *Psychotherapy Networker*, Vol. 26, No. 5, p. 40.

51 Elizabeth Loftus and Katherine Ketcham. *The Myth of Repressed Memory: False Memories and Allegations of Sexual Abuse*. New York: St. Martin's Press, 1994.

52 Mark Pendergrast. *Victims of Memory: Incest Accusations and Shattered Lives*. Hinesburg, VT: Upper Access, Inc., 1995.

53 Martin and Deidre Bobgan, "Psychoheresy and Inner Healing," Parts 1, 2, & 3, *PsychoHeresy Awareness Letter*, Vol. 15, Nos. 1, 2, & 3, http://www.psychoheresy-aware.org.

54 http://www.examiner.com/x-20682-Boston-Skepticism-Examiner.

55 *Ibid.*

56 Begley, *op. cit.*

57 *Harvard Mental Health Letter*, Vol. 26, No. 4, p. 8.

58 *Ibid.*

59 Omar Rodriguez, "Afrocuban Religion and Syncretism with the Catholic Religion," http://scholar.library.miami.edu/emancipation/religion1.htm.

60 John T. McNeill. *A History of The Cure of Souls*. New York; Harper & Row, Publishers, 1951, pp. 45-46.

61   Martin and Deidre Bobgan. *PsychoHeresy*. Santa Barbara, CA: EastGate Publishers, 1987, pp. 11-25.
62   Robert C. Fuller. *Americans and the Unconscious*. New York: Oxford University Press, 1986, p. 6.
63   *Ibid.*, p. 21-22.
64   Bobgan, *op.cit.*, pp. 27-41.
65   Alexander W Astin, "The Functional Autonomy of Psychotherapy," *The Investigation of Psychotherapy: Commentaries and Readings,* Arnold P Goldstein and Sanford J. Dean, eds. New York: John Wiley, 1966, pp. 62-65.

Chapter 7: In Cahoots?

1   Association of Biblical Counselors Conference, May 14-16, 2009.
2   www.psychoheresy-awareness.org/mainpage/html.
3   Martin and Deidre Bobgan, *Person to Person Ministry*, Santa Barbara, CA: EastGate Publishers, 2009, also available as a free ebook at http://www.pamweb.org/ppmbk_online.html.
4   www.christiancounseling.com.
5   Phone call to Lelek's office on February 24, 2009.
6   http://www.christiancounseling.com/en/cms/?144.
7   http://www.ccef.org/counseling_rates.asp.
8   Martin and Deidre Bobgan, "Biblical Counseling: Simoniacs and Pharisaics?" *PsychoHeresy Awareness Letter*, Vol. 3, No. 1.
9   Phone call to NANC on May 3, 2009.
10   Martin and Deidre Bobgan, "Pay for Prophecy?" www.psychohersy-aware.org/payproph72.html; "Biblical Counseling: Simoniacs and Pharisaics?" www.psychoheresy-aware.org/bcsimony.html; "NANC & the APA," www.psychoheresy-aware.org/nancap65.html; "$$Simony & Biblical Counseling," www.psychoheresy-aware.org/simonybc.html; "Charging for BiblicalCounseling," www.psychoheresy-aware.org/charge75/html; "Shut Down the'Biblical Counseling' Movement?" www.psychoheresy-aware.org/shutdown.html; Martin and Deidre Bobgan, *Person to Person Ministry*, Santa Barbara, CA: EastGate Publishers, 2009.
11   Commentaries consulted are: *Believer's Bible Commentary*, Thomas Nelson Publishers; *Jamieson, Fausett, and Brown Commentary*; *John Gill's Exposition of the Entire Bible*; *Matthew Henry's Commentary*; *Matthew Poole's Commentary on the Holy Bible*.
12   William MacDonald. *Believer's Bible Commentary*. Nashville: Thomas Nelson Publishers, 1990, p. 712.

13   Matthew Henry. *Matthew Henry's Commentary in One Volume.* Grand Rapids: Zondervan Publishing House, 1961, p. 1846.

14   John Gill. *Exposition of the Entire Bible.* e-Sword, Version 9.5.1, Rick Meyers, 2001-2009, www.e-sword.net.

15   Matthew Poole. *Commentary of the Holy Bible*, Vol. 3. Peabody, MA: Hendrickson Publishers, 2008, p. 568.

16   *Strong's Exhaustive Concordance.*

17   Gill, *op. cit.*

18   Henry, *op. cit.*, p. 1947.

19   MacDonald, *op. cit.*, p. 1096.

20   Eva S. Moskowitz. *In Therapy We Trust: America's Obsession with Self-Fulfillment.* Baltimore: The Johns Hopkins University Press, 2001, p. 83.

21   "$$Simony & Biblical Counseling," http://www.psychoheresy-aware.org/simonybc.html.

22   Debbie Dewart, "Charging Fees for Biblical Counseling? Relationship, Responsibility, and Remuneration," http://www.christiandiscernment.com/View%20and%20Print.htm.

23   http://www.ibcd.org/counseling/i-would-like-to-receive-counseling.

24   www.bcecvisalia.net/contact.htm.

25   Jeffrey A. Kottler. *On Being a Therapist*, Fourth Edition. San Francisco, CA: Jossey-Bass, 2010, p. 126.

26   *Ibid.*, p. 120.

27   Bobgan, *Person to Person Ministry, op. cit.*

28   *Webster's Encyclopedic Unabridged Dictionary of the English Language.* New York: Gramercy Books, 1996, p. 293.

29   *Ibid.*, p. 1415.

30   *Ibid.*, p. 1094.

Chapter 8: Overcoming Problem-Centeredness

1   Martin and Deidre Bobgan. *Person to Person Ministry: Soul Care in the Body of Christ.* Santa Barbara, CA: EastGate Publishers, 2009.

2   Martin and Deidre Bobgan. *Competent to Minister: The Biblical Care of Souls.* Santa Barbara, CA: EastGate Publishers, 1996, p. 92.

3   Martin and Deidre Bobgan. *Christ-Centered Ministry versus Problem-Centered Counseling.* Santa Barbara, CA: EastGate Publishers, 2004, p. 80.

4   Bobgan, *Person to Person Ministry, op. cit.*, p. 167.

5   *Ibid.*, p. 179.

6   *Ibid.*, pp. 185-197.
7   Robert B. Hughes and J. Carl Laney. *Tyndale Concise Bible Commentary*. Carol Stream, IL: Tyndale House Publishers, Inc., 2001, p. 606.
8   *Jamieson, Fausset, Brown Commentary.* E-Sword—the Sword of the Lord with an electronic edge, http://www.e-sword.net.

Chapter 9: Ministering Biblically

1   Martin and Deidre Bobgan. *Person to Person Ministry: Soul Care in the Body of Christ*. Santa Barbara, CA: EastGate Publishers, 2009, p. 173.
2   Adam Clarke. *Adam Clarke's Commentary on the Bible.* E-Sword—the Sword of the Lord with an electronic edge, http://www.e-sword.net.
3   Albert Barnes. *Albert Barnes Notes on the Bible*, E-Sword, *op. cit.*
4   John Gill. *John Gill's Exposition of the Entire Bible*, E-Sword, *op. cit.*
5   Clarke, *op. cit.*
6   Gill, *op. cit.*

Chapter 10:The Believer's Daily Walk

1   Kent L. Norman. *Cyberpsychology. An Introduction to Human-Computer Interaction*. New York: Cambridge University Press, 2008, p. 284.
2   "Television & Health," Internet Resources to Accompany *The Sourcebook for Teaching Science*, http://www.csun.edu/science/health/docs/tv&health.html.

FREE *E*BOOKS

by Martin & Deidre Bobgan available at

www.psychoheresy-aware.org

PERSON TO PERSON MINISTRY: SOUL CARE IN THE BODY OF CHRIST is about a Christ-centered approach to nurture the spiritual life of believers and to equip them to fight the good fight of faith and thereby confront problems of living through exercising faith in Christ and the Word. This book also reveals the innate sinfulness of problem-centered counseling, shows how problem-centered counseling leads Christians into feeding the flesh and quenching the Spirit, and gives reasons why Christians must abandon the problem-centered approach.

12 STEPS TO DESTRUCTION: Codependency/Recovery Heresies includes essential information for Christians about codependency/recovery teachings, Alcoholics Anonymous, Twelve-Step groups, and addiction treatment programs. They are examined from a biblical, historical, and research perspective. The book urges believers to trust in the sufficiency of Christ and the Word of God instead of man-made programs.

AGAINST BIBLICAL COUNSELING: FOR THE BIBLE is about the growing biblical counseling movement and urges Christians to return to biblically ordained ministries and mutual care in the Body of Christ. It is an analysis of what biblical counseling is, rather than what it pretends or even hopes to be. Its primary thrust is to call Christians back to the Bible and to biblically ordained ministries and mutual care.

CHRIST-CENTERED MINISTRY VERSUS PROBLEM-CENTERED COUNSELING reveals the origins and faults of problem-centered counseling, describes Christ-centered ministry and how it differs from problem-centered counseling, and encourages local congregations to minister as God has called them to do, without intimidation from or the influence of the psychological or biblical counseling movements.

CRI GUILTY OF PSYCHOHERESY? responds to *Christian Research Journal*'s 4-part series, "Psychology & the Church" by Bob and Gretchen Passantino. This book demonstrates that CRI leaves an open door to integrating psychotherapy and its underlying psychologies with the Bible and gives biblical and research reasons why this open door constitutes psychoheresy.

FREE *E*BOOKS

by Martin & Deidre Bobgan available at
www.psychoheresy-aware.org

COMPETENT TO MINISTER: THE BIBLICAL CARE OF SOULS is a call to believers to use the Word of God empowered by the Holy Spirit to minister to one another in the Body of Christ. It addresses such issues as: What can churches do for people suffering from problems of living? Does the Bible offer another unique way to minister to believers? What can Christians do to help and encourage one another.

THE END OF "CHRISTIAN PSYCHOLOGY" explodes myths about psychotherapy and demonstrates that "Christian psychology" involves the same problems and confusions of contradictory theories and techniques as secular psychology. Teachings of major psychological theorists are described and analyzed. This book presents enough biblical and scientific evidence to shut down both secular and "Christian psychology."

FOUR TEMPERAMENTS, ASTROLOGY & PERSONALITY TEST-ING reveals the source of the four temperaments and demonstrates the tragic weaknesses of personality inventories and tests. Personality types and tests are examined from a biblical, historical, and research basis.

HYPNOSIS: MEDICAL, SCIENTIFIC, OR OCCULTIC? examines hypnosis from scientific, historical, and biblical perspectives and shows that hypnosis is the same whether practiced by benevolent medical doctors, shamans, or occultists. Exposes both obvious and hidden dangers.

JAMES DOBSON'S GOSPEL OF SELF-ESTEEM & PSYCHOLOGY demonstrates that many of Dobson's teachings originated from secular psychological theorists whose opinions are based on godless foundations. Dobson uses the Bible along with unbiblical ideas. Self-esteem and psychology are the two major thrusts that too often supersede sin, salvation, and sanctification. They are another gospel.

LARRY CRABB'S GOSPEL evaluates Crabb's integration of psychology and Christianity. The book demonstrates that, though he sounds biblical, his teachings are dependent on unscientific psychological opinions. It also reveals Crabb's increasing influence in psychologizing the Christian walk and turning churches into personal growth communities through his mixture of psychology and theology.

FREE *E*BOOKS
by Martin & Deidre Bobgan available at
www.psychoheresy-aware.org

MISSIONS & PSYCHOHERESY exposes the mental health profession's false façade of expertise for screening missionary candidates and caring for missionaries. It explodes the myths that surround the psychological testing used on these hapless men and women. It further reveals the prolific practice of using mental health professionals to provide psychological care for missionaries suffering from problems of living.

PSYCHOHERESY: THE PSYCHOLOGICAL SEDUCTION OF CHRISTIANITY exposes the fallacies and failures of psychological counseling theories and therapies for one purpose: to call the church back to curing souls by means of the Word of God and the work of the Holy Spirit rather than by man-made means and opinions. Besides revealing the anti-Christian biases, internal contradictions, and documented failures of secular psychotherapy, *PsychoHeresy* examines various amalgamations of secular psychologies with Christianity and explodes firmly entrenched myths.

THEOPHOSTIC COUNSELING: DIVINE REVELATION? OR PSYCHOHERESY? evaluates the counseling system recently devised by Dr. Ed Smith, who claims direct revelation from God, but whose system is a combination of theories and techniques gleaned from Freudian and other forms of psychotherapy, ideas and practices from the inner healing movement, and enough Scripture to make it sound biblical. With his numerous testimonies of cure, Smith's system is gaining in popularity among Christians.